Social and Political History
of The German 1848 Revolution

RUDOLPH STADELMANN

Social and Political History
of the German 1848 Revolution

TRANSLATED BY JAMES G. CHASTAIN

Ohio University Press / Athens, Ohio

© 1948 F. Bruckman KG, Munich
for the German original edition
2nd edition 1970

English translation © 1975 by James G. Chastain
ISBN-8214-0177-7
Library of Congress Catalog Number 74-27711
All rights reserved.
Printed in the United States of America by
Oberlin Printing Co., Inc.
Designed by Harold M. Stevens

Table of Contents

Introduction

When this book first appeared, it was hailed
by Karl Griewank of Jena as signifying "a
decisive step toward a new general interpretation" of the social
revolution of 1848. Stadelmann attempted to write a sociological,
a socio-political, and above all a socio-psychological history of
the revolution. For many readers, the most important aspect of
the work was its pioneer role, a stimulus to strike out boldly on
a new path. "Every historian," Griewank assured, "who concerns
himself with a sociological understanding of historical transformation will obtain rich stimulation from Stadelmann's work."[1] Stadelmann's history must be classified as sociological because it deals
with the role of social groups, more specifically the artisan, laboring,
and peasant classes. His goal was to discover how the "common
person experienced the upheaval and how he interpreted what was
happening." His task then was to investigate such matters as the
"emergence of a new stratum in society and its active entry into
political life" from the vantage point of the man in the street.
For this new history, he looked not merely to what occurred in
the lobbies of the representative assemblies and in the audience
halls of royal palaces, but also in the voluntary associations and
mass demonstrations, in petitions and street songs, in the secret
diaries and actions of forgotten contemporaries.

This book has additional significance as a document of historio-
graphical nature, which may be as important to some as its informative content. Until the Second World War Stadelmann closely
corresponded to the model of the German "mandarin" professor.[2]
This book, however, was written during the intellectual ferment
that followed the war. It attested Stadelmann's personal reexamina-
tion, his rethinking, his entire outlook which changed radically

with the psychological shock of contemporary events. Stadelmann exemplified a widespread eagerness to ask new questions of history after being part of a generation that followed false prophets. He began to write a new sort of history concerned with the masses, rather than continuing his earlier preoccupation with a narrow intellectual history, *Ideengeschichte*, rooted in the pure idea. He himself was the product of the spirit of late Weimar Germany; therefore, his book documented the distance that one member of this generation traveled toward political reeducation. The publication also reflected the tensions of the cold war, and its extreme strictures of Marx and Engels were sometimes an unfortunate product of the time in which the book appeared. The perceptive reader might indeed argue that Stadelmann belonged to a tradition of social interpretation of German history which actually dated back to Marx and Engels, and that this book owes a great deal more than Stadelmann perhaps realized, or was willing to admit in 1948, to the work of the forerunners of social history. The book itself was part of the great post-war interest in the history of society that in the United States produced important studies like Priscilla Robertson's *The Revolutions of 1848: A Social History*.

Rudolf Stadelmann is remembered by posterity as an historian who "mastered the sources in the smallest details and knew how to analyze them in the entire context." However, he was hardly just a highly learned professor isolated in research and teaching, unaware of physical reality. The son of a Protestant minister from peasant stock, Stadelmann combined the robust with the refined, the outdoorsman with the aesthete; living with his family on a country estate, he had the muscular frame of a gymnast and horseman with the hands of a manual worker and the thick neck of a peasant, yet his friendly eyes looked out from behind the thick lenses of a scholar. In a short autobiographical sketch written before his death on August 17, 1949, at the age of forty-seven, he described himself upon his arrival to teach at the University of Freiburg in his late twenties as a "passionate kayak paddler [who] had just written a sensitive book on the decadence of the 15th century." One writer concluded that the "tension between a down-to-earth, simple vitality committed to actual existence and a psychologically sensitive understanding for the historic periods of decadence and crisis, for the uncertainties of transition and historical consciousness" characterized his entire way of thinking. Without losing sight of the lofty world of the pure idea, Stadelmann was also historically rooted in concrete facts, able to stand back from the documents for broader insights and new interpretations, yet he always remained a "realist."[3]

The focus of Stadelmann's archival research begun in the summer of 1947 was the history of the artisan class. In addition to his book, Stadelmann's research produced an unfinished study which was published posthumously with the collaboration of Wolfram Fischer.[4] His background in intellectual history brought an awareness of the power of ideas to influence events, although he never viewed ideas as impersonal agents: instead he saw them working through individuals and specific social classes. Stadelmann placed this work in the context of a typology of European revolutions, including the English Revolution of the 17th century, the French Revolution, and the Russian Revolution. His goal was "to discover what was typical in the course of revolutions and to investigate the sociological as well as the psychological motivating forces of upheaval." He wished to write a book similar to Crane Brinton's work on the French Revolution, the *Anatomy of a Revolution*, which would discover the "social and political powers of the abortive German revolution."[5] He therefore looked beyond the specific facts of 1848, which, as he noted, had previously been recounted in greater detail by Veit Valentin, and instead generalized about the nature of revolutions. A closer investigation of Stadelmann's work shows that an interest in revolution is the unifying factor that underlay all of his historical writings, thus this study is actually the culmination of all of his earlier efforts. Stadelmann had always emphasized the constructive power of revolutions, thereby placing himself among the progressive writers in spite of his long-standing interest in decadence and the writings of Jacob Burckhardt, which were typical of his generation of "mandarins." Stadelmann recognized the positive side of revolution, arguing that everything truly creative was "revolutionary." This force originated in the depths of society and thrust forward bringing a new and passionate enthusiasm. Stadelmann thus praised not only the liberalizing effects of traditional revolutions but, in addition, he considered the Reformation and the German uprising against Napoleon forms of the popular movement, which could also be called "revolutions."

Since Stadelmann's book on 1848 represents such a radical departure from the traditional interpretation, it is hardly surprising that some readers will feel that Stadelmann achieved only partial success. It struck Robert Bezucha that the volume was "fraught with an intellectual tension between old and new history, between the conventional manner of discussing the Revolution of 1848 and the social conflicts which revealed themselves through it." To some extent Stadelmann's work anticipated what George Rudé recently identified as the "new 'labor' history" that developed after World War II. "Its most distinctive characteristic," wrote Rudé, "has been to abandon the old institutional, Labor-Movement oriented, narrative history of the past and to turn towards a more rounded *social* history of both labor and 'the people' at large." Like Stadelmann these historians put a "new emphasis on people as opposed to institutions."[6] Stadelmann shared some of the concern of the "new 'labor' historians" for turning away from the old concentration on a narrow institutional and organizational approach to the study of non-elites toward a study of the foundation of voluntary associations whereby one could gain a more meaningful understanding of the crisis than with conventional history. Rudé and Stadelmann, however, differed in that the latter retained his traditional interest in intellectual history. Upon investigating the plight of the lower orders, Stadelmann expressly broke with the interpretation which saw the revolution originating in objective conditions of misery or the rise of social classes, and carved an individual niche in historiography for himself. He turned his back on the study of actual conditions of poverty by denying that they were the true source of revolution. It was a psychological, a subjective consciousness, more than indigence, he felt, which brought historical change. The revolutionary ideologist on various levels seemed to him the decisive impulse for revolutionary action. He characterized his own interpretation as "ideological," arguing that "subjective consciousness underlay change more than objective conditions." He rejected as naive the popular assumption that great poverty caused the revolution.* For Stadelmann the salient fact was less the actual

*He in fact argued that the conditions of workers who revolted in 1848 may have even improved shortly before then. Although the data he cited are from the work of the famous Marxist historian, Jürgen Kuczynski, of the German Democratic Republic, his conclusion has been accepted by few leftist historians; yet

condition of deprivation than how it was perceived by contemporaries. While great need had always been present, this had not created a revolution—or even a consensus that this was wrong. A more important shift than the rich becoming richer and the poor becoming poorer between 1789 and 1848 was a public cognizance that this state of poverty was evil and should be changed. As the Enlightenment effected the Great Revolution, this sensitivity influenced the ruling class, where a secret fear grew ultimately into a bad conscience; the political class doubted its own mission, making resistance to the revolution difficult. An important fact distinguishing 1848 from 1789 in Germany was thus a discovery of the exploitation of the lower classes. The recognition of the suffering in the lower orders was the work of intellectuals who created a sensitivity to the fate of the poor. Stadelmann concluded that in the beginning was the idea. An ideology had to be framed and distributed before any revolution was possible. He found that this was the work of doctrinaire, middle class intellectuals, especially academicians, who used their academic posts to attack the bureaucratic absolutist state during the first half of the 19th century. "The way to the revolution," he concluded, "originated not in the most dire poverty, but rather among subtilized thought and philosophical programs." The revolutionary ideas were spread by "an uprooted intermediate social stratum" which did not "belong essentially to any class and that intellectually disputed the ruling social order." Yet for these thoughts to be transformed to action, they had to find receptivity in a revolutionary class. Here Stadelmann found a key element in social history: the psychological condition of the peasants and artisan journeymen. The journeymen "were the rootless element in society," who were "torn between two worlds." Although they could no longer aspire to become masters, they "fought with all their energy against merging with the factory workers." They were the "true carrier of the revolution," while the "urban proletariat was historically mute in comparison."* The

it is really no more than an aside to his principal point that the actual state of poverty was far less important historically than the perception of its existence by contemporaries.

*Investigators have recently followed in Stadelmann's footsteps and questioned the traditional concepts of a lower middle class. As Robert Bezucha latterly pointed out, these young historians challenge the assumption of the *Manifesto* that the "declassed" artisan was ruined by the destruction of guild protection, as the *Communist Manifesto* pointed out, when he was sacrificed to a liberal "industrial freedom" which gave him only the right to starve.

Stadelmann called attention to the fact that Germany was basically an agricultural area, hence the significance of rural upheaval in 1848. He noted the importance of the discontent brought by over-population, causing growth among the lowest class, indeed creating a new class of proletarian landless farm laborers which had not existed before the 19th century. This was an area that had been too often overlooked by writers on 1848, who usually focused on the urban centers. Here his methodology was especially appreciated by Griewank. "From an abundance of individual material he sought, always presenting particularly and at the same time typically, to make the events descriptive of their more or less conscious motives. From a wide knowledge of the sources and secondary literature he allowed an astoundingly rich material to speak and strove to form out of this a fertile and complete historical picture." The investigation of rural conditions was a particularly difficult task. Stadelmann had to deal with the great diversity of situations in the various German states. Before 1871 there was no Germany, but several separate Germanies, the thirty-eight sovereign states of the German Confederation. Germany's history has been regional, disjointed, complex, and multiform. Writers on 19th century Germany had to deal with a rural predicament which differed greatly from one locale to another. Here one must contend with local history which alone could afford a manageable area for testing generalizations for the greater geographical district. Here history could be removed from vague generalities and placed closer to the documents.

artisans should be lumped together with small manufacturers and shopkeepers in a "reactionary" group attempting to "roll back the wheel of history," while the proletariat was the "universal class in whose hands lies the future." Robert J. Bezucha, "Current Research on the Social History of Nineteenth Century France," *Annual Proceedings of the Consortium on Revolutionary Europe, 1750-1850*, II (1973) (Gainesville, Florida, 1975); Joann Scott, in a paper at the Society for French Historical Studies of March, 1971, concluded that "Generalizations about artisans are at the stage that generalizations about the 17th century crisis and the 18th century agricultural revolution were ten or twenty years ago." Quoted by Bezucha, *Ibid.*

For much the same reasons Stadelmann, in his search for the typical pattern, chose to include outlying districts for his investigation; he selected, for example, the instance of political associations in provincial Königsberg rather than in Frankfurt or Berlin. He defended this practice for two additional reasons. In 1848 the social profiles of the larger urban centers did not differ significantly; Berlin was at the time merely larger than Königsberg. In addition, during the revolution town and country acted in unison, so that events in the more remote localities closely paralleled those in the larger towns without the difficulties inherent in dealing with larger figures. "The best explanations," free from extraneous considerations, Stadelmann concluded, came "where the law of large numbers did not have an impact from the outset." Thus he chose the court chamberlain of the dwarf principality of Ballenstedt to demonstrate how a revolutionary psychosis set in during 1848 to transform the chamberlain's assumptions radically—and what is more, against his own best interests. At the inception of the revolution the defensive powers of the reaction were paralyzed; even court officials like Kügelgen were "seized by the experience" and overcome by "a mixture of intoxication and perplexity." "At the moment of the revolution's birth," Stadelmann noted, "no white army existed." All were swept away as they entrusted themselves to the great wheel of history—at least long enough to overthrow the various German governments in March. Yet the revolution eventually miscarried.

Stadelmann evaluated the relative importance of a number of factors for the failure of the upheaval of 1848. Part of the difficulty was the German tendency toward lawfulness. The attempt to build a German state based on the power of the liberal idea was frustrated by the "inborn submissiveness," the "ignorance of the essence of power" exhibited by the man on the street. This could be noted in the formation of political parties, one of the permanent results of the revolution and the subject of a recent book by Werner Boldt.[7] The reactionaries were more successful in creating mass political organizations than the moderate spokesmen of the March revolution. A more commonly recognized reason for the lack of fruition in 1848 was the German parliament of 1848, the first common representative assembly in German history. Stadelmann, however, defended the record of the German parliament and placed primary responsibility on the personality of Frederick William IV, the mentally unstable King of Prussia, for the failure of the assembly's constituent labors. If the Prussian throne had been occupied by a "Coburg prince," who had inwardly accepted the liberal March ministry, Stadelmann suggested, the Berlin revolution might not have been in vain. Instead, Frederick William rejected the crown proffered by Frankfurt as "carrion," a "dog collar" which would chain him to the 1848 revolution. Neither a Frederick the Great nor a great statesman was necessary in 1848; apparently a Coburg prince with a capable ministry in Berlin would have sufficed, Stadelmann concluded.

This view of the Prussian monarch was to a great degree a reaction to a school of 20th century historians.[8] Most recently Alexander Scharff of Kiel attempted to refurbish the tarnished image of the Prussian monarch by blaming the revolution's miscarriage on the European powers' threat to united Germany. When the book appeared it was most widely questioned on this particular point: did the neighbors of the German Confederation seriously contemplate armed action to prevent German unity? Stadelmann dismissed the evidence as insufficient to prove that revolutionary France and tsarist Russia posed a serious problem of a common alliance against Germany. My own research as well as that of Frederick de Luna's in the French archives suggests that Stadelmann's conclusion was correct.[9] France indeed did not at any time seriously consider a war against united Germany, and Lamartine's overtures in the early spring quite specifically concerned only the strained relations between France and Russia caused by the Polish question. My work in the French military archives substantiates Lamartine's public and private statements that the imminently anticipated Polish war would be fought with Germany as an ally. Stadelmann's conclusions concerning the absence of a foreign threat to German unity have been supported by intervening historical research.[10]

The reasons for the revolution's failure would not be found by studying the diplomacy of the year, but only by investigating the social undercurrents. Stadelmann rejected the long-range chances of success for a mid-19th century revolution based on a *coup d'état* of a few determined individuals. In this time frame, an uprising could have had a lasting effect only if the masses had already rejected the old order and were ready to accept what the insurrectionaries offered. Success of the 1848 German revolution ultimately depended on its universal support. The old political fabric could be destroyed "when it had lost its vital inner force." Besides a widespread rejection of the old order, a revolutionary class had to be defined. This, Stadelmann believed, was the "socially uprooted intermediate stratum," not the lowest order, not the most down-trodden, but the socially declining lower-middle class, who pro-tested the degradation of their social status, their "declassment" from the great middle class into the factory—they were at the forefront of the urban revolutionary struggle, not the factory prole-tarian with "nothing to lose but his chains." Likewise in the country-side, it was the slightly better-off who led the protest, not the totally dispossessed, rural proletarized and landless workers. The lower-middle class was the source of social unrest, of discontent, of candidates for emigration. What they protested in 1848 was their enslavement by economic *laissez-faire*-inspired "industrial freedom" which destroyed the protection the old craft guild system had once offered. Seeing their livelihood endangered by the capitalis-tic factory system, the artisan workers revolted in March to restore the guilds. Their motivation was never class consciousness, an idea "enormously premature" in 1848, but guild consciousness among the revolutionary masses. It was the struggle of quality wares against the machine-made article, an upheaval of artisan cottage industry against mass fabrication. There was not a basic contradiction, Sta-delmann argued, with capital, a storm on the bourgeois state, or even against the bourgeois social order. The development of a class-conscious proletariat, inspired by the Marxist movement of Bebel and Liebknecht, was a generation away, and the workers, mostly artisans, considered themselves part of a common middle class.[11]

It was the second stage of the revolution, the social demands of the communists, Stadelmann suggested, that drove the entire bourgeoisie, including the small artisans and peasants, into the arms of the old forces of order and destroyed the revolution. The bourgeoisie feared radicals like Frederick Engels, abandoned the revolution which was fought for the middle class, and allowed it to be crushed by the forces of reaction. The liberal movement in Germany was neither strong nor confident enough to survive, and this failure burdened German history for a century. The organic development toward freedom and parliamentary democracy did not evolve naturally but was cut short by reaction, which isolated Germany from the common Western European liberal form of parliamentary government. The middle class in the summer and fall months of 1848 was disturbed by those points of the communist program that attacked the foundation of the bourgeois state. In addition they feared that Frederick Engels, as he fought in Elberfeld with the bourgeoisie against the reactionaries in May of 1849, was only waiting on the fringes to use the arming of the people to turn the masses against the bourgeoisie after the common aristocratic enemy was conquered—as Lenin toppled Kerensky in the Great October Revolution. Thus the civil war of May, 1849, frightened the bourgeoisie to the point that German democrats were burdened with the red flag of communism for a half-century.

In spite of reservations, Stadelmann concluded that 1848 was a revolution, be it a strange sort of revolution. People were transformed as during the Peasant Revolt of the Reformation and in the November Revolution of 1918. The example of the court chamberlain of Ballenstedt showed how events could create a psychosis, changing individuals, causing an inebriation that would lead them to do things foreign to their own nature. It was a German sort of revolution: a revolution of Herr Piepmeyer with a concern for law and order, a struggle for liberal rights, but generally within an obedient and non-political frame of reference. It left behind disappointment and a mistrust of ideals. As A. J. P. Taylor wrote, "1848 was the decisive year of German, and so of European history. . . . Never has there been a revolution so inspired by the limitless faith in the power of ideas; never has a revolution so discredited the power of ideas in its result."[12] In its place a realism set in that prepared the way for Bismarck and a conservative and violent solution to the German question. The bankruptcy of 1848 cleared the path by discrediting the middle class liberals, causing them to lose confidence in themselves, and leaving them ready to sacrifice liberty for unity.

Social and Political History
of The German 1848 Revolution

I

SOCIAL ORIGINS OF THE REVOLUTION

There are three theories that attempt to explain the historical origin of revolution. The oldest is most common in textbooks and among the pamphlets of revolutionaries themselves. It is based on a simplified conception of the suppression of freedom and the welfare of the people. A ruling government becomes so intolerable by its inequitable basis or despotic oppression that the downtrodden rise with violence against it to force a change in the social and political structure. The cry for freedom, according to this outlook, is clear proof of the corruption in the old governmental form. The question of whether or not the former system at the moment of its demise was unchanged from an earlier period when few questioned its validity is hardly asked in this naive theory of revolution, and yet only this consideration would yield a valid reason for the creation of a revolution. The fallen governmental system and its social form cannot really bear alone the weight of guilt; otherwise, it would be impossible to understand why the revolution had not broken out long before, perhaps at its inception. Most abuses complained of in the *cahiers* of 1789 by the French voters had existed for a hundred or two hundred years. In many cases three, six, or even twelve generations had suffered under the conditions without their causing a revolution. Now everything suddenly was seen as absolute oppression, injustice, vexation, and abominable power that under Louis XIV was the pride and the accepted character of the nation-state. One could try to explain this astounding fact

3

through the employment of exact and well-documented investigations of what gradual or decisive changes the *ancien régime* went through, when it deteriorated into abuse and degeneration. Thereby, however, the historical inquiry shifts ninety degrees. Strictly speaking, one would not view the *ancien régime* as the cause of the French Revolution, rather one has to depict the corrupt *ancien régime* as the point of departure for the events, and must search less for the roots of the revolution than for reasons for the depravity of the old ruling order.

Another cause is often suggested. The reason for rebellion is not sought in the structural changes of the old order, but in the appearance of new historical factors and standards. With this we turn from the simple theory of oppression as the true cause of revolution to a new explanation. This second view of the origin of historical crises explains the political upheaval as the result of the emergence of new social strata, either a new social class comes to power, or an ethnic element which until now has stood in the shadows now forces itself to the top, or perhaps simply another type of human being arises, attracting those similar to it, repelling those foreign to its nature, and in this manner a kind of historical natural selection is conjured up which explains the change in morals, norms, outlooks and institutions.[1] The French Revolution is explained by this method as the rising of the Mediterranean man against the Germanic ruling class or the English Revolution of the 17th century is designated as the emergence of the middle class. In the German 1848 Revolution the sociological cause is found in the emergence of the fourth estate, in the disorderly breakthrough of the proletariat into the half feudal, half bourgeois world of the Metternich era. Since the stimulating work of the Viennese national economist Ernst Viktor Zenker (1897) and the comprehensive book on the revolution by the Frankfurt historian Veit Valentin (1930), the attention of research has increasingly focused on the social undercurrent during 1848. Although the classicist of sociological historical interpretation, Karl Marx, himself never spoke of anything more than a petty bourgeois movement, the tendency is widespread to perceive the March Revolution as the first expression of the social crisis in the industrial epoch. In view of the problems of procuring documentation for a history of the working people and the arbitrariness and chance of statistical information, one accepts into a historical work the descriptions of poverty given by famous pioneers of social justice with some hesitation. Some statistics used by Dronke, Violand, and Ketteler cannot be substantiated by archival verification. But the task remains to use a sociologically oriented history of social orders to investigate the question how a new class arises and enters actively into political life. One must seek the events not merely in the audience chambers of royal palaces and in the lobbies of parliaments, but there where the less conventional history was acted out: in the clubs and mass demonstrations, from petitions and popular songs, from the secret diaries and from the ordinary life of unknown contemporaries. Any evidence from the days of crisis is helpful which gives us a glimpse into the way that the common person experienced the upheaval and how he interpreted what was happening.

If we pursue the sociological explanation of the revolution to the documentary sources, then the historical interrogation is again shifted. It demonstrates that the subjective consciousness underlies change more than objective conditions, and that this psychological change causes manifestly stronger impulses for historical action than real conditions. So we are almost forced to write a third type of revolutionary history. One could call it ideological. It originates in the observation that oppression creates discontent and opposition only where it is perceived as an injustice. A new need will make itself known only when it is awakened. And the consciousness of oppression, the feeling of a need for change begins in general with teaching, infectiously, through imitation, in any case through the infiltration of ideas, whose origin one can describe more accurately. The miners of the Erzgebirge, in Westphalia, and in the Rhineland have suffered for centuries under the harshness of their place of work, under insufficient sanitary conditions, under the exploitation of the human work force and every kind of danger, certainly more than the rebellious peasants of the 16th century or the industrial worker of the 19th century. But they did not revolt, because the miner lived in a fixed social order where these conditions belonged to the normal state. From time to time some of his comrades were killed by firedamp. He had to lie on his back to pick out low seams. Coal dust covered his homes and gardens. The beneficiaries of the mine lived far away in a city palace and did not share with him under any circumstance the toil and torment

5

of physical labor. In every epoch since the end of the middle ages the objective conditions of even the best-directed mines would have sufficed to explain a revolution. But neither during the Fuggers' era nor in the era of high capitalism has a revolution broken out in mining districts. In this highly stratified world, the bacillus of rebellion never penetrated to make the fate of men unbearable.

A susceptibility for subversive ideas is much more noticeable where an uprooted intermediate social stratum is formed that does not belong essentially to any class and that intellectually disputes the ruling social order. The bourgeois-aristocratic writers in France of the 18th century are as significant examples as the proletarian intellectuals of the 19th century. How this uprooted, questioning intelligentsia acted, which political and social goals it pursued, depended not so much on its actual economic position as on the ideas which they realized as writers, agitators, as itinerant demagogues, fanatic prophets, and with which they aspired to awaken and organize the others, to arouse the quiet masses, the passive afflicted. For these messengers of the revolution, the ideological message was the essential meaning of life. Their journalistic or conspiratorial or other propagandizing activity would awaken in certain classes or groups of people a need which under certain conditions could be transferred to revolutionary action. The Lutheran preachers of the Reformation, who wanted to induce the congregation to select their own pastors, injected into the peasants of 1525 one of the main demands of the Peasants' War with this theological-political idea. The *Philosophes* of the 18th century Enlightenment first spoiled the taste of the French bourgeoisie for the inherited institutions of an absolute state. It is not by chance that before 1848 the doctrinaries of the middle class, professors, intellectuals, and journalists, delivered the political slogans, that tailors and cobblers (that is, members of trades affording time for reflection) played a dominating role among the activists of the common people. The path of the revolution is formed not by the strongest arms nor by the most extreme poverty, but rather among subtilized thought and philosophical programs. A survey of the history of the origins of the great revolutions makes it seem as though the mandates of an idea had taken command of the body politic for a certain historical role. The ever-present economic and social needs seem then to be no more than the humus in which the seeds of ideas can develop with a prospect of success among the masses. One could view the economic situation as the constant and the intellectual currents, ideals and utopias as the variables in the equation of history.

*

The view has long ago been rejected that the German revolution of 1848 arose from an especially drastic multitude of grievances and from a critical development of social injustice. The conditions under which especially the little man in Germany lived in the 1840s were almost without exception far better than those of the last decades of the 18th century. If it were true that a ferment in a country was caused by prevailing social conditions or more or less scandalous habits of the ruling class, then the disposition of Germans to imitate the example of the French Revolution around 1790 would have been incomparably greater than in 1848. But not the beacon of 1789, but rather the weaker example of the Paris February revolution incited Germany and evoked the sudden collapse of the political regime. The far more enveloping events sixty years earlier ran up against a bourgeois spirit which, after a few vacillations, clung almost without exception to obedience to princely authority and valued the governmental form of enlightened despotism more highly than a Jacobian prototype.[2] How can we explain the variation in effects of the foreign impulse other than as a difference in intellectual upbringing among this same citizenry? Because from a social viewpoint it is the same middle class which determined public opinion in 1800 and lived through the *Vormärz* epoch. It was certainly no worse off than it was fifty years before. The German territorial state had not become more oppressive during two generations, but on the contrary, more civilized and more just. In fact, the life of the common person had made during this interval decisive progress in security, comfort, cleanliness and in human dignity. The standard of living had reached a high level and stability which it probably had never experienced in all the previous centuries and which a hundred years later has been partially lost again. It is not without reason that a parish chronicle from Saulgau written in 1851 noted of the *Vormärz* epoch: "The years between 1830 and 1845 were among the happiest in

7

the history of the world!"[3] This is only proof on a popular social level of what Leopold von Ranke expressed for the culturally oriented social stratum in his famous description of the Restoration as "halcyon days." Consultation of the reminiscences of a self-made man like the Berlin trade school director Friedrich Klöden overpowers us with the improvement in outward living standards during this period. What crudity, hardship, and brutal harshness in a Berlin caserne district or East Prussian country towns in 1790! What comfort and Biedermeier safety, what security and "policing" in 1840! It was no dazzling prosperity, but a noticeable well-being had arrived, in which one could no longer even conceive of the terror caused by a Schinderhannes and the Prussian military recruitment drum. No longer did princely castles exist where two thousand persons at court and a thousand horses in the stables were maintained at the cost of the subjects, as the Elector Karl Theodor of the Palatinate once had. There were no longer court parties like those of Karl Eugen, whose Ludwigsburg fireworks cost 300,000 Gulden. There were no longer higher civil servants like that Prime Minister of Saxony, Count Bruehl, who could show his guests 500 different suits, 100 silk dressing gowns, 843 snuff boxes, and 1500 wigs, that he had squeezed out of his poor, tiny land.[4] The personal extravagance, unscrupulous trade in human beings, the evil financial machinations, and the absurd war games of the 18th century had vanished. Although in a few states like Bavaria, Electoral Hesse, and Brunswick scandalous goings-on in the princely household remained to be censured, still in the majority of the castles the expenses were far less provocative and the means of income procurement had long since ceased to be so shocking as during the earlier absolutist age.[5]

As at the top so also among the people, the conditions improved perceptibly. There were far fewer subjects beaten than in the 18th century. There were also a great deal fewer school children beaten than under the authority of the old village school teachers, who, as a rule, had been recruited from among the ruined craftsmen, discharged soldiers and village musicians. When in 1779 an old school teacher of a Swabian town, after fifty years of service, compiled a "conservative estimate" that in his life he had given 911,527 paddle licks, 1,115,800 blows on the head, 136,715 slaps, and 124,010 switchings,[6] this barbarian pedagogy was not entirely a thing of

8

the past; but the new teacher training colleges and the more humane adjustments in elementary schools pushed the old ways strongly into the background. The educational system of the *Vormärz* era not only raised the secondary schools and universities of Germany to an unprecedented level, but also offered a multitude of new possibilities for trade circles interested in technical training. The pedagogical enthusiasm of the Pestalozzi era and the crusading urge of the enlightened state converged to expand trade schools and opportunities for further professional training. For the apprentice, shop clerk and journeyman, for a fine craftsman, locksmith, and spinner, the progressive-minded territories, like Hamburg, Berlin, Frankfurt, Saxony, and Wurtemberg, offered a wealth of promising beginnings. There was a great deal offered that benefited the learning ability, the energy, and the desire for advancement of the petit bourgeoisie in the Sunday schools and evening courses, in occupational and drawing lessons, in the voluntary associations and adult education institutes, in journeyman and artisan associations.

The lot of the worker class, with the exception of the transitional misery of cottage industry, was materially better off than under the stagnant economy of late mercantilism and the continental blockade. One can easily detect the growing prosperity in the figures of artisan statistics. In 1800 the preponderant majority of master craftsmen lived on such a bare subsistence level that they could not employ a journeyman. By 1846 conditions in Prussia had altered to the degree that for 457,000 masters there were almost 385,000 journeymen. While as late as 1819 only 51% of the independent workshop owners could maintain a helper, by 1846, 84% had expanded their business enough to employ help.[7] Regarding paid wages and compensation, it is much more difficult to note an improved economic position. The buying power of money varied from year to year, and the price of bread changed with the conditions in the grain markets. It does not mean very much, therefore, that a roofer under the Darmstadt construction wage scale of 1777 could earn a maximum weekly wage of 7.50 Marks, while in 1847 a spinning master in Breslau collected 18 Marks, and machine workers, silversmiths, and printers received substantially higher sums.[8] Since 1846 and 1847 were years of great scarcity and moreover threatened by growing unemployment brought about by a rapid population increase, the wage conditions in town and country were often wretched. From the Rhineland and Silesia, from cottage worker districts in Saxony and the textile city of Vienna, even in Bavaria and Hesse, contemporary pamphlets of the 1840s contained calculations that the yearly income of day laborers and unskilled workers remained under a subsistence minimum.[9] But among factory workers, wages in general rose faster and conformed more closely to the cost of living than among craft workers and casual laborers.[10] One would therefore be mistaken to blame the introduction of industry for a universal deterioration in living conditions. In general, public prosperity certainly rose, and the independent industrial worker was not among that portion of the population who suffered most from the economic changes. When the writings of Wichern and Hasemann, the statistical formulations of Reden and Reuter, and a multitude of essays by national economists and the reform tracts often mentioned that since the end of the 1830s, wages had lagged behind the general evolution of prices, that a glut of working power drove up the profit of employers and left many proletarians without bread, that the large factory owners profited ruthlessly from the predicament in the job market, in that they hired younger, cheaper hands and dismissed the better paid fathers of families, the reliability of this description cannot be doubted, even if they chose one-sided examples to shake up consciences. But one should not forget that centers of industrial production were also frequently perceived by contemporaries as a deliverance from the overpopulated settlements of tenant farmers in the environs, and the workers coming from the countryside considered themselves as rich people with their cash wages compared to their rural village neighbors.[11] In the *Vormärz* era, the combination of some agriculture with regular factory work already had become a widespread and especially advantageous pattern for solving the problem of population density. Industrialism was not only harmful, but also beneficial in dealing with the problem of rapid growth of humanity, which was noticeable in all parts of Germany since the end of the 18th century, although except for Silesia it had not caused an acute crisis anywhere.

The triumphant course of the machine age was actually consummated especially slowly in Germany and was in no case revolutionary. In 1841 only 240 steam engines existed in Austria-Hungary, used mostly in mines, spinning mills, and in cloth manufacture. The quantity was greater in Prussia; on the eve of the revolution the number perhaps exceeded 1200. Even there only an extremely small proportion of the population worked in large factories with a staff of over 500 men. A middle-sized firm like Krupp employed around 140 workers in 1846; a Prussian or Saxon machine factory might involve 250 people. Factories on a large scale existed only in Bohemia, where the Liebig woolen factory in Reichenberg had already brought together 8,000 workers. Under no circumstances is it really possible to speak of an industrial proletariat in the modern sense. on German soil. True working masses were first created in the great railway construction of the 1860s, and among these excavators we encounter also the first men who consciously thought of themselves as proletarians, as the moving memoirs of the central German, Karl Fischer, testify.

It is difficult to answer the question of how large the fraction of factory workers was in relation to the total of those employed in industry. The statistical records are especially vague here, because the lawmakers purposely neglected to determine where the boundary between workshop and factory, between handwork and manufacturing was to be drawn, and left local authorities to make the distinction. Hermann Schlüter's figures are commonly accepted as a description of conditions in 1846.[12] According to these, in Prussia, for 457,000 masters and 385,000 journeymen there were around 550,000 factory workers.[13] Even if these data are accepted—they seem to present a strong statistical dislocation of questionable cases and dwarf operations on the side of "factory" work—there was still a relation of eight to five in favor of crafts, while in 1925 the ratio had changed so radically that the relationship was three to one in favor of the factory worker. Not much is explained sociologically with this crude statistical breakdown. Even when a half-million in Prussia and close to a quarter-million in Saxony are claimed as factory workers, and when within all of Germany a figure of a million independent workers is computed, this is not to say that all of these masters and journeymen who flowed into manufacturing plants were already proletarians. There were among them the established home worker, cottager, piecework master, married journeyman, and penniless artisan, who always kept open the option of opening his own shop someday. A modern business census would probably include very

few of these. Thus a recent work on the beginnings of industrialization in Baden pointed out that in 1840 only 10,000 men can be
spoken of as factory workers. Even when we include the 4,000
cottage workers, there were ten times as many masters or journeymen employed in crafts.[14] The statistics of 1836 in Wurtemberg
indicate similar percentages.[15] Even in the old industrial districts
of the Wupper and the Ruhr, in Aachen, Gladbach, and Crefeld
west of the Rhine, one must realize that conditions were very patriarchal and relaxingly rural, as Blechen's lovely painting depicts.
Certainly the chimney smokes, but right next to it flourishes the
romantic idyl, and urban slums do not yet exist at all. The actual
development of large industry only began in the 1860s, and the
1848 revolution hardly signified a turning point in economic history.
During the period when Disraeli in England, with the approval
of the readers of novels, could speak of "two nations" growing
up, irreconcilable with each other, between which no communication, no sympathy, no mediation, and no common moral law
existed, whose thoughts and feelings were as far apart "as inhabitants
of different planets," in Germany this class division did not yet
exist. Capitalist and proletariat were not yet deadly enemies; they
still all belonged to a common middle class world, so to speak,
and it had not been many years since rich businessmen, who took
finished products from the spinner and weaver in exchange for
raw materials and tools, had stood on the same social level as
their pieceworker. Alphons Thun in his brilliant book on the industry
on the lower Rhine[16] showed very clearly how the knifesmith, sword-
smith, sharpener, and scissormaker in Solingen regarded themselves
as almost the social equals of the established wholesale dealers
to whom they weekly delivered their goods; their education, social
life, their respectability competed with the bourgeoisie, although
these specialized workers were far behind the merchants in terms
of income. These were old master families, in which the manual
ability of the father was inherited by the son. Many cultivated
a taste for music, ordered books of fine literature and held public
office.[17] In the Berg town of Remscheid the way of life was freer
and more prosperous, even more suited to the daily mutual relationships of master and helper, and the craft character of the famous
export industry even more purely preserved.[18]

Close by, certainly, existed textile areas where joblessness, child

12

misery, and the employment of women predominated, and the wages were shockingly low when the market for goods was poor. The Crefeld silk workers rioted in 1828 when all fourteen firms except one cut salaries by fifteen percent, after the competition from Zurich at the Leipzig Fair supplanted Rhineland silk cloth. But, except for a procession during the night and a few broken windows, nothing happened. For decades this was the only time that indignation was released. It was not a social revolt, but rather a stormy wage demonstration like those of the craft journeymen that were repeatedly recorded in the 16th to the 18th centuries.

When in 1848 the centuries-old cover of patriarchal habit was raised for a moment, it was especially clear what the oppressed silk weavers wished and fought for. On March 27, 1848, with the Mayor presiding, they negotiated an agreement with their employers that the looms at which they worked would revert to the ownership of the individual weavers, who would again be recognized as independent craftsmen. They wished to organize a guild, and decided among themselves that no master could have more than four looms operating. Their ideal was the old corporate craft guilds, and the workers did not forget even the orphan daughters of the guild masters: the factory owners could engage only them; other girls could not be employed.[19] The incident in Crefeld is a moving document of social history. The return to guild-controlled industry and small workshops: this was the essence of the revolutionary ideas of the silk weavers on the Rhine. There is no question here of a modern proletarian class consciousness, of a socialization of the fruits of labor, of a sharing in the management of the work, of profit, and in a common means of production. They made the means of production, where feasible, the private possession again of the master and left the retail organization to capital. They defended themselves with every means against large industry and tried to save small business in the form of domestic industry. The generation of 1848 was thoroughly social-conservative in its thinking and aspirations, not to say petty bourgeois. Any other contention is a later construction or an anticipation of a condition that at the time existed at most in England, not even clearly in France and Belgium. In spite of the growth of factories, the introduction of the steam engine, and the lively traffic on the newly built highways and railroads, the social structure of the industrial class basi-

13

cally remained artisan, as also in the generation between the Congress of Vienna and the fall of Metternich nothing changed in the general occupational structure of Germany.

Naturally, since the end of the 18th century a gradual cleavage had set in between the guild master on one side, who often observed his privileges and specialization very rigidly, and the independent factory owner and small entrepreneur on the other side, who often were much more mobile, more successful, and had stronger capital reserves, yet whose social origins were often in the sphere of journeymen who had failed to become masters. The enlightened state had long ago recognized the significance of this independent industry and shifted its support to it, especially under the motivation of the economic teachings of Adam Smith and his German disciples. Thus a grotesque reversal set in. The government between 1815 and 1848 was essentially more progressive, liberal and emancipated in its economic policy than its tradesmen themselves, who were typically craftsmen and journeymen, instinctively aspiring toward a return to corporative unity with guild regulation and the independent existence of small masters. Even in the revolution, industrial freedom was not the slogan of craftsmen, but the battle cry of the bureaucracy, who on an increasing scale since the Prussian law of 1810, and finally in all the states of the German Confederation, intended to eradicate the restrictions of the guild spirit, to accelerate initiative, to enliven backward technology, and to promote prosperity. Werner Sombart noted that this progressive bureaucracy lacked the chorus of liberal free enterprise, because in Germany no large business class existed. The governments were faced by a singular opposition of tradesmen, who certainly wanted to stand politically with the party of movement but fought economic liberalism tooth and nail. The craftsman's impulse for social survival forced him over to the other side, where the state-licensed authority protected the independent master against competition and shoddy workmanship, against mass production and capital accumulation, against being absorbed into either the proletariat or the bourgeoisie, and guaranteed the social unity of the lower middle class. Industrial freedom necessarily divided the tradesmen. A few could rise to become rich manufacturers while the great mass inevitably had to become dependent hired laborers. It is comprehensible that many individuals, including the unemployed handworkers or poorly paid journeymen who could not marry, strove to leave the restrictions of the guild for the freedom of factory work. It is a surprising testimony to the health of the body politic in the first half of the 19th century that the overwhelming majority struggled against the new game rules of industrial freedom with an astounding, instinctive certainty.

Everything has in itself a good and bad side. And always some group is literally pulverized by such a good-evil matter. The actual mourners of the development and those finally perplexed by the dilemma were the journeymen. They really wished to become masters, to partake of the honors of the guild, to exclude inferior goods, and to maintain the quality of their craft. But simultaneously they wanted to be released from the red tape and chicanery of the old guild monopoly, to trump their masters and to keep in step with progress. They were torn between two worlds. The old corporation refused to allow them to advance because they would take work from the elders, and the guild regulations offered enough manipulation to keep the gifted journeyman in his place. In the modern factory economy of large firms using machines and the production of mass goods, they had to sink to the level of skilled workers and could no longer rise above the social class of wage labor. Thus the journeymen were the restless element in society. That is to say, they were uprooted. They could no longer earn their bread as independent masters, and still they fought with all their energy against merging with the factory workers. In many places regulations and privileges forbade guild journeymen to work in the same area as the non-guild hack even when they were employed in the same factory. Many of these journeymen stepped quite consciously into the industrial age and were the first leaders of wage earners. They proudly called themselves workers like their French colleagues and proposed placing the state at the service of the working class. Numerically, few followed their example, and the history of the 1848 revolution shows how difficult it was for them to tear themselves from the guild ideal. Even a majority of the radical Frankfurt journeymen's assembly, which admitted day laborers and factory workers, opposed industrial freedom and favored the guild principle.

Nevertheless, the conflicting fate of the journeyman, torn back and forth between guild authority and manufacturing freedom,

15

between craft and factory, had created a sociological breeding ground which united political enlightenment with social desperation. These intelligent, uprooted individuals, who had innocently fallen between the grindstones of progress, as a social component probably became the actual carriers of the revolution. The urban proletariat was historically mute in comparison. Just as the inhabitants of the London slums never began an insurrection, one could expect little from the hovels of German cities that played such an important role in the social paintings of the day. Details of life in worker suburbs of Berlin and Vienna were certainly ghastly:[20] damp dwellings where a line through a room was the division between one family and another, the ragged beggar children and colonies of thieves who made the area around the city walls unsafe, the factory girls who as street prostitutes in the evening hauled benches and cushions into the center of the city, and the cave men who lived for months in the sewer pipes. One must be careful, however, to avoid exaggerations. When we look closer, there were only two such notorious "family houses" standing in Berlin's "Voigtland."[21] The dregs of society in all European cities from Milan to London had already been living similarly since 1770; they had survived four revolutions in Paris without improving essentially their mode of life. A social-political crisis does not develop from such conditions, no matter how hideous and pitiable.

The brutal accompanying phenomena of industrial wage labor were a greater weight on the social structure: extortionist wage scales, child labor, excessive work hours, deficient hygienic facilities, lack of factory inspection, epidemics, moral neglect. What the official reports and a multitude of social reform pamphlets develop in detail here is shameful. But the historian of the revolution ought not to make the mistake of trying to find, so to speak, the main cause for the revolutionary crisis in these grievances without waiting to observe where the weight of empirical observation lies. In fact there were districts in Germany too, like the Solingen light metal industry, in Elberfeld, Crefeld, and Aachen, where the notorious truck system, which was the subject of such bitter controversy in England, was customary. The businessman, who brought raw materials and semi-finished goods on a large scale to cottage laborers in small workshops to be fabricated, often joined his wage payment with a merchandising business, in that his workers were forced

16

to take a portion or all of their salaries in over-priced goods, on which the jobber took his percentage a second time. The employee was compelled either to get rid of the merchandise in turn at a loss or to receive, instead of his daily bread, luxury articles like clothing, coffee, rice, flowers, or especially brandy, items that bore no relationship to his actual needs.[22] But more careful investigation shows that this "payment in goods" did not originate in advanced industrial capitalism of the 19th century, rather it was a survival of an abuse that already existed in the 15th century and is documented since the 17th century in many heavily settled home industry districts. Those responsible were frequently small marginal producers or Jewish retailers, while the large firms and official corporate organizations of tradesmen combated and censured the practice in strongest terms. The degeneracy of the payment in merchandise incited men to revolutionary action only in a few isolated cases in March, 1848. So in general, the grievances about working conditions and the lack of social legislation did not remotely play the part in the unrest of 1848 one might have expected from widespread cries of distress for social reforms of the 1840s. One must also conclude that the welfare state of princely bureaucracy attacked these problems with greater energy than the free-trade theory of western lands allowed. No one would go so far as to commend the *ancien régime* of Metternich's time for its industrial inspection and its assistance to workers. But one must admit that the state apparatus in these thirty years before 1848 concerned itself not less, but rather decisively more with the economic situation of its subjects than in earlier years. To be sure any broad effect by the bureaucracy, who on the whole were judicious and even eager to help, was hindered since state intervention and control of entrepreneurs would have been a contradiction to the bureaucracy's own doctrine of support for absolute industrial freedom and the self-regulation of the economy. For this reason, they employed those legal regulations hesitatingly and with a kind of inner schism when they were obliged to intervene in the free contractual relationship between employer and employee. In the struggle against the truck system in the Harz and Silesian districts it is significant that mayors, district magistrates, the provincial diets and the boards of trade (not to mention even such a respected producer of armaments as Peter Knecht, who was a personal friend of the Prussian heir) had long ago pointed out the scandalous conditions and had placed themselves on the side of the exploited. But for doctrinaire reasons the district governor of Düsseldorf and the ministers in Berlin delayed the matter and only in the months before the outbreak of the revolution did preparation begin on a law that finally, on February 9, 1849, prohibited payments in kind in Prussia. In the question of child labor, the Prussian bureaucratic state had intervened earlier and in 1839 the employment of children under nine years of age was discontinued, while the work-day of those aged nine to sixteen had been restricted to ten hours. Even though much had not been improved at all and some only as the direct result of the trade law of 1849, the beginning of industrialism and the imperiled domestic industries can only with great caution be regarded as the inciting forces of the revolution. Those affected were almost completely inactive. The population of Wuppertal, for instance, that lived under depressed conditions and was subject for an entire year to the communist propaganda of Moses Hess and Frederick Engels, proved to be unreceptive to the message of class struggle. There is explicit testimony showing that in the secret communist meetings conducted by Engels and Hess in Elberfeld there was a complete absence of the worker population.[23] In the March Days of 1848 they could not be aroused to the barricades, indeed hardly be moved to demonstrations, and not even workers of Vienna and Berlin went into the streets on their own initiative.

The only thing that perceptive contemporaries could observe in worker circles as in all other layers of society was "an obscure urge toward changed circumstances." But such a vague urge for improvement touches with its ghostly wingbeat not only those who fare badly, but—at least in the form of anxiety—also those who at the moment were well off.

Indeed it is astonishing to what extent after the mid-1840s the secret fear of a precipitous overthrow of the *status quo* sent spine-tingling chills through the ranks of the ruling classes. This evoked that veritable flood of suggestions for reform, political pamphlets, and charitable societies that were concerned with social questions around 1845. Probably here in the spiritual insecurity and pangs of conscience, in the foreboding and the shivering of the living generation, we can find the actual roots of the March events. Order which can no longer exist in good conscience is no longer order.

A world in which the giant shadow of revolution emerges is no longer a normal world. Within it all charity, all good will, all zeal for reform, and all confessions of inadequacy change nothing. This order is admittedly not necessarily consecrated to destruction; the final results of the revolution of 1848, which in a large measure confirmed anew the old order, proved this. However, such a period of insecurity and bad conscience exposes the patient to a fever which dashes through it and causes it to shiver. The crisis will be the more purifying and healthier, the less it is interrupted in its initial stages by medicinal cures. But its power is greatest as long as it still is in the offing. The threat of disease paralyses all resistance and all self-confidence of the old order. In the moment when the fever breaks through and seems to triumph, energy for action, the defiance and honor of the *ancien régime* awaken anew. Then begins the struggle between old and new, which in history has always been reconciled in favor of a diagonal line. But the historical wonder no longer exists, and the magic of the revolution is already broken. This only lasts as long as all are held under the spell of its irresistible approach.

There were many symptoms that awakened a presentiment of the inevitability of a catastrophe among contemporaries. Technology, the railroads, the masses, the lack of religious faith, the misery, the attacks upon property brought the guardians of the bourgeois-feudal social order in the German principalities into confusion. It was felt that the actual signal of the crisis, the trumpet sounding before Jericho, was an event that was almost beyond human competence and responsibility: the famine of 1847 in upper Silesia. There in the Polish territory of the Prussian eastern province, 80,000 fell ill of spotted fever and almost 16,000 perished. The acute cause was a potato disease that had continually affected crops adversely since 1845 in the whole of Germany and in the fall of 1846 had entirely deprived the impoverished rural population of its chief means of sustenance. Why precisely did this epidemic among the rural workers in this case become a crisis of public confidence for the state, the administrators, and the society? This question heads deep into the structure of the rural eastern districts and can only be understood in connection with the peasant question. What sort of impression it left behind is testified by the statement of General von Natzmer, a confidant of King Frederick William

19

IV and a typical representative of the *ancien régime* in Germany. During the preparation for a charity lottery, which was organized in Berlin to aid the famine districts, he remarked, visibly shaken, that "in the conditions of Silesia lie the seeds of a coming upheaval of existing conditions, because too much is involved."[24]

Shortly before, Silesia had been the stirring showplace of mass social misery, and also at that time the roots of the disturbance led not to the locale of the factory, but rather to the rural workers. It is obvious that the classical account by Wilhelm Wolff of the rising of the Silesian weavers in 1844 pushed agrarian conditions into the foreground. The rural spinner of yarn, the calico weaver, and the linen weaver of the Silesian mountain districts had been struggling against the fetters of their dependency since the end of the 18th century. Hereditary subjugation had actually been thrown off since St. Martin's Day, 1810, by the Stein Law. But for the majority of the cottagers, the ground rent and the payments in kind, the oats for the dogs, the tariffs on goods, the hunting payment and similar fees remained in force. The authorities, the village community, the money lender, and the state took from him in one or another form through taxes, interest, labor payments, and other dues, a full third of his paltry cash income, and he was left at most 40 Talers per year for heating, light, repairs, clothing, and education for his children. What made his condition absolutely unbearable, however, was not the advance of the machine and the industrialization of the land, but rather, on the contrary, the deficient utilization of manpower. The growth in population and the excessive supply of cheap labor, the difficulties with markets, the outmoded artisan workshops, that had almost ruined linen production and then also cotton spinning, had depressed wages for many decades. The buyers of yarn, cotton cloth, and fustian in the districts of Langenbielau and Peterswaldau at the foot of the Eulen mountains, where the disturbances broke out, offered only fifteen silver groschen for a ball on which a weaver and his entire family had to work for nine long days. Where the house weaver was in some measure tolerably treated and the traditional pay of thirty-two groschen was continued, even during the excitement of the revolt, a distribution of a supper and a small gift of money to each participant was enough to move the mob into a retreat, yes, even to shouting hurrahs for the factory owner. Only before the home of the family Zwanziger, who had accumulated an ostentatious wealth within a few years, could they no longer be held back. The household goods, the clothes and the prized coaches, the provisions and business papers were destroyed, trampled, torn apart, and scattered in the wind. A crowd of three thousand poor weavers swept like an avenging army into the neighboring village and there demolished yet a second estate. However, no manufacturer was personally mishandled, no fires were set, no bakeries were stormed, even though the mood against the grocers was no less heated than against the factory owners, and repeatedly, as in the old days, there were complaints of short weight merchandise. A few companies of soldiers quickly put down the turbulence, but the impression on contemporaries was deep and lasting. The desperation of an economic stratum who had fallen debilitated, without guilt and without protection, into the most bitter poverty, who so obviously had been given into the hands of the rich capitalists, illustrated in a singular manner the problem of "pauperism," which precisely at this time was beginning to be discussed relentlessly. Wilhelm Wolff, the unorthodox doctoral candidate in classical philology at Breslau, had already, the year before, directed attention to the miserable living quarters of the provincial capital and had founded the "society for the education of helpless proletarian children," which counts, councillors of commerce, doctors, and generals joined. In 1845 he had pronounced the revolutionary phrase directed against the tradition of two thousand years of Christian civilization: that not the more or less complete practice of charity, but only a radical transformation of the social order could create change. "The blame does not lie in the manner and style of caring for the poor, but in our entire situation. All of society to its foundation is judged and sentenced as long as any kind of 'poor relief' exists."[25]

This recognition did not grow from the wretched districts of Silesia alone. It is far more the result of theory and the tide of European events than of local experience and observation. Saint-Simon, Blanqui, Fourier, above all however their gifted German exponent Lorenz von Stein had brought a greater awareness of the rise of the proletariat with their teachings and books than had the actual conditions in Germany. The system of dialectical materialism, which Frederick Engels studied in the industrial conditions of England and Karl Marx in the course of the revolution

21

in France, had not spread during the *Vormärz* era beyond a small circle of collaborators on the *Rheinische Zeitung*. But French socialism already exerted an appreciably profound effect among the German middle class, and after 1842 the voices increased demanding a reform of politics, above all basic, preventive measures against "pauperism," against the mental and physical indigence of the masses, and the indifference of society to the distress of the disenfranchised. Friedrich Harkort, one of the most competent and open-minded entrepreneurs of the lower Rhine, had already in 1843 imploringly called for a closing of the open gulf between the haves and the have-nots through an emphasis on education of the people. "Consider the millions in England, Ireland, and France, in all of the large cities, who are prepared to set the world on fire, since they have nothing to lose, and our warning will appear justified."[26] For the sociologically backward, handicraft-Biedermeier Germany, these "millions" were at the moment certainly still a prospect of the distant future. But for men like Harkort it appeared exactly the time to act to prevent the catastrophe which had already broken out partially over the hungering rural and industrial districts of western Europe. Doubtlessly, with the prevailing political system, with the enormous expenditures for the standing army and prisons, for theater palaces and expensive court costs, with the disenfranchisement of the lower classes from all political responsibility and from all mental development, one could not handle the social questions. This recognition spread far during the *Vormärz* era into liberal circles, and it was also finally one of the driving motives behind the increasingly passionate discussions about the Prussian and the German constitutional question.[27]

One must, in conclusion, again emphasize that only as an ideology did the social causes of the revolution gain importance. Not the state of social distress itself, but rather the penetration of an awareness that distress existed had a revolutionary effect. And this realization of a social problem did not first move those affected, but the observers. Wherever a political-radical tendency is noticeable in artisan and journeymen societies, in gymnastic groups and reading circles during the 1840s, it was bourgeois intellectuals, journalists and lawyers, former theologians and book dealers, that lit the fire. Democracy was not a demand of the working class, rather the social question was an essential part of bourgeois democracy.

The number of journeymen and artisan masters or even of factory and agricultural workers who were involved in an active criticism of the existing conditions was very small. We almost know them all by name or can find their traces in the lists made by the police during the *Vormärz* era, who got the subscription lists of the notorious newspapers from the small post offices, from which they knew precisely the members of the secret cells of the opposition. If one seeks the anonymous masses who subterraneanly determined events between 1815 and 1848, then one must seek them less in the industrial circles and much more among the peasant class. There a social ferment had indeed accumulated, originating in specifically German conditions, based on outdated abuses, which the enlightened bourgeois authoritarian state with a Josephist imprint had failed to solve.

II

THE PEASANT QUESTION

At mid-century a full two-thirds of Germany's population, in Prussia even as much as four-fifths, was still employed in agriculture. The remaining third was divided among craft trades, factory work, commerce, professions, officials, and domestic service. Germany could justifiably be described as an agrarian country, and the social conditions on the land were the foundations of German life.

The great question that occupied all the states of civilized Europe as far as Russia from the second half of the 18th century to the mid 19th century was the great process of peasant emancipation. This dismantling of feudal conditions in the west had also begun long before in some way or another in the individual German territories, partly through the example of the crown lands administration, partly by legislation, partly through free agreements between lord and peasant. This gradual and many-sided movement in the feudal eastern territories before 1848 was carried out more systematically and produced more historical agitation than in the western and southern feudal areas where conditions were more tenacious and the contrasts between lord and copy holder more concealed. The burdens that fell on the peasant class were very likely for that reason found on the west side of the Elbe to be more oppressive, because the peasants were more aware, and the nobility and feudal authorities no longer functioned as the governing power. The rural population, who had already been somewhat influenced by thoughts of citizenship, could not understand why they should remain "subjects of subjects" after Napoleon Bonaparte had already fortunately mediatized the dwarf states. The struggle over the extent and the legal foundation of various duties and historically stipulated obligations was therefore carried out with more bitterness in southern Germany than in the districts of patrimonial manorial domains, where the proprietor of 1200 estates still universally enjoyed a reverential authority as police, judge and jury, as village lord and patron.

The rural revolution did not break out in 1848 in the districts that lagged behind in granting rights to peasants, but rather where the community constitution and citizenship privileges were greatly modernized and hence the discord between political rights and agricultural dependence was most pronounced.

Peasant liberation originated not only in the new challenge of human rights, which the Enlightenment had popularized, whereby every individual demanded personal freedom, safety of property, and the joint responsibility for the community, rather it also corresponded to modern economic views and agrarian policy, which had been introduced from England, especially in the regions of manorial estates of eastern Germany. It had been discovered that a man managed the land more profitably and more efficiently when he strove for the condition of free wage and labor, than when he performed his plowing and manual labors against his will and in the old manner with crude implements. So the capitalistic tendency reinforced the legal development. Since the dissolution of the old situation of forced labor was joined with many advantages of a more intensive use of the nobility's estates, the eastern landlords, who were proficient in business matters and managed their property themselves, struggled less against the changes than the patriarchal noblemen in the south-west, who lived from revenues and held with greater tenacity to outmoded historical rights. It also could be observed that the rural population threw themselves with rare eagerness into their new slavery as free wage laborers, because they saw only what they gained and not what they lost and exchanged for very questionable progress; because from an economic standpoint, this improvement actually consisted of deeper penetration by capitalistic business methods into the rural labor situation.

The legal emancipation of the peasant class occurred in three stages and in three different directions: first, the abolition of hereditary servility, which meant the personal liberation of the serf, who until now had been tied to the soil; second, the improvement of the peasants' property rights, meaning the surrender of the full property rights in return for proper compensation in money or land; third, the elimination of labor obligations (*Fron* or *Robot*) and the simplification or abolishment of tributes (produce or money). Without a doubt this development meant radical improvement for those middle-sized farmsteads (in Prussia amounting to about fifty *Morgen* and up), equipped with draught animals and a horse-drawn vehicle. If the newly independent peasants, after paying for their emancipation in land or money, summoned up the economic strength to endure free competition with the large agricultural enterprises, they had survived the worst, and in many districts they enjoyed a prosperous and satisfying existence. The goal attempted by the far-sighted, conservative agricultural policy of men like Stein, Vincke, and Stüve was largely attained, and a strong, self-confident and stable agricultural middle class was created which supported the state. For the smaller farms, however, the loss of the old patriarchal situation very frequently became a disastrous forfeiture. The charity in hard times, the prescribed reduction of taxes in bad harvest years, the obligation of the lord of the manor to furnish his bondsmen with seed corn and alms, the protection from attachment and being bought out, state protection from confiscation of peasant lands as estate property: all this henceforth ceased. Where emancipation was carried out, the former small tenant (*Fronbauer*) sank to the level of day laborer, because he could no longer maintain himself on his diminished holdings. The lord of the manor became the employer, the contract was drawn up for a year or a sequence of years. The agricultural worker retained, as before, a piece of land and the allotted dwelling, perhaps with the right to graze a cow on the pasture, but he could not have more than an acre of field land and another acre for a garden, because he was not to exist from his own farming, but rather he was to be dependent on wages from work on the large estate. The motivation was not an evil desire for domination, but an economic necessity as long as the conditions on the estates remained unchanged, and this solution was therefore recommended by well-informed reformers like Thaer and Sack even before the decrees of Hardenberg.[28] Otherwise where should the establishment get its work force after the peasants' feudal obligations of transport, road making, harvesting and threshing were abolished? The safest and healthiest answer was still the settlement of field hands as crofters or "*Insten*," who received modest acreage as partial payment and otherwise worked with their entire families as day laborers on the estate. Often the lord of the manor had an obligation to find jobs for the emancipated rural workers to protect them from unemployment and the loss of wages. From a social standpoint this newly created class of cottars or crofters (*Insten*) was worse off than the copy holder with a small and entailed holding, which nevertheless still was private property, but economically they lived in a more tolerable position than the deeply indebted serf who had to obtain a draught team and menial workers in order to fulfill his feudal obligations. According to an inquiry made by the Prussian state economic board in 1848,[29] those day laborers dependent but securely settled on the estate were in a better position than the "cottager" or "colonist," who had rescued a tiny piece of land from the emancipation period, but who could not live off its proceeds and sometimes had to seek other sources of income. Above all the cottagers (*Instleute*) were in a far better situation than the third category of agricultural laborer, the renters or hirelings (*Einlieger* or *Heuerlinge*), who enjoyed neither fixed terms of employment nor property rights. These so-called "independent" rural workers usually maintained only a marginal existence, and they were exposed to a precarious life which assumed catastrophic forms during periods of scarcity. In the Rhineland they suffered frequently from lack of work. In the east, where workers were constantly in short supply in the 19th century too, their income varied considerably with the season and business conditions.

It was in the nature of things that the enormous population growth noticeable throughout Europe after 1780 and persisting in rural districts until the March revolution, almost without exception caused growth in the lowest class of rural renters, since relatively few were drawn off by emigration abroad and into cities. In 1785, around 200 peasants and 360 cottagers lived in the sixteen villages in the district of Wollmirstedt. In 1842 there were 203 peasants compared to 320 cottagers, which shows even a slight decrease in the established land-owning element. In their place, by 1842, 984 renters, who did not even exist as a category fifty years before, lived in the sixteen villages.[30] The historical development of the population thus worked toward the evolution of a rural proletariat. In some places the members of this unfortunate social layer were

27

called "anxiety workers" ("*Angstarbeiter*") because they had to be concerned from month to month with work assignments, and as contracted day laborers without a piece of land, they enjoyed neither the advantages of serfdom nor the advantages of freedom. The legal and economic circumstances accompanying peasant liberation supported this sinister trend of the increased rural population. After the regulation of landed property, which the Stein reforms introduced into Prussia, the division of the formerly dependent peasantry into an autonomous middle class and a homeless proletariat was unavoidable, and it is to a great extent naive to blame this merely on the mistakes of legislators like Hardenberg. Certain groups of this peasant class, who were caught between the rural middle class and the agricultural proletariat, and who could not go backwards nor forwards, strata which had become neither entirely free peasants nor entirely free rural workers, played a similar role in the agrarian sector to that of the artisan journeyman in the industrial realm, standing between master and factory worker. They became above all the source of social disturbance and discontent, bacteria of a transitional period, which decomposed the social order by announcing demands which cannot be defined as being bound more to the future or to the past.

However, those who comprised the lowest rung of the social ladder in the open country, the *Instleute*, day laborers, and casual workers, were nowhere the cause of disturbances during 1848: instead they held back exactly like the unskilled factory workers during the revolutionary period. Silesia offers a noteworthy example of this. The day laborers and Polish rural workers in upper Silesia, who shortly before had experienced a typhoid epidemic which provoked the compassion of physicians and publicists throughout the world, remained quiet in 1848. The spinners and weavers of middle Silesia, who four years previous to 1848 drew the attention of the entire middle class through their uprisings, did not take part in the March Revolution. In their place the well-off peasants of lower Silesia, the rich millers, innkeepers, and "rustical proprietors" from the fertile districts of Leignitz and Glogau seized the flag of insurrection. The vassals of Count Schaffgotsch, the peasants of the Hirschberg Valley, the *Dreschgärtner* of German districts in upper Silesia joined the revolution and demanded a new hunting law, a new law on encumbrances, the elimination of the manorial

28

jurisdiction, and a constitution for the peasant community. Nearly everywhere the insurgents were prosperous peasants and village mayors.[31] The decisive agrarian demands of the Forty-eight revolution were requests of the peasant middle class. These were for the completion of peasant emancipation, which had come to a standstill halfway. But among them are hardly any demands which reveal the monstrous weight of the question of rural labor.

The most inflammable situation was in Silesia, because the peasant emancipation had not been carried out there, in contrast to the old Prussian provinces, and the process of regulation and redemption was checked by all sorts of limitations. In this part of the country only a quarter of the peasants possessing draught teams had reached satisfactory settlements of their property rights by 1848.[32] Others felt cheated by the discharge of services and taxes, or they were excluded, to their disadvantage, from the use of forest and meadows. Reasons for dissatisfaction existed sufficiently not only in Prussia, but also in Austria, in middle Germany, and in the south-west German states: comparison with a more fortunate neighbor, complaints about the hardship caused by high payments, taxes, fees, and tithes.[33] The peasants of middle and south Germany were brought to an obstinate, insubordinate, and rebellious condition through one or more of many problems: the poor availability of credit, general circumstances, the splintering of lands through hereditary division, the lack of feed and bedding straw for cattle-breeding, the bad harvest years, and the running of errands and humiliating work on the roads under the supervision of the game warden. Even in the years before 1848 it was clear that the districts outside of Prussia lacked a clear discharge law for the various feudal dues, tithes, and payments, and that the peasants would not be internally placated until the hunting privileges and the nobility's freedom from paying taxes were eliminated. This exemption of large landholders from property taxes, which in Prussia had been traditional only in the provinces of Brandenburg and Pomerania, was perhaps the most offensive privilege that the new age would abolish. It was contested not only because of envy, but also for the sake of justice, a concern which had run in the blood of the peasants for centuries.

Social differences in the country were definitely felt far more intensely than in cities. The "serving class" and the ruling class faced one another very blatantly and clearly. Although the descriptions of the contrasts between life styles in huts and palaces may be exaggerated in some accounts, and regions did exist where the noble lords even shared their passion for the hunt and hunting rights with the artisans and innkeepers from their villages,[34] it has been confirmed by many witnesses that small local tyrants were accustomed to reaching for a club when their "people" did not obey them. One has an idea of the echo that must have been generated in the age of *Biedermeier* humanitarianism by an account like that traced out by Wilhelm Wolff in his pamphlet, "The Silesian Billions." The son of a Silesian cottager, who through great sacrifice and privation became a student and tutor in Breslau, describes with great bitterness from his own youth the conduct of noble Junkers and men of rank who were more concerned with the brooding nests of their pheasants than with the human dignity of their peasants. "From the garden the pheasants spread far into the woods and sought nesting places. Woe to the woman or maid who rashly came too close to such a nide and disturbed the hen! If the lord or his huntsman caught sight of her, the memory of noble pheasants would remain with her for life. We ourselves in our youth witnessed how a young robber knight, serving as an apprentice in land management to another high noble, cultivating inherent noble passion, for this reason brutally abused a peasant woman and crippled her without being troubled by anyone. They were poor people, and to complain meant a lawsuit, which cost money, and also called for some trust in justice. . . . "[35]

Trust in the justice of the ruling governmental circles and the current methods of government was shaken not only among the poor people, but even more vividly and stubbornly among the politically-minded men of the bourgeois middle class, and this crisis of confidence became the actual cause of the revolution. It was a belated settlement of accounts of the bourgeoisie with the traditions and ramifications of princely absolutism and was therefore by no means a social, but a political movement.

III

THE BOURGEOIS OPPOSITION

As the March wind of 1848 swept through the underbrush of the old state and cleared the soil for a new beginning, the aversion old Germany had provoked for the past thirty years among her neighbors was actually exposed for the first time. Even though the German people had fought, during the Napoleonic wars, side by side with the freedom-loving countries of Europe and was accordingly respected, a generation of political standstill since the Carlsbad Decrees was sufficient to close Germany out of the western European community of political ideas. In the Swiss press above all, on the occasion of the upheaval in Germany at the end of this period, a repugnance, a contempt, and a moral-political judgment of rejection now came to the surface, showing an alarming degree of alienation. The liberal *Appenzeller Zeitung* wrote after the victory of the March Revolution in Berlin, half encouraging, half deprecating: "until now it was thought that this people was made up of 'lackeys, parasites of the state, poets, intellectuals, philosophers and slow-witted beer-drinking types (*Biermichel*).' Now, to our delight, we are instructed otherwise."[36] The world of the German Confederation was for the politically enlightened and progressively inclined bourgeoisie in the west, who already enjoyed either a republican government or a constitutional regime, an incomprehensible dark spot, a backwater of reaction, in which, strangely enough, the cradle of the systematic and historical sciences existed, but which otherwise was a place where perfidious princes and dissolute dancers, narrow-minded bureaucrats and prodigal courtiers carried on their frivolous game, in which foreign policy was directed according to Russian instructions and private life was

31

examined by Metternich's spies, in which justice was always obse-
quious and the police without shame, in which the press was muzzled
and free expression of opinion was prosecuted, in which excessive
taxes were levied for a standing army, yet no constitution offered
protection from the arbitrariness of power, and people had not
even managed to throw off the feudal bonds.

This portrait of Metternich's Germany was, as we know today,
exaggerated in several respects and did justice neither to the intentions of the great European statesmen nor to the conditions in
numerous individual German states. Certainly political life in both
Prussia and Austria was entirely suppressed, and elsewhere, where
constitutions were permitted, it had also been in a desperate state
since 1830. The censorship and control of the mails was almost
as base and cynical as in Russia, where the Grand Duke Constantine
possessed a choice collection of confiscated letters, that he had
bound in leather and exhibited in his private library as piquant
reading matter. But no one who investigated the state administration
could deny the trustworthiness and prosperity among the unpolitical
subjects, the honesty and integrity of the average civil servant,
his technical qualifications and unprejudiced selection. Men like
the father of Prussian industrial policy, Privy Councillor Beuth,
and reformers like Finance Minister Motz or President von Schön
had few peers among European administrators.[37] And when in
Wurtemberg the autocratic Minister von Schleyer, son of a Tübingen
petty bourgeois, who had worked his way up to the highest post
in the country, explained at every opportunity that the land had
never known such wonderful times, the leader of the opposition
could not contradict him.[38] Even Electoral Hesse could call itself
a law-respecting state (*Rechtsstaat*), in spite of all the constitutional
controversy and court scandals, because it had a secure group of
civil servants, and measures of the administration could be disputed
in carefully constructed judicial proceedings.[39]

The picture of the Metternich era, as liberal public opinion liked
to depict it, was seen from the outside and without an understanding
for Germany's particular historical development which, toward the
end of the 18th century, had not led this solitary land from the
common level of continental absolutism into a class or egalitarian
revolution, but rather into the dead end of enlightened despotism.
This political system of humanitarian princely service had once

inspired the admiration of Europe; now, in rapidly changing times, it no longer pleased anyone, and the Germans themselves continued to suffer under it, since they could not find a suitable alternative. The situation was stagnated by the remarkable characteristic of Germans which Karl Friedrich Moser criticized long before the outbreak of the French Revolution: "Every nation has its great motivation: in Germany it is obedience, in England—freedom, in Holland—trade, in France—the honor of the kings."[40] The inclination toward obedience in the low and high ethical sense of the word, the habit of accepting all directives coming from a superior who possessed more insight, a greater general grasp of the situation and more responsibility, had driven deep roots into the German consciousness through experience and fate, by teaching and custom. This internal dependence on a strong command had not merely hindered the over-due revolution for decades, but also in 1848 prevented a real counter-revolution from arising. The officers and civil servants, the Junkers and nobles, the peasants and soldiers waited in vain in the early months of 1848 for the clear word of a legitimate king to sacrifice themselves for the royal cause. That it did not occur or only occurred when the *élan* of the revolution was already exhausted meant that a cleansing crisis in the epochal year of German national history never took place. The antitheses of revolution and counter-revolution smoldered worse than before under the cover of the quickly restored order.

During the thirty years from the Carlsbad Decrees until Metternich's fall, opposition to the rulers grew even in Germany, setting a goal of the conquest of absolutism and the feudal social structure. How strong this opposition had secretly grown was first actually realized when, to general astonishment, the throne suddenly began to totter and the opposition itself had to help prop it back up. Within this body of subjects, until 1848, those factors which other more politically progressive lands had already differentiated according to parties and philosophies, remained an undivided whole. Democratic and liberal tendencies, republican and class motives, enlightened and romantic concepts, arguments of proponents of free trade and the guilds merged with one another. Men of conservative leanings were forced to associate themselves with the liberals to be distinguishable from the officials of the governing party, and the students of Rousseau were often hardly discernible from the

33

liberal adherents of Burke, who strove for the existence of a historically established parliamentarism. Without the multitude of foreign
prototypes, the development of political thinking in the German
restoration era was inconceivable. But this profusion is also intimately connected to the disunity among the German opposition.
They learned from the pure democracy of Switzerland and from
the constitutional doctrine of Benjamin Constant, they took up
Mirabeau, Sieyès, and the texts of the Great Revolution, and above
all the German theoreticians of liberalism derived essential characteristics of their political doctrine from the Belgian constitution
of 1831 and from the rich source of English constitutional history.
Very little was entirely original, but in several instances solid bases
for development are visible, and an astounding wealth of political
ideas spread throughout a cross section from Constance to Königsberg.

The liberals of Baden and East Prussia were mostly committed
to abstract theories. In this case, the intellectual-historical connection with the Enlightenment was the driving force, with Rotteck
and Schlosser on one side and Kant on the other. The Palatinate
and Rhine Hesse felt the aftereffects of the radical current of the
Giessen "Blacks"—of Follen, Büchner, and Weidig. It is here that
the Jacobin strains, the idea of the omnipotent communal state
and the desire for social equality were first heard in Germany.
In Nassau and Electoral Hesse, administrative liberalism was more
usual, which mainly struggled for a constitutional state (*Rechtsstaat*)
and an independent court of justice. It represented the belief that
the right of the people to resist was sufficiently protected by a
chamber of notables and a law granting them the right to approve
taxes. In Swabia and Westphalia the roots of the liberal tree were
buried deepest in the native soil. The resistance to absolutism in
old Wurtemberg reached back to the representative assembly of
the 18th century, and the dualism between rulers and ruled lay
deep in the blood of the Swabian burghers. Moreover, the struggle
of Uhland and his friends for the good old law of country-wide
representation had no bias toward wealth. Like old Jahn, Uhland
the romantic was also an advocate of the poorer orders, the common
man and the modest artisan, who still possessed enough of the
unspoiled, honest intelligence, the straightforwardness and willingness to sacrifice, the customs of their forefathers and the peasant

experience, to find the right way in the concerns of the community. This romantic democracy of Uhland,[41] which expected from the simple people, who had grown up believing in estates, the same creativeness in political matters that, according to romantic theory, it had shown in tales and folk songs, of course, may not have much more to do with modern mass democracy than a common name; and its forming a front against autocracy, bureaucracy and aristocracy has acquired another meaning in the sociological reality of the modern territorial state. Already in the ideological duel during the *Vormärz* era, this antiquated opposition to the triumphant march of the thoroughly organized administrative state, to centralism and absolutism, to secretaries and councils was somewhat backward and romantic (as Hegel once correctly rebuked). But it betrayed at the same time so much inextinguishable, healthy civil sensitivity, so much pride in man and in the independent dignity of the clan that one would like to overlook the lack of insight and tactical skill in their political daily work. Uhland's Swabian associates in the struggle, Paul Pfizer and Friedrich Römer above all, men of the highest competence, were soon pushed in another direction by the existing conditions. As young men they found their way to the Prussian intellectual state and later all too quickly to liberal ministerial absolutism. The poet himself really felt little impetus to step down into the arena of parliamentary struggles and take part in the tedious proceedings of the chamber "with good grace," (even in the St. Paul's Church), after the delightful moment of the first impulse was over. He admits himself that he did not have the disposition of a professional politician, as he started to train himself to be, considering it unavoidable in the *Vormärz* era— "only as a volunteer, as a citizen, as one of the people, did I enter into it."[42] So for several reasons this conservative Swabian people's democracy was unable to establish itself more firmly, although it perhaps might have shown an organic path from the smallest to the greater and greatest community.

The teachers of self-government and self-administration had greater success in Westphalia and in lower Saxony. Here it was the prosperous landowners and *Landrats*, factory directors and mayors, business men and city fathers, not men of letters, professors and poets, that proposed the attack on the authoritarian state. Even a figure like the old Friedrich Harkort in Wetter on the

Ruhr, the active industrialist and headstrong social reformer, who as early as 1825 pushed for the building of railways and in 1837 sent the first Cologne Rhine steamer to London, was similar to Uhland in his belief in the "healthy sense" of the people. But he wished to develop and to educate them, and in this sense, he wanted to reform the elementary schools and have better elementary teachers hired. He wanted to spread political education in a rational way and to cause a breakthrough of the humanitarian spirit of the age. Exactly like Baron vom Stein, he was convinced that "An enlightened people aware of the needs and conditions of the state develops a greater public spirit, is less likely to be agitated, obeys the law more spontaneously than a tumultuous, raw mass."[43] For this passionate protagonist of state reform from the top down, the spirit of competition and the spirit of association, the liberal and social ideas of the times, were something thoroughly conciliatory, never antithetical. The thought of a revolution was abominable to him; never had he considered anything else for the Prussian monarchy than a thoroughgoing reform. He did not wish to create a constitution from the top down, through a limitation on the power of the king and a supervision of the bureaucracy, but rather from below by the creation of more healthy rural and urban working conditions. "Honor must be united with work," and one must be able to acquire property through labor. The land was to be divided so that every peasant family procured its share, which it could cultivate with its own strength. The industrial worker would be guaranteed the free development of his talents. His dwelling must be provided in the country, and comfortable conditions for transportation created for him. Organizations for mutual support must be formed, and those sharing in the work should also share in the profits of capital. Above all the children of the poor must be given back their right to a youth: play, joy, friends, knowledge, and freedom. Then out of a spirit of self-help and fraternity, from the dignity of work and from the cooperation of workers at all levels, a citizens' state of Germany would rise that would be able to breed a satisfied people.

Such a profound social program was infrequent in the liberalism of the *Vormärz* era. One feared any proximity to the socialist utopias that were introduced from France and England; this was particularly true in north-west Germany, which was very sensitive to everything abstract and removed from life, all that was imaginary and without a solid foundation. Experienced liberal fighters like the Westphalian Baron Georg von Vinke or the patrician of Osnabrück, Karl Stüve, who behaved incomparably courageously, the one in the United Landtag of 1847, the other in the constitutional struggle in Hanover of 1837, professed openly a philosophy of historical law, aristocracy, the land, and everything established and existing. Stüve was even mistrustful of the lack of constraint in absolute freedom of the press and, in spite of his intense struggles, preferred not to allow it without limitations. Vincke was in every fiber a born aristocrat, who scorned seeking political power for everyone. But he held it a chivalric duty on every occasion to step in to protect the poor and the weak, as expressed in the old meaning of the word "representation." Both of these, the most famous statesmen north-west German liberalism produced, were convinced that the self-government of the nation originated in the village communities and the cities, that the communities needed their own finances and their own police to exist. The duties on land had to be dissolved, the taxes divided equally, and the village mayors must be freely elected before it made sense to discuss a constitution. But they never forgot for a moment that a submissive people cannot be made politically mature by having its interests limited to municipal accounts, the acquisition of fire engines, and the installation of fountains.[44] Germany in general and every territorial state in particular had to become a constitutional state. This constitution should not be based on social orders, that is, founded on the old class-structured privileges, rather it must become representative, the governed must take part in free and secret elections. Only such an active participation by those who were previously just subjects of the legislation of the state could annul the tutelage, which in wide circles was increasingly recognized as a disgrace.

In north German territory it was the Rhineland where this sentiment was most widespread and was dictated with the greatest impatience by the economic developments. Here the consciousness of the bourgeoisie approached a level among the industrialists, bankers, merchants, and ship owners that was already an established tradition among the free Hanseatic cities. They felt, as free citizens of a rich city, more than equal in birth to the servants of emperors, kings, and princes, and demanded a role in the government that

37

this social self-estimation implied.[45] Without a doubt, until the calling of the United Landtag in 1847, the forms of criticism and struggle in Rhine-Prussia were much more confined than in states which already possessed a constitution and a central house of deputies. Men like Camphausen, Hansemann, and above all the industrialist Mevissen were able to assert themselves more strongly in public only in the last years before the outbreak of the revolution. But even at the end of 1830, the businessman Hansemann could present the King of Prussia in Aachen with a petition in which he earnestly noted that one could not artificially maintain or reestablish by laws or decrees a social order which was dissolving as a result of the development of a bourgeois society.[46]

But it was not this attack by industry and trade against the state of 12,000 manorial estates which led liberalism to victory, but rather a united front of ideologists, the theoreticians of the constitutional rule of law. Indisputably, the voices of the universities, the leaders of the student associations, and especially the numerous professors found an older and wider response than the Rhineland businessmen, in spite of all the problems of censorship and police chicanery. As spokesmen for a national citizenry and at the same time the unity of Germany, they demanded a proper participation of the middle class in the construction of political life. The unison of political objectives and journalistic methods was most advanced among lawyers and national economists, historians and literature professors all over Germany. The historian of both west European revolutions, Friedrich Christoph Dahlmann, drafted an abstract for their political doctrine. His unfinished work of 1835, "Politics traced back to the foundation and dimension of existing conditions" (*Die Politik auf den Grund und das Mass der gegebenen Zustände zurückgeführt*), outlined in unforgettable, pensive sentences, inspired by Hegel and Burke, the fundamental ideas: the concept of royal sovereignty, the character of the social orders in the empire, the right to resistance, the freedom of the individual responsible only to God, the historical dynamic of the constitutional idea. "The mission is to establish the state in the consciousness of the people" (*Die Aufgabe ist, den Staat im Volksbewusstsein zu vollenden*): that was the Hegelian watchword of the *Vormärz*, the inheritance of the reform period, which old liberalism continued and which, in the general consciousness, became a higher, idealistic faith in progress. Certainly the local color of leading localities and cadres was distinguishable everywhere. Dahlmann and Sybel in Bonn, Haym and his circle in Halle, Droysen and Beseler in Kiel, Häusser and Gervinus in Heidelberg, Fallati and Mohl in Tübingen had maintained their own respective political tones. The attempt at a collection of all "good patriots," the fusion of proponents of the liberal idea from Aachen to Königsberg and from Kiel to Passau ensued from this direction. It was called for by the organ of professorial liberalism, the *Deutsche Zeitung* of Gervinus and Mittermaier. But they never succeeded in shaping all these individuals into an ordered platoon, and to the majority of these learned politicians, the transition from academic study to journalism, from the office desk to parliament, remained all their lives a sacrifice to patriotic idealism, never to an elementary will for power.

The patriotic striving of the liberals of the *Vormärz* era could never separate the question of Germany unity from the question of a German constitution, and the German constitutional question was intimately tied to the state of domestic political life in the individual territories. Also the question of unity was decisively ripe for a revolution. The German national consciousness was, if not awakened by the expansionist policy of the Napoleonic French Empire and the counter-blow of the Great Coalition, at least immensely stimulated. It had received a lesson, in the mobilization of popular powers by the Jacobin vigilance committee and its conduct of total war, which was deeply understood at least by the men of the Prussian uprising, by Scharnhorst, Gneisenau, Clausewitz, by Jahn, Arndt, and Friesen. Under various forms and refractions they continued this militant nationalism of the Napoleonic period during the years of peace after 1815. Men like Blücher, Clausewitz, or Stein from the beginning did not agree with the intellectual movement among the gymnastic societies (*Turnerschaften*) and the college student associations, and they placed themselves on the side of Metternich's authoritarian government. It was not the standing army and the reactionary circles which had created the sensitivity of the national feeling of honor and a passion for national borders; rather it was the liberal echo of the wars of liberation and the institution of a reserve army (*Landwehr*); it was (as in France) a vulgarized romanticism and a popular late idealism that was also grist for the mill of the national state idea in Germany. Experiences like the bellicose speech of Thiers in 1840, the common moments of celebration like the Reformation day, the anniversary of printing and the Cologne cathedral festival, the conventions of the gymnastic and singing societies, the gatherings of scientists, the congresses of south and middle German opposition deputies of the people in Hattersheim (1839), Hallgarten, Leipzig, and Heppenheim (1847) contributed to increasing and keeping alive the aspiration for alliance of all Germans. The stagnation of the German constitution and the impediment to any organic reform because of Habsburg interest of state; the unintelligible borders of the German sovereignty and the overlapping of state and national borders in Luxemburg and Holland, in Silesia and Posen, in Bohemia and Croatia; the limited economic unity, the internal tariff barriers, the anarchy in weights and measures, the variety of legal codes and the lack of freedom of movement; the dependency of German safety on the good will of both major powers and the neglect of Germany's military state; the realization of the lack of a fleet, of a colonial policy, of protection for German merchants overseas; the stream of German emigrants to the United States without any guidance or spokesman; above all the subordination of the dynasties in Berlin and Vienna to preemptory orders of the Tsar and the absence of Germany among the Great Powers: all of this, individually and as a whole, in combination with the powerful European tide of events, which was also felt with great sympathy in Spain and Italy, in Denmark and Poland, in Hungary and Greece, had to generate the need for political consolidation and national integration among the politically awakened Germans. It was plainly the liberals, the men of the political opposition, who upheld this new German nationalism; like the liberals in Poland and Italy, they stepped forward as martyrs to the national idea. The poet of the German anthem, which was written in 1841, was a free-thinking German literature scholar who lost his post as professor in Breslau a year later because of his progressive political beliefs.

There is no mistaking that in the 1840s the national idea did in some cases take on a pan-German flavor. Fiery apostles of the *Zeitgeist* like List and Harkort called attention to the mouth of the Danube and the German settlements in Wallachia. The *Augsburger Allgemeine Zeitung*, whose *grossdeutsch** inclination was

---

*grossdeutsch: German state including Austria, as opposed to *kleindeutsch* solution which excluded Austria from Germany.

clearly directed against Prussia, published articles discussing a loose association of Holland, Denmark, and Switzerland, even the "Celtic-German Belgians," with the German Confederation. An exaggerated, nervous importance was ascribed to the thought of a two-front war with France and Russia. And the comprehensive ideas of a middle European federation of Frederick William IV and his advisor von Radowitz assisted this sort of expansionistic movement, which was widely circulated in Austria by a rather extensive journalistic network.[47] The more closely the moderate liberals adhered to a *kleindeutsch*-Prussian nucleus for their future national state, the more they were immune in general to such extravagances of phantasy. Not through expansion, but only by consolidation into a solid political substance could all German difficulties be overcome. There were men, and not only from the left wing of the progressive party, who comprehended that the principle of national autonomy also brought obligations. They removed themselves from "the darkness and selfishness of the Teutomaniacs" (Varnhagen), and became familiar with the idea that a victory of this principle in Europe would mean as much sacrifice as profit for the people in the middle. It was impossible for one to wish to retain the Poles, the Czechs, and the Italians as involuntary members of the Reich, while at the same time demanding self-determination for the Germans in Schleswig, in south Tyrol, and in German Austria. "Europe reconstructed according to nationalities, everything foreign will fall away; if we could regain everything German, we would be richly compensated": thus Helmut von Moltke summarized the liberal credo at the moment of the March Revolution.[48] We have no reason to doubt the honesty of this avowal. Only as in Posen and Prague the concrete national political responsibilities dramatically piled up did intellectuals begin to disagree, and even in far-left circles doubts were expressed that fanaticism for justice favoring the foreign peoples long established within the Reich might not be a misjustice against the safety of one's own people.[49]

The idea of the national state in general should not be condemned from such historical inconsistencies. What was right for other peoples also had to appear equitable for Germany. Public opinion also demanded for the German nation a united state capable of performing legal acts, in which economic life could be carried on without restraint and the sovereignty of the people could be respected abroad. They wanted finally to overtake the advantage that England, France, and Spain had already won three centuries before. The *Ancien Régime*, that the liberal wished to clear away with reform and that the democrats wanted to fight with fire and sword if necessary, had not been created by the Vienna Acts of Confederation and the Treaties of 1815, but dated from 1648 and the Treaties of Westphalia. Down with Metternich! That meant at the same time: down with Münster and Osnabrück, down with a subtilized system devised manifestly only to the Germans' disadvantage of the balance of power between Habsburg and Brandenburg, between emperor and empire, between Protestant and Catholic territories. Germany set to work to overcome the results of the Thirty Years' War in the field of political formation a hundred years after the initiation of efforts towards healing the economic and spiritual scars of that catastrophe. If the foreign powers identified themselves with the political system of the greatest defeat in the history of Germany, then they inevitably had to collide with a national revolutionary energy. The first alarm for the politicizing of the liberal middle class in Germany was, according to the testimony of the entirely unpolitical Rudolf Haym, the defiance of national feeling and connections between peoples by a dynastic law of succession to the Danish crown in the Schleswig-Holstein affair.[50]

In spite of this, it is false to trace the cause for the outbreak of the March revolution back to goals of foreign or national policy held by German intellectuals, as a recent English presentation attempted.[51] What caused a deep and apparently implacable rage against the police and military state in this *Vormärz* generation was constant petty pestering by the gendarmes and border officials, the secretaries and the bureaucrats who harassed individuals and victimized trade and traffic. Because the arbitrary action of the lower and higher police authorities especially touched the itinerant craft journeymen and students, these two groups of the population were the real pioneers of the revolution. However, what bore down on all citizens without distinction was the disgrace of constraint. This was called to mind daily by the blanked passages of the censor in the newspaper, by the never-ending measures of conscientious state officials and teachers, by the struggle between state constitution

42

and the Diet legislation over the exercise of censorship. The milestones on the road to civil war were the great court trials of Friedrich List in Wurtemberg, of Rector Weidig in Darmstadt, of Sylvester Jordan in Electoral Hesse, of Eisenmann in Würzburg, of Jacoby in Prussia. The heaviest grievance of the nation was and remained the suppression of the freedom of expression. In terms of numbers there were actually not so many, a few hundred perhaps, that sat in prisons or were involved in degrading trials. But they were all known, and their cause was taken to everyone's heart. If Austria and Prussia, the German Confederation as a whole had allowed public opinion free expression, then, from all that we know, Germans would not have relinquished the path of peaceful reform.[52] However, the reckless handling of constraints on opinion allowed a ferment to grow in the German states that sooner or later threatened to find its solution by violent means. Curiously, a pacification again materialized after the impassioned beginning of the year 1847, when the convening of the United Landtag in Prussia and its disappointing conclusion caused the heaviest strain on internal political life since Sand's assassination of Kotzebue. Even the economic crisis of the year, which had sent a horde of beggars and unemployed into the streets, had not led to an explosion.[53] Admittedly the situation in the spring of 1847 was unsettling for a time. In Berlin, in Stuttgart, in Ulm, in nearly every large city there were bread riots, broken windows, cannon drawn up, barricades, bayonet attacks, wounded and dead among the demonstrating masses. But the majority of the petty bourgeois residents placed themselves on the side of the forces of order and did not resent the flow of blood. As far as they were able, the public and municipal administrations took pains to mitigate the existing privation, and these exertions were generally appreciated. The half-measures of the governments were less easily forgiven, especially the half-measures of a romantic king toward whom Germany had looked with hope for years. The scrambling change of ministers, the mistaken or intentionally misdirected concessions of the monarch, generously bestowed and autocratically withdrawn rights created in the period of the United Landtag an atmosphere of discontent and mistrust that could lead one to fear the worst. But the storm ebbed almost completely; people returned to their accustomed edifying or romantic reading and in the following winter, even at the princely courts,

43

they enjoyed the mild political jokes of the Munich leaflets. By the end of the year 1847 public agitation came to an almost complete standstill. The social concerns were far less ardent than in 1844 and 1845. The demands of the peasants had remained the same for decades, and the points in the liberal program were not intensified.

The sparks of the revolution ultimately fell unexpectedly and suddenly on a bourgeois world which certainly long ago had come to a sort of silent agreement on the desirable demands, but had increasingly pushed the radical outsider to the side and avoided any climax. In north and south, men were united on a program that essentially called for plentiful reform but did not mean an actual revolution. The damages caused by the bureaucratic authoritarian state were acutely realized: the social climbing and obstinacy, the caste spirit and the hollow smugness of the state officials, the stupidity and mania for detail (*Rechenhaftigkeit*) of the machinery of state, the surveillance and snooping in opinions of cultural life. All men of good will agreed on what was needed: freedom of the press and a popular suffrage law, elimination of the pen-pushers, and a clear division between justice and the administration, the emancipation of the land from its manorial fetters and an incorporation of the aristocracy into the communal bourgeois constitution, the reform of criminal law codes and cutting down the budgets for the army and diplomacy, a shortening of the civil list and the abolition of pensions. It was still only a minority who grasped the subtle goals of the liberalism of the *Vormärz* era: the activation of the citizen, the energetic and responsible cooperation of great masses of the voters in the responsibilities of the state, and self-administration on the local level. But even these people who had their minds made up only wanted a cooperation, a division of power between the people and the government, between the legislation and the administration, between the chamber and the king. An aspiration to establish, over and above this liberal dualism, an absolute responsibility of the governed, an actual popular sovereignty, was only outlined by a very small circle of radicals, and even they had no clear conception of which organs must develop first to support a true self-government, let alone having—as Tocqueville did in France—a clear idea of the necessary weaknesses and sources of errors existing even in democratic institutions. The awakening bourgeois opposition was united from the furthest left to the moderate constitutionalists only in the will and determination to finally break with any regimentation by the old political powers. The opportunity for this was to arise suddenly and contrary to all expectations.

IV

THE MARCH EVENTS IN GERMANY

There was a connection between the nature
and manipulation of censorship and the fact
that European events were more quickly known and more passionately discussed in Germany and Austria than internal German occurrences during the generation before the outbreak of the revolution.
This receptivity to the outside barometric reading was connected
not so much with the cosmopolitan leanings of German liberalism
as with police orders to limit public opinion to meagre court and
cultural news. But forcing attention to foreign events was also
dangerous for the government, because, in an epoch when the principle of progress and the principle of preservation were reflected
everywhere in political affairs, every triumph by the tendency to
freedom in Europe necessarily also had repercussions in Germany.

The first challenge by the *Zeitgeist* occurred in 1846 in Cracow.
This old capital of Polish nationalism and shelter for the tombs
of Polish kings had been placed under the protection of the dividing
powers in 1815 as an independent free state. When the revolutionary
Polish propaganda tried to create a stronghold there, the Russian,
Austrian, and Prussian troops entered Cracow and annexed the
free republic to the Austrian monarchy. The old powers of the
restoration appeared to be advancing; the idea of national self-
determination and freedom was insulted at a focal point of European
sympathy. In the same year, 1846, the national sensitivity of the
Germans themselves was awakened at a painful spot. Christian
VIII of Denmark announced in an open letter of July 8, 1846
that according to the royal law of 1665 female succession also
was valid in Schleswig. The Estates of both Elbe Duchies, in the
face of this, maintained their own dynastic law of inheritance and

demanded independence under a Duke of Augustenburg. German public opinion, with the University of Kiel in the foreground, threw itself into the national border battle with the passion that the discussion of the Rhine frontier had excited a few years before. They saw in the reckless employment of dynastic reason of state by the Danish ruling house an encroachment of the old authorities. The fact that Metternich supported the legitimate power of princes, and thus Denmark, generated a deep alienation between the emperor's court and German patriots. Even the German Diet spoke out for the right of the Holstein Estates.

But only the third European testing ground allowed antagonism to develop clearly and fully: the *Sonderbund* war in Switzerland. Not without the interference of the Great Powers, Austria and England, in the matter, an armed struggle broke out on Swiss soil between two camps. The victory of the radical *Tagsatzung** over the Catholic cantons brought a European echo like the triumph of Palmerston over Metternich, like a duel between Lord Firebug and Prince Midnight. It was not a religious conflict, nor a dispute between federalism and union, but rather about the great domestic political concerns of the time: freedom or authority, progress or backwardness, republican virtue or the Holy Alliance. Not since the July Revolution had such an example arisen. The impression was strong not only in Germany but also in Italy, where the rage in Sicily and Calabria ignited the fire which signaled the February Revolution in Paris.

Sufficient kindling material was also on hand in Germany. In the large cities the hungry proletariat gathered during the year of famine for demonstrations and riots. The leaders of the political opposition in the west and south gathered at meetings. Bavarian clericalism, against all expectations, went over to the camp of the king's opponents to bring an end to scandal over the Spanish dancer.† In Prussia the tension and disappointment was greatest. Frederick William IV adjourned the United Landtag without even guaranteeing it the right to meet periodically. The aggregate eight Prussian provincial estates might be an old-fashioned ornament

---

*Tagsatzung—former assembly of Swiss cantons meeting in Baden and Frauenfeld under the presidency of Zurich, abolished in 1848.

†Lola Montez (1820-61)—Spanish dancer of Irish-Creole extraction, mistress of Ludwig I; meddled disastrously in Bavarian politics, leading to the king's abdication.

of the crown, but would not be allowed to become an independent political factor. When the king, under the pressure of an angry mood outside and within the state, finally called the appointed committees to Berlin (January 1848), it was already too late for this method of frugal concessions. After February 24, the day when the throne of Louis Philippe was publicly burned in Paris on the Bastille Place, the German governments were overwhelmed by an irresistible wave. Everywhere there were passionate petitions, meetings, marches, burning enthusiasm among all layers of the people, fraternal festivals, arcs of triumph, and societies. The most remarkable part was that the governments gave in as though in silent agreement without any resistance and acknowledged the justice of the revolution before acts of violence actually occurred.

The question whether the March revolution was an independent achievement of the German people or a dowry of the Paris workers that surprised prudent Germany is almost as old as the revolution itself. To be fair one must distinguish between the starting point and the setting of goals, experience itself and the direction of a revolution. Without the dramatic events in Paris and without the flight of the French king, certainly at this moment there would have been no revolutionary psychosis, no March ministries, and no national assembly in Germany. After the suppression of the hunger revolts of 1847, which took place with the approbation of the citizenry, conditions in the individual German states seemed more consolidated than ever, and the liberals themselves were completely surprised by the triumphant sweep of the revolution. But the other side is also true: all of the points of the program that the March men offered in Germany had been prepared, developed, formulated on the spot, and accepted in wide circles of public opinion. The goals they sought were known by every citizen in Germany who had not entirely closed his ears to political discussion. This is why the incidents in every German capital were so remarkably parallel and achieved, on the most dissimilar historical bases, almost the same result. What the new era in Germany should accomplish had been explained clearly enough for years by the minorities of the chambers, the oppressed writers, and the liberal deputies in election meetings.

This actually also answers a second question much discussed by contemporaries: whether the revolution could be attributed to a group of conspirators or to an imperceptible "meeting of minds," to the intrigue of agents and emissaries or to the "spirit of the time" and its puzzling effect on men living at the same time.[54] During the *Sonderbund* war and once again in May, 1848, an interesting correspondence was carried on between Frederick William IV and his astute London ambassador, Prince von Bunsen. Bunsen said, with some justice, that "faith in conspiracies," in careful preparations according to a pre-arranged plan of revolutionary action by definite activist groups, whether described as Jesuits, Free-masons, Jews, anarchists, or democrats, was refuted by the Swiss occurrences. The king, on the basis of his own experiences in Berlin, returned to this thesis and claimed obstinately that for two weeks long in Berlin non-Prussian foreigners "prepared everything systematically for the most infamous revolt that ever disgraced a city."[55] The evidence he offered was anything but convincing. He maintained that sods of grass and stones had been seen being taken into the city for the barricade struggle, and a stream of "rabble," French galley slaves, Poles, restless south Germans, Milanese counts, and rich Mannheim merchants, altogether ten to twenty thousand unreliable elements, were systematically drawn to Berlin and hidden there from the police for the great putsch. Conservative opinion has tenaciously held to this naive thesis of the conspiratorial character of revolution. It was nothing but a poorly devised means to delude themselves of the seriousness of the revolutionary experience. Precisely the Berlin events between 13 and 19 March were a compelling example of the unintentional, almost obligatory course of critical events, where individuals recognizable by name played only an incidental role; the substance was carried out by a silent concurrence of anonymous groups and masses. The German revolution is only one component in a great European wave that did not break until it reached the borders of Russia. The revolution apparently broke out a few years or decades too early, and the countries that at that time resisted the infection, like Belgium, Holland, and the Scandinavian states, developed more fortunately and organically. But the direction that the current took once it broke out had already been prescribed.

On February 12, 1848, consequently almost two weeks before matters came to a head in Paris, the Baden representative Bassermann moved in the Karlsruhe chamber that a German parliament be called of representatives from all of the state legislatures to embark on the reform of the confederation in a parliamentary manner. Under the impression of the storming of the Tuileries, a large popular assembly met in Offenburg on February 27, where the Baden representatives Mathy and Hecker gave notice of the basic demands of German liberalism: freedom of the press, trial by jury, constitutional government in all the individual states, and the calling of a common parliament for the confederation. A week later the dangerous international situation brought the leading men of the south German opposition to a conference in Heidelberg, which agreed on two points: that Germany should recognize the new government in France to prevent a war with the neighboring state, and that a commission of seven men must make preparations for the election of a national assembly. Already a week before this Heidelberg meeting, Heinrich von Gagern broached this question of a federal authority, and thereby touched upon the cardinal problem of a German revolution. A princely head, a central Reich ministry, and a national representation should be placed at the top in Germany and the Diet should work in its own way toward such institutions. A contemporary observer correctly stressed[56] that this sequence of fixed goals documented the independence of German liberalism from French example. While in France a republican-socialist movement won the victory and immediately used it for internal political innovations, the March Revolution of the liberal opposition in Germany indicated that the nation needed a monarch-ical-constitutional leadership and that the problem of constructing a state stood in the foreground. The monarchical tendency also held the upper hand during the Heidelberg assembly, although Hecker and Struve energetically pushed the idea of a German republic. It was Heinrich von Gagern who shifted the question of the formation of a German state onto the diplomatic track, when he supported a tour of the German courts by his brother Max and sought to win the governments for his constitutional-unitary solution with a Prussian head.

The decisive first victory of the revolution was won on March 13 in Vienna. There also it was the liberal bourgeoisie, the industrial societies, the judicial-political reading circles, the students of the university, and the academic intelligentsia who traced out the goals and determined its dimensions. Perhaps in Vienna a more intense social resentment existed among this bourgeoisie than in the rest of Germany. Perhaps here the attitude of the ambitious son of poor parents dominated, who could not rise in the world against the protection and the prejudice of the ruling class, was not allowed to become "a useful member of human society," and now inwardly brushed aside all historical prerogative and innate rights of domination by becoming a radical democrat.[57] The demands in the Austrian Empire, however, were also for freedom of the press, trial by jury, supervision of the state budget, and a constitution. Metternich felt his position so secure that he failed to take security measures. When the cry "Metternich must go!" rang out of the crowd which had besieged the meeting hall of the Lower Austrian Estates, and a deputation of citizens repeated this demand before the Privy Council, he withdrew quietly in order not to endanger the throne and the monarchy. The monarch, the archdukes, the court, the civil service, and even the bench of counts in the Estates were happy to find a scapegoat with which they could perhaps purchase their continued existence. With great effort, order was maintained, and a new ministry was formed under an enlightened aristocrat, Franz von Pillersdorf, who soon proved to be rather incapable. An academic legion, a bourgeois national guard, and the calling of a parliament were conceded. The Transleithan half of the empire* gained extensive independence, its own ministry, a separate administration, complete freedom of the press, and a democratic parliament. The Magyars demanded in addition their own system of taxes and a separate army. The Czechs pressed for a Bohemian legislature, the Croatians desired a south Slavic kingdom, the Italian provinces revolted, Galicia became a seat of disturbances, and the King of Sardinia invaded Lombardy. It seemed then only a question of weeks or days until the Danube Monarchy would break apart into its historical and national components. The internal fragmentation of the surviving regime and its ideological irresolution were made more than clear by the events of Metternich's resignation. The man that only yesterday was able by his incalculable prestige to hold together an entire empire found just two of the many hundred flatterers and climbers of the court society really loyal and now had to flee through Bohemia and Saxony to Holland. The Arch-

*Hungary—the Leitha River separates Hungary and Austria

bishop of Olmütz, who owed his whole existence to Prince Metternich, forbade him residence in his city, and in the country inns he could only with effort be protected from the excesses of the population. The sick state chancellor himself no longer believed in the possibility of resistance and therefore rejected any attempted defense: "It is no longer a question of politics, but the social question." He had always seen the approaching torrent of social upheaval and built dams against it. Now that it had broken through, his advice was to capitulate, and he did not desire a return to any official post. The social forces were stronger; now the monarchs must "honorably enter into the new order of things, free from any ulterior motives." The old statesmen and the old principles, in his opinion, were no longer viable; they were worn out. The state chancellor, in the spring of 1848, had no adequate conception of the absolute authorities' power of recovery. There was therefore some truth, as legend maintained, that he gave up the fight prematurely.[58]

Under the influence of Prince Metternich's flight and the perplexity of the Prussian monarchy, the republican current grew visibly, especially in Baden. The popular assemblies in Offenburg, Freiburg, and Heidelberg of March 19, 26, and 27 stood under the growing influence of the radical deputy Struve. Also in the Frankfurt inns, where the men of the committees preparing for a national parliament gathered, the republican idea emerged, which deeply surprised all of those coming from the north. Struve spoke there also in the circles of the future parliamentarians of the necessity of giving the German people a republic, because this governmental form was the only antidote to reaction. The dictatorship of the radical minority as the only effective way to protect the accomplishments of the revolution surfaced clearly in the conversations. But the voices who wished to allow the will of the entire people to speak under any circumstances predominated, and they had every reason to doubt that the general will was favorably inclined toward a republic. The achievement and protection of the freedom of conscience had long been the most important concern of the liberals. Now they could not begin, after their victory, by perverting this freedom of opinion, whether by a republican *coup d'état* or only an armed reinforcement from the country. Any direct action was wholeheartedly rejected as illiberal, although the borders of legitimacy had actually been breached by the preparation of a national parliament.

It was a very random and haphazard group which met in the Frankfurt preparliament (*Vorparlament*). From Austria only two representatives appeared, and no one knew who had delegated them. From Prussia came 141 men, who were mostly men the municipal councilmen in various towns had chosen from among themselves. From other states "all former and present members of estates and participants in law-giving assemblies" were invited. But the north German states of secondary importance sent only a few delegates. Under a weak president, and uninformed concerning parliamentary procedure, there were many humiliating scenes of disorder, helplessness, and dilettantism. A clear division into left and right of the more than 500 delegates who met standing up in St. Paul's Church was impossible. Rumors from the street of the invasion by armed Darmstadt citizens or of the approach of German workers from Paris disturbed the assembly. Only the democratic left under Struve's leadership possessed an explicit program, but they numbered no more than 18 members. This small minority aware of its goals proposed freely elected presidents in the various states and a federal constitution for all of Germany following the example of the North American free states; for the moment they supported above all the creation of an executive committee and transfer of executive power to the assembly. The overwhelming majority of the representatives certainly wished a parliament for the Reich, but no republic. The minister from Darmstadt, Heinrich von Gagern, progressively emerged as their leader. With his aims he imperceptibly shifted the character of the revolution. His aspiration was to overcome the absolute void of the German nation in foreign policy; his means consisted of an "agreement" of a sovereign national assembly with the 38 sovereign governments of the German Confederation. The priority measures were limited, in the view of the majority, to control of the purged Confederation Diet by a committee of the preparliament, the so-called committee of fifty. As it became apparent that the majority of the assembly wished an agreement with the princes on the future Reich constitution, the radical minority under the leadership of Hecker withdrew from the preparliament. The forty unconditionals who followed him insisted upon the establishment of a committee of public safety and requested that the preparliament declare itself a permanent popular revolutionary committee. But this radical group was checkmated in the St. Paul's Church with so little difficulty, that Hecker was only voted the fifty-first for the committee of fifty, and Struve was ranked even lower. The national liberal majority also dealt highly contemptuously with the social demands of the left and their program for a bill of basic social rights. Proposals favoring the poor, which Venedey and others suggested, were received by the liberal Römer with an approving gesture as he turned to the full house, "All of you certainly share sympathy for these people, and I request that we give evidence of this by rising." A few minimum requests of the radicals were then passed. Aid for the unemployed, reform of the factory laws, state schools for all social classes, and protection of emigrants from exploitation were to be included in the basic law of the German people.

After four stormy sessions the preparliament dissolved itself on April 3 in favor of the committee of fifty, to which six Austrians were elected to emphasize the pan-German character of the committee. The committee had no more mandate than the earlier assembly, and it also had no real power of regulation. Its political role resulted from a mesmerizing of the governments and the lack of will in the old Diet, from the petitions and confidence of citizen assemblies and individual persons, certainly from the theory of the sovereignty of the people that every speaker, every organ used to authenticate itself. Basically the resolutions of this committee were only its "views," as one of its members correctly noted.[59] But the Prussian government as well as the Diet obeyed without resistance the suggested election law, the appointed dates, and the fiery Schleswig-Holstein policy of this irregular, popular assembly. Only against Hecker's rising in Baden, against the anti-German disturbances of the Czechs in Prague, against the separatism of the new government in Vienna and the Polish intrigues in the Grand Duchy of Posen did the Frankfurt revolutionary central prove itself to be fully powerless. And yet here the sovereignty of the people first collided with the actual difficulties of their revolutionary action. Should they unleash armed rebellion or leave all of the thirty-four thrones untouched, should they support the national movement among the Slavs or maintain the historical shape of Prussia and Bohemia, should they destroy the Austro-Hungarian monarchy or renounce the Germans in Austria? These were the really decisive questions of the historical moment and definitely of greater importance than deciding whether fifty or seventy thousand souls should be included in an electoral district and if the national assembly could open on May 1 or 18. Not even the relationship between the Frankfurt committee and an improvised federal authority was put in order. The plan of Welcker, the new deputy to the Diet from Baden, for a triumvirate from the Diet to be entrusted with the military-diplomatic leadership in national matters failed, because of the insuperable mistrust of most members of the committee for the organ of the old regime. And yet this solution was only logical. If the governments of the individual German states were not set aside and the dynasties were not to be touched, then one could only form a new central government together with them, and meanwhile could only create a central organ out of the Diet.

When the committee dissolved itself on May 18, to be sure, perhaps nothing had been bungled in Frankfurt, but also nothing had been decided. The constitutional questions were all saved for the national assembly that was organizing on the same day in the Church of St. Paul. The committee of fifty had been unable to place itself at the head of the revolution; Frankfurt had not become the capital of the German movement. This peaceful merchant city of barely 40,000 inhabitants remained what it has always been, a convivial and exciting convention center with garlands, flags, and pennants. The focal point of German destiny, even in these first weeks, lay unmistakably in the two capitals, Vienna and Berlin. But since there were *two* capitals nothing consequential for unity, for the future national state of Germans, could take place there either.

The government in Berlin, already in the first days of March, expected a greater collision in the royal capital and made certain military preparations which were more provocative than anything yet. But a vehicle for the revolutionary activity did not emerge. The Berlin city council and the municipal senate were more than fearful. The committee of the United Landtag which had met since mid-January for consultation in drawing up a draft for a criminal law allowed itself to be dismissed without resistance and consoled with only a promise that the king would call an assembly of estates every four years. The Berlin artisan society, against which denunciations had already been submitted and which had also included, for several years, very radical intellectuals as members, since 1846 was again more engaged in the intellectual development of its members than in a political struggle. The university students certainly held stormy meetings among themselves, but did not dare to be the first to act. The only place where one heard strong language was in the coffee houses, in "the Tents," on the edge of the zoo, where the Berlin petty bourgeois was accustomed to spend his Sunday afternoons, and now the musician's stage could serve as a podium for speakers in larger popular gatherings. In the coffee and beer halls of this park, students, writers, office clerks, young artisans and workers, also "well-fed assistant professors" and newspapermen stepped before their fellow citizens and began their political speeches with very generally-acknowledged complaints against the old system, about the "33 years of ignominious subjugation" and the dawning of a new era.[60] The concrete political demands were initially quite modest and limited to the immediate convocation of the United Landtag and establishment of freedom of the press. Political ignorance in Berlin was occasionally astounding. Freedom of the press was understood by some as the freedom no longer to be "pressed," that is no longer to pay taxes, or as the chance to place classified ads without paying from now on! The leadership in forming a revolutionary opinion was most likely among the correspondents of the *Zeitungshalle*, where a number of intelligent Jews were employed as writers and the question of emancipation, of the equalization of all religious confessions, played an important role. Many circles already openly considered civil war, since posters appeared asking the soldiers, in case of a conflict, not to shoot their unarmed fellow citizens. On the whole, though, Berlin was astonishingly quiet and loyal.

Then on the evening of March 13 the crowd was greatly agitated. They observed the cavalry concentrated around the Brandenburg Gate, militarily securing the castle and armory, and it was rumored that the government would make use of the old prohibition on assembly to disrupt the gatherings in "the Tents." The first incidents occurred during this evening, and this striking out with the naked sabre prepared the coming conflict between the military and civilians that most eyewitnesses denoted as the "actual pivot of the Berlin Revolution."[61] The first attempt to build a barricade had already been made in the Grünstrasse. On both sides it was still more goading, ridicule and loose play than a serious feeling of civil war; however, among the citizenry the brutality of the mounted military evoked understandable resentment, and their derision of the uniform had to cause serious consequences, given the sense of honor among the troops of the line. On the evening of March 14 the first deaths occurred, and the raw fury of the soldiers, that was especially observable among the Potsdam guard cuirassiers, in turn infuriated the people, who sought to revenge themselves by throwing stones and insults. On March 15 the first rifle shots were heard from troops who were clearing the castle square of demonstrators, apparently without higher orders, and on the 16th the first volley sounded, which unleashed tremendous indignation among the Berliners. But the king's favorable reception of two delegations from the Cologne and Berlin city councils improved the disposition of the capital visibly, and it was actually only a feeling of gratitude that led a mass of well-dressed citizens to the castle square on the afternoon of March 18 to applaud the king.[62] It had become known that the king had approved a law freeing the press from censorship and a license for the convocation of the legislature, and this was to be announced before the castle. With this the most important demands had been met. The agreement on a written constitution in Prussia had been made, and the promise of a transformation of the German Confederation given. This was of course not everything that was wanted, but it constituted a basic step forward, for which the moderate and thankful Berliners were honestly happy. Suddenly a threatening cry arose from among the joyful crowd, before whom the king had shown himself twice on the balcony in a vain attempt to make himself understood: "Pull back the military! Away with the military!" According to Gutzkow's testimony[63] the call came from no more than twenty well-dressed men, who originated the cry in chorus. They did not actually wish to incite, but rather to obtain a pledge of the concession from the king. It irritated the citizens that a reinforced sentry of the First Guard Regiment had closed the usual passageway through the castle gate. The sight of uniformed soldiers perhaps also recalled the victims of the last few days. It was out of place, in this historical hour of reconciliation, to be held in check by flashing bayonets. Thus a residue of bitterness and exacerbation remained at the root

57

of the celebration; the people hardly knew how to account, even to themselves, for their deep mistrust.

A high officer attached to the king related very vividly in his memoirs his encounter with the spokesman of the masses surging against the castle courtyard. "I pushed through the soldiers to the front and tried to speak with the civilians at the forefront in order to find out what the people actually wanted. One individual among them, a book dealer whom I knew personally named Schneider (as I later learned, an out and out democrat), came with me through the soldiers into the courtyard so that I could speak with him in quiet, which was not possible with the howling and thronging of the masses. But even from him I got only evasive answers, out of which emerged a general wish that the military should draw back and a citizen guard take its place; then any reason for disturbance would be gone, and the people would withdraw."[64] The information was highly significant and in truth exhaustive. The king should trust himself to his citizens, become a civil king, and disavow the military state. At the outset it was certainly only a small group of reputable townsmen and politicized heads of families, who clothed this desire for an established revolutionary precedent in a demand for the formation of a national guard. But when, against all expectation, the order was given from the castle for dragoons and grenadiers to clear the square, suddenly the entire crowd, that stood there by thousands in the warm spring sun on the castle square and was driven back by the bayonets, recognized its actual objective. Without any sort of clarification of the constitutional relationships, this revolutionary excited mass of people, torn back and forth between jubilation and indignation, with its threatening cry "Away with the military!" was determined to cleave the root of the Prussian monarchy. The King of Prussia was in fact, above all, the commander in chief of the military forces and unrestricted master over a well-prepared, magnificently disciplined, and ardently royalist army. Before anyone could speak of suffrage and the power over the budget, about constitution and chambers, he had to force the king to be a partner down at the level of common citizenship. The army in Prussia was not only the weapon of reaction as in the Habsburg empire or the Tsar's domains, but rather the actual substance of the state, the soul of the monarchy, the basis of its legitimacy as well as its popularity, that which distinguished the Prussian community from all other states. A Hohenzoller without an army was not just a citizen king, but only a shadow king, and the question of what power then ruled in the state had to be decided first. The demand for the withdrawal of the military from the nerve center of the state (castle, armory, and state bank) was of greater consequence and meant more than the demand for the resignation of Metternich or for the abdication of Ludwig I of Bavaria. It went deeper than the political wishes of the opposition in the secondary states, who only demanded new ministries and new chambers. The call for the retreat of the army meant an actual revolution, that is, a change in the foundation of the state and in the constitution of authority. This is why the decisions of Frederick William IV and his entourage in the next twelve hours were so fateful, and later, when the monarchy reflected on its military foundation, were so humiliating for all participants, and such a blind spot in their consciousness. Only the threatening challenge of the bourgeois revolution reawakened in the Prussian monarchy and its servants a feeling for the military root of the sovereign's dignity and brought this conviction to the surface. The administrative state of Frederick William III had already taken other, more modern paths, and it is questionable whether it would have ever given cause for a revolution.[65]

The royalist side initially seemed to succumb entirely because of irresolute decisions and fanciful castles in the air, sentimental spells and panicky consternation. A central command was absolutely missing. The king was subject to various influences and could not establish a line of policy. The military party and the camarilla used a favorable opportunity to place the Commander of the Guard Corps General von Prittwitz in charge of all troops residing in Berlin. Under his order the dragoons rode from the lists onto the castle square, and a battalion of the Kaiser Francis Regiment soon afterwards moved forward out of the middle gate to reduce the pressure there. When an excited gesture set off two shots during this maneuver, the crowd dispersed to all sides shouting: "To arms! Betrayal! They're murdering peaceful, unarmed people on the Schlossplatz!" Everyone rushed into the residential districts of the inner city to build barricades, mold bullets, gather paving stones, and to open the street battle. Also a hundred University of Berlin students—from a total of 1500—threw themselves into the thick of the uproar and brought weapons from the fencing hall of the university. They believed nothing less than that the king had attempted a *coup de main* in order to rescind everything at the exact moment when he had promised the decisive concessions. No remonstrance could have any effect against this mass psychosis, and soon after three o'clock in the afternoon, in several places, especially between Alexanderplatz and the castle, a real civil war broke out. That the first aimed shots of this day came from the side of the people has never been denied by the revolutionary histories or memoirs. Debtors, convicts, and workhouse inmates were freed. Poles joined the ranks of the revolutionary multitude. Armed artisans climbed the church towers and rang the alarm in all parts of the city. The student Arnold von Salis, member of an old aristocratic family of Graubünden, proceeded with a few friends into the Borsig locomotive factory to bring succor from the muscular machine makers with their heavy iron rods and hammers. Only after they were paid their weekly wages, under no circumstances in blind revolutionary intoxication, but rather, self-assuredly and soberly, they promised help, where alleged betrayal had occurred and comrades had been shot down. The fighting went on almost all night. Outstanding among the often very weak line of troops defending the barred streets and blocks of houses were the journeyman turner Gustav Hesse as a cannoneer, and the metal fitter Sigrist as the defender of the barricade at the Cölln city hall. But it was not merely men in working smocks and craftsmen, but also well-dressed students, journalists, respected shopkeepers, the veterinarian Urban, the prosperous members of the rifleman's association, officials, teachers, homeowners, in short, "citizens of all classes," who took a hand in this struggle, barricaded their homes, as sharpshooters chose a certain uniform button as target, and in distant parts of the city enlisted the military posts. Around 1000 prisoners captured by the victoriously advancing troops were brought to the castle, and then, under brutal ill-treatment, taken in the night to Spandau; many street fighters were finally cut down in the corners and in the attics of houses being searched. It was not so much a struggle between king and people as a settling of accounts between the military and civilians. Fraternizing with the fighting troops hardly ever happened; Prussian discipline and the solid military formation withstood all the strain. And yet it seemed that General von Prittwitz's fear that discipline was crumbling caused him to give a pessimistic report of the military situation and motivated the king to end the struggle. From a purely tactical standpoint, towards morning the main streets were nearly all under the control of the military, and the 15,000-man-strong garrison was master of the situation throughout. But in Paris, Louis Philippe, on the evening of February 23, had over 37,000 trained troops at his disposal and yet the next morning lost his throne and dynasty. When one recalls the experience of the Paris street battle, it was perhaps not so surprising that in Berlin on the nineteenth around seven o'clock in the morning a proclamation of the king "To my dear Berliners" was distributed, and the order was issued to the troops to retreat into the casernes. The sensitive personality Frederick William IV from the beginning winced before the thought of a bloody sacrifice. Albrecht von Roon reported that the order for a street battle was wrested from the king bit by bit, and each time he wailed, "Yes, all right! Only no shooting!" In his proclamation he promised with sentimental words that all troops would draw back from the streets and squares, when "my true and dear Berliners" cleared away the defended barricades and sent delegates to him. "Hear the voice of your king, inhabitants of my true and beautiful Berlin and forget what has happened, as I want to and shall forget it, for the sake of the great future which will dawn, with the grace of God, for Prussia and, through Prussia, for Germany. Your benevolent queen, genuinely a true mother and friend, who languishes in great suffering, joins her intimate and tearful request with mine. Written in the night of 18 to 19 March 1848. Frederick William."

While the king actually capitulated needlessly to a far from successful revolution, he created the impression for himself and his capital that it was exclusively his fatherly goodness and charity which on the morning after the night of terror returned the prodigal son to grace. Frederick William had been crushed by the bloody events since March 13, and probably had already decided to make a new attempt at peace before the military report of that night. In addition, the situation in the provinces was a cause of concern; General Wrangel had even been forced in Stettin to allow the formation of a citizen guard and to distribute live munitions to them. In the evening hours of March 18, moreover, Frederick William received the disturbing report of Landrat von Vinke and read a memorandum by Radowitz, which drew the lesson from the Paris street battles that the troops should be withdrawn from Berlin before their restraint was destroyed by extended combat in the streets. This motive tipped the balance for the king as with Prittwitz. They feared for the morale of the soldiers massed in the inner city, if they were exposed much longer to the temptations of the revolution. Certain misunderstandings in the transmission of orders, irritation and defiance of the commanding officers, who preferred to pull back entirely from the unclear situation rather than occupy an untenable position, likewise exerted an influence in the surprising withdrawal of the soldiers from before the barricades, from the castle square, and finally from Berlin itself. Something false came over the king's entire behavior from this moment on. That he in truth capitulated before the revolution and had surrendered himself was shown in the course of Sunday, when the bodies of the fallen, the murdered, and barricade fighters shot under martial law were carried from all sides into the castle court, and the king and his wife had to step out on the gallery to the clamor of the crowd to lament and to honor the victims of military tyranny. While the regiments left the capital with drums beating, a citizen guard was quickly armed, beginning sentry duty already in the night of March 19 at the king's castle. It is possible that the entire maneuver of the withdrawal of the troops was intended differently or at least was understood differently by men who took part in carrying it out. If the king gathered his armed power outside of the capital and could flee himself beyond the ring of insurgents, with one blow he could have been master of his decisions again and could dictate his conditions to Berlin. Actually General von Tümpling related in his account that immediately after the retreat of the troops, a carriage with six horses drove up to the main gate, and the royal pair, ready to leave, already were standing on the steps. At this instant, the first of the fallen was carried into the castle courtyard, and the people, as though they sensed the intention, lay some of the dead bodies in front of the lead horses to prevent the departure. Tümpling was able to persuade the king, on the steps, to turn back before a new trial of strength developed. If this information is accurate, then it offers new evidence of the overthrow of the crown on the morning of March 19. The second travel plan, which included preparations at a side door of the castle opposite the court apothecary, would have been the equivalent of a secret flight of the monarch; it apparently was foiled at the last moment by the fears of the queen.[66]

In other places too the Prussian military state capitulated to the revolution. As General von Wussow took a reconnoitring walk through the capital, on this Sunday afternoon he heard everywhere the maledictions of the population directed against the person of Prince William of Prussia, who, they charged, was mainly responsible for the violent acts of the soldiers. They demanded his abdication of the throne, and the overly anxious Chief of Police reported that his life was endangered. As the brother of the king was not entitled to individual political dealings, the heir to the throne and his wife could only leave the castle by a side door in the evening of March 19 disguised and in secret, to enter a waiting carriage near the castle apothecary, that had been kept in readiness there for hours in case the king himself fled into exile.[67]

An apparently leaderless, anonymous commotion in the street had, within a few hours, dragged down the authority of the strongest military state of Europe. The question is understandable: who was responsible for the action? Was it foreign agents, Frenchmen, Poles, south Germans, foreign students and "emissaries," who threw bribes around and thus created a following among the scum of the streets? Was it workers and students, who, as in Paris and Vienna, formed a revolutionary alliance and dragged the hesitant middle class behind them? Was it a secret movement that was organized in cafes and wine cellers, in beer halls and saloons? Was it artisans or intellectuals, professional revolutionaries or solid citizens? Out of what elements was the crowd created that, not merely at the castle, but in countless other outbreaks of barricade battles, gathered in bitter mass confrontations? When we examine the accounts of the contemporary witnesses,[68] it is overwhelmingly clear that the population of Berlin took part in its entirety. The Russian Ambassador Baron Meyendorff, certainly a trustworthy witness, in his report written to Chancellor of State Nesselrode on March 20 surely gave the most striking characterization of the street troops, and the Russian Military Attaché Count Benckendorff corroborated him as eyewitness: "One cannot deny that a large majority of the citizens took part in the rising; even the homeowners supported the building of barricades and the tearing up of the cobblestones before the advance of the army; the paving stones were carried by women and small children onto the roofs of the houses . . . . All the citizens believed in the betrayal and cursed the king."[69] It was obviously a panic that had taken hold even of the quiet burghers on the afternoon of the fateful day. It can hardly be denied that Polish directors, recognizable by dashing shakos and other parts of uniforms, served as experts in street riots. That individual intellectuals and editors added fuel to the distaste for the military state was obvious. The names of Swiss and Russian students can be found in police files. But simple statistics of the dead prove that participants came from all levels, and every social class took part approximately in its proportionate number. If we must point out one group, then it was the young handicraftsmen who stood in the first line. Among the journeymen who lost their lives in the barricade struggle, the greatest percentage was of cabinetmakers, then the tailors, and, after a larger interval, the locksmiths. These were obviously exactly the professions on the border between independent artisan and dependent wage labor. The furniture trade had forced the cabinet workshops to be transformed into factories. Only the manufacture of ready-to-wear clothing was still available to the tailor, and the locksmith journeymen were employed in thirty-five machine factories that already existed in Berlin. It was no proletariat who were pushing for a revolution here, but rather those threatened in their social position. Not long before they had demonstrated against clothing and furniture stores, because these deprived the independent craftsman of his bread.[70] These German artisan journeymen, who may have spent a portion of their years of travel in Switzerland or Paris, supplied the mass of soldiers for the revolution. But they were neither the commanders nor the misused of the insurrectionary movement. Nowhere had they stepped out of the circle of the entire citizenry, who here in Berlin as out in the provincial cities, in the Mark Brandenburg as in the Rhineland, in Prussia as throughout Germany, experienced the stages of the revolution with an astoundingly uniform rhythm. Berlin, which during the entire crisis remained monarchical at heart without experiencing any excesses, attacks on private property, or personal acts of revenge, was drawn into the whirlwind relatively late. But it is understandable that a large city of 400,000 where a great deal of intelligence, desire for progress, impatience, hunger, and wish for sensation was collected, could not avoid for long the political fever that had taken hold of an entire nation.

Since March 20 the city was in chaos. The shop signs of providers to the court, that bore the name of Prince William, were destroyed. His palace *Unter den Linden* that was to be plundered was only saved when a young man wrote with chalk on the wall: "Property of the nation!" The aristocracy of the capital fled to Potsdam with everything they could carry. The king circulated, surrounded by princes and·generals, under the black-red-gold flag, and embraced the popular ideals of Germany: freedom and unity. Though he forbade the cry "Long live the Emperor of Germany!," he could not prevent one of the king-makers of the day, the veterinarian Urban, who marched bareheaded with long curls and a flowing beard beside the royal group, from carrying in his hands a painting of the imperial crown. Frederick William IV at this moment had completely taken over the role of the "leader of the entire German people" and had honestly decided to unite Prussia with Germany. He believed in the "rebirth" of the nation, as his manifesto the morning of his parade through the streets announced. With great moral courage he stepped before the officer corps of the guard regiments on March 25 in Potsdam and embraced the new civilian revolutionary state. "In Berlin such an outstanding spirit reigns over the citizenry that it is without equal in history. I therefore wish that the officer corps likewise would seize the spirit of the time as I have, and that they all from now on will prove themselves to be loyal citizens of the state just as they have been loyal soldiers." Bismarck described how the Brandenburg-Pomeranian aristocracy objected to this betrayal by the highest feudal lord of the Prussian monarchy's tradition by banging their sword scabbards and with hardly suppressed grumbling. Frederick William, according to them, had not been forced, but rather had voluntarily taken the step to a constitutional civilian state. It is comprehensible that among men of the old Prussian mentality the thought arose that another member of the royal house might be supported who would give the redeeming order to counter-revolution.

The guards remained in Potsdam and the three other regiments were transferred to the capital, where popular speakers proposed a reconciliation of the citizen guard and the military. On March

30 a festival of rejoicing took place as the new garrison entered arm in arm with its brothers-in-arms of the revolution, decorated by the cheering Berliners with green branches. But even if individual soldiers of the Pomeranian regiment mingled in the newly opened democratic clubs and the left became less an enemy of the military— the cleavage which had opened in the character of the Prussian state could only be papered over with illusions on both sides. In truth, even in the heart of the government the struggle between a civil and military condition for the kingdom had never really been settled. Frederick William IV was not really capable of realizing the character of a responsible ministry and to transfer to it the management of the country's affairs. Time and again he interfered in an absolutist manner by giving direct orders to the subordinate organs in the governmental apparatus. In relations with the military commanders of his army, he did not even allow anyone to advise him, although according to the spirit of the March regime, a responsible minister of war would have to serve as the constitutional authority. Already in mid-May, a very serious conflict occurred between Minister Camphausen and the king because of this. The entire ministry of state placed the principles of constitutional monarchy before the king's eyes and demanded the forbearance of the king from carrying out independently any act of state not executed by a minister. But Frederick William wrote a pompous letter the same day in answer to the prime minister, in which he developed his royalist point of view[71]—and there it remained. In May already there was no longer anyone who could break the bizarre stubbornness of the romantic dilettante on the throne. Even the street demonstrations that flared up again violently on May 12, when the recall from England of Prince William, the "grape-shot prince," became known, were not enough to bend the will of the crown. The ministry of state, made ill at ease by the provocative gesture, feared far more the displeasure of the king than the deputations from a "political club."

The uncertainty in the situation of state conditions was transferred to the new popular assembly, which had been chosen in preliminary elections by indirect procedures, as it met in Berlin on May 22. They themselves were not certain whether they constituted merely an assembly of agreement—as the king called it—or a constituent assembly. Finally it designated itself somewhat vaguely as a national assembly and avoided a basic conflict over the division of roles between the government and the popular assembly in the drawing up of the constitution. The Camphausen ministry sought to strangle the chamber with a multitude of subordinate drafts for laws, to prevent accomplishment of its actual task. The revolution in Prussia thus soon came to a dead end. An energetically constitutional ministry did not emerge, the chamber failed to wrench political leadership into its hands, and public opinion was divided. Bourgeois and worker fell out among themselves, and in June there was even a street battle between the citizen guard and an army of workers. The raid on the armory brought another turbulent night for the Prussian capital and showed how easily the organs of authority could still be hypnotized by a riot. The authorities, whether civil or military, were frozen into complete inactivity. But the people themselves did not know what to do with their strange power, did not know how to use this terror that they spread. To be sure, during the night barricades were again built and weapons plundered from the arsenals, but many of the often valuable historical weapons were traded the next morning for a few silver groschen and returned to the museums by well-meaning citizens. No one resisted as the leaders of the storming of the armory, some students, intellectuals, and machine workers, were arrested and publicly tried. After the Paris June Days, when the bourgeoisie proved victorious, in Germany there was really no longer any chance of a proletarian attack. But there was also no one who could carry it out. The small putsches and riots in the streets, the howls and whistling of the crowds before a hated palace or an unfortunate representative only increased the common desire for a return of law and order and prepared the ground for reaction. Berlin quickly became "gemütlich" again and took on its old character: obedient, unpretentious, sober, witty, and easily swept away with military music and parades. Actually, the surprising compliance of the king in the March Days had probably strangled the *élan* of the Berlin revolution.[72]

V

PSYCHOLOGY OF THE REVOLUTION

The decisive scenes of March, 1848 were acted out in the triangle of north Baden, Vienna, and Berlin. Frankfurt was only an intersection of lines of force, but not a stronghold of revolution. In the remaining capitals, in Cologne and Leipzig, in Bremen and Königsberg similar events took place, but entirely on their own terms and spontaneously. Eyes were always turned toward the three centers where victory or defeat, reform or upheaval would be decided. On March 1 it was Karlsruhe, on March 13 Vienna, and on March 18 the uncrowned capital of Germany, Berlin, where the fate of the revolution was weighed. This does not rule out the possibility that the historian can study typical sides of the German revolution better in a provincial city than in the great focal points. We know that the leading large cities were only slightly removed from the social profile of the small middle-class town. But since the perpetrators of the revolution were not the proletarian masses, but rather respectably bourgeois, one will find the best information where the law of large numbers was of no consequence from the beginning.

It has been perceptively observed that the spark of the French revolution really would never have burst into flames in Germany if on the decisive days of March a beaming spring sun had not brought a crowd into the streets and before the castle. The peculiar mass-psychological occurrences, especially observable in Berlin: the fraternization, the solidarity, the increasing moral and physical power of the individual acting in large units, the quick accommodation and emulation, the avalanching propagation of a panic, the precipitous reversal of mood, the interlacing of exultation and mistrust, of homage and hate, of fear and threat—all of this perhaps would never have developed if the citizenry had been scattered to their four walls by pouring rain.[73] However, one always goes astray in trying to explain historical events by elementary mass-psychological reactions alone, however important it is on the whole to be aware of the social pathological tendencies.[74] Often very coincidental causes set the spirit of the times in movement, and often it disguises itself under really shameful forms of expression. But the infection itself presupposes a historical readiness that resides on a completely different level than the laws of emulation, herd instinct, mass terror, and demagogy would suspect.

The fact that the year 1848 was a true revolution for the Germans, an earthquake which set the entire external and internal fixtures of a people atremble is, of all contemporary documents, to be found most vividly portrayed in the letters of Wilhelm von Kügelgen, which follow the events and sentiments of this year in a small central German court city with extraordinary faithfulness and clarity.[75]

Kügelgen was in truth no revolutionary type. The Baltic aristocrat, who had spent a rich and happy childhood in Dresden, was a man of the *Biedermeier,* of bourgeois joy in learning and humanity, whose working day and holiday were intimately tied up with the idyllically limited life of a small German princely court. He was court painter and reader to the Countess of Anhalt-Bernburg and was later named a regular chamberlain to the mentally ill prince in the tiny town of Ballenstedt in the Harz mountains of central Germany. Accustomed to changing his dress several times a day to appear properly at the different meals, receptions, reading and tea hours at the court, he hardly had a thought for the constitutional conditions of the tiny state, that was burdened by censorship and taxes, oppressed by land laws and bureaucratic despotism, and belonged to the most backward lands of Germany.[76] He possessed an inexhaustible supply of fine cigars and was provided at every festive occasion with a new box. He drove each afternoon in the princely carriage drawn by four horses to some scenic spot and had a snack served him overlooking the landscape of the Brocken. He had no trouble making ends meet, except when the annual expenses for unavoidable Christmas presents accumulated in excess. His amiable irony found a bright side even in the small pleasure of handing out medals, and he did not allow himself to be depressed by the crying financial needs of the country.[77] Kügelgen, who stood close to the pietistic circles of Herrnhut and deeply experienced the unique melancholy of the Ranke period,* found himself thus in absolute harmony with his surroundings. He bought a stately home with garden and adjacent buildings and had himself named professor by his crazy sovereign. In the year 1847, when the first storm warnings of the revolution ascended on the peaceful horizon of the German *Biedermeier*, his children reached the age to be presented at court. From a personal and social-egotistical point of view a man like Kügelgen could not wish anything better than the continuation of existing conditions. Not even the daily association with a mentally disturbed ruling prince could excite doubt in him concerning the wisdom of the constitutional monarchy. His ideal state was a ministerial government with two chambers and an unwritten ministerial responsibility that forced the monarch to retain only "good," that is capable, honest, and dependable, officials in office.

And yet this bourgeois-aristocratic courtier, who "seemed to belong to Ballenstedt like the organ to the church," was one of the finest seismographs of the revolutionary tension which was spreading through Prussia and the adjoining territories since February, 1847. "It often seems to me as though the entire nation were standing before a dreadful abyss," he wrote on the day that he learned of the calling of the United Landtag by Frederick William IV.[78] From the beginning, there existed two complexes of conditions which made him tremble: the presence of an extreme "proletarian class," who could easily be swept away to desperate lengths by restless elements, and the blindness of the ruling social class, who only increased the discontent and ferment dangerously with totally insufficient palliatives. Kügelgen was convinced at the beginning of the year 1847 that the king could only rule absolutely if he were idolized by his subjects and that Frederick William, the champion of this monarchy, had already forfeited his popularity. He

---

*Herrnhut—community of Moravian Brethren 40 miles E. of Dresden, founded by Count Zinzendorf in 1722 and exemplified by deep personal devotion to Christ.

Ranke, Leopold von (1795-1886)—German historian who combined pietist Lutheranism, the ideals of Fichte, and the philosophy of humanity from Goethe and Herder.

70

realized that days of grace for the monarchy since the July Revolution had not been used to advantage, and now, when the King of Prussia spoke his imprudent words of the "piece of paper" that ought not come between God and country, Kügelgen was convinced that Germany too stood before a violent upheaval in its form of government and had to travel the same painful path that England and France had already endured in the 17th and 18th centuries. The flood gates of the future opened up. Kügelgen saw the deluge approaching. He still believed that his place was in the tiny boat beside his "little count" where he would be engulfed by the violent times. He did not yet know that he himself in his light skiff would be raised to the crest of the billows. And still it was he who became a true witness of the revolution, who could explain what he himself had suffered.

On the eve of the revolution there was a large number of intellects in Germany who were stricken with grave misgivings and pessimistic prophecies, with a weariness with progress and a general European malaise. The thought of emigration to Australia or North America fascinated not merely the younger sons of peasants, but also the aristocratic landholder, officers, bureaucrats, and writers. Jacob Burckhardt came out at this time with the unhistorical, purely aesthetic world of Italy and classical Rome. Ernst von Lasaulx discovered an unhappy parallel between the present and the decline in late antiquity. August Vilmar observed with perspicacity the end of German idealism. Kierkegaard and Grillparzer formulated, each in his own way, the collapse of humanity. Artists and poets, almost without exception, felt at mid-century a barrenness and stagnation in their inspiration. This originated not only in an awareness that their works were mere imitation, but also from a paralysis perhaps originating in the sickly future of social and political life. Wilhelm von Kügelgen expressed in words this peculiar feeling of the times in January, 1848, without an apparent reason. The ambiguous sensation of the cultivated, bourgeois, saturated existence and its approaching end, this already no longer entirely fulfilled idyll made him melancholy. "I apprehend that it is the most humane period that Germany has experienced in its history and am also inclined to think it the most moral by far. However, I believe that we stand on the eve of some sort of great end, because all former conditions and all former guiding ideas either have already been extinguished or certainly are in the process of dissolving. What comes after this I do not know and have not the slightest notion, but I suppose that the disaster will be very terrible."[79] The consciousness of an internally disturbed order was current, although viewed objectively, no walls had collapsed and only a few small doors had been broken down. Was the bourgeois-courtly culture of Goethe's time ripe for a downfall or was it only threatened by an ideological attack from outside, by the approach of western European ideas, by unbelief, atheism, utopianism, by the mania for progress and the acquisitiveness of an emancipated society, by the "wish-of-thé-masses-to-live-better" (Jacob Burckhardt)?

In this divided time, in which the romantics looked back to the faithful age of the crusades, the idealists to the harmony of the War of Liberation, and the statesmen to the intelligent rationality of the 18th century, in these critical 1840s, when the first railroads were built and civil safety was enhanced by gas lanterns and hard sidewalks to a standard never before known, in which the criminal statistics visibly declined and the newly rich factory owners began to ride in their own carriages, in this halcyon epoch, in which contentment and satiety, resignation and the pride in progress lay so close to each other, there was something in the air, and no contemporary could withdraw himself from this atmospheric pressure, whether he was in his heart a royalist, constitutionalist, or socialist. A bolt of lightning could strike at any moment and everyone was prepared to perceive it as a just act of history.

Because of this, from the beginning the powers of defense were paralyzed that in the course of action awoke as the counter-revolutionary forces. At the moment of the revolution's birth no white army existed. Even the soldiers of the king, the bureaucrats, the ladies of the court, the lackies were seized by the experience of the revolution and gave themselves over to the spell of the novelty that befell them, with a mixture of intoxication and perplexity. Wilhelm von Kügelgen, the court painter and chamberlain of Ballenstedt, who still in April, 1847 wished to be swallowed by the tide at the side of his absolute prince, had entrusted himself as gullibly to the great wheel of history as Lafayette in Paris and the German citizenry in 1918. One really had no choice if he lived through the events with perceptive senses. He stood under the impression of higher powers, and even the leading minds in Germany fell into the enthusiasm for freedom and the ecstasy of the historical experience, as once Schiller and Hutten had known it. The finest document of this enthusiasm was formulated by a free-lance writer in Heilbronn, who shortly before had written an unforgettable biography of Ulrich von Hutten. David Friedrich Strauss, the heterodox theologian, who investigated the mythical character of the gospel and denied the essence of immortality, wrote on February 29, 1848 to his friend: "What times begin, dearest Rapp! And I believe we fundamentally can only win. I at least do not know what I might have to lose, that would be worth discussing. During the night, after the news of the proclamation of the republic broke, it was my first thought as I awoke repeatedly; with a start the supposition occurred to me in the first moment that it might be a dream, and I quickly tried to assure myself of the truth and my complete wakefulness. What was always our most intimate thought has now been fulfilled."[80]

The more moderate Germans, whose most secret wish had not really been realized with the republican form of government, believed at first that they could remain outside of the wave. But they too were prepared to be affected, perhaps through a national war against France, by the stormy world happenings. They almost were looking forward to this liberating war, as it would foster unity and bring a constitution that had been promised them in 1813. The nation had to be welded together by a common experience, perhaps by the threat of expansion of the new French revolution, while at the same time it extorted democratic institutions from the frightened princes. "If we now only remain quiet, we shall peacefully and lawfully obtain everything that we could reasonably want," wrote Kügelgen on March 4.[81] But immediately afterwards, the Cologne socialistic demonstrations of March 3 disclosed the irresistibility of the revolutionary wave and destroyed this hope for a peaceful national reform.

It is no accident that precisely this Cologne incident, that as an actual entity and demonstration of power was dispersed by the military with little effort, made such a deep impression on German public opinion. Unlike what occurred in Baden and Hesse, the assembly of masses here before the Cologne city hall revealed the democratic undercurrent and concealed socialistic program of the revolution. What Gottschalk, Willich, and Hock—a doctor, a first lieutenant, and an author—demanded in their petition before the Cologne city council was not just the arming of the people and universal suffrage, freedom of the press and the right of assembly, but the actual principles that the constitutionalists and liberals deeply loathed: the immediate transfer of lawmaking and administration to revolutionary committees, "protection of work and security against human needs for all," state education for children and the complete abolition of fees for schools, in short, socialistic guarantees and the immediate establishment of a radical sovereignty of the people.[82] Here the conflict seems to be delineated which soon thereafter inexorably divided the revolution: the opposition between liberalism and democracy, between bourgeois and proletariat. The unexpected and early emergence of extremism brought a deep division within the midst of the moderate bourgeoisie, which was so prepared to let itself be carried up and moved along by the wave of revolution. The only remaining choice seemed to be either for "gutter rule and barbarism" or "authority and government." Every "good and upright person," that is the *vir bonus* of the *Biedermeier* political community, could not doubt which he had to choose. At the very moment of the greatest open-mindedness for a reorganization and rebirth of politics, the apparent last phase of this revolution showed for a moment as through a rift in the clouds. What must happen when a people, who so recently were filled with the idea of an unbloody and lawful reform, with the thought of idealistic reconciliation with a purified monarchy, now at the height of its political enthusiasm with reform is shown the dreadful sight of social cataclysm? Would it not have been a sign of a miserable lack of instinct if the citizens had not offered the deepest resistance against such profound attacks and surprises as were discernible for a moment in Cologne?

The momentary alarm at the red signal flame from Cologne did not hamper Germans in the most distant corners of the Reich from living in the weeks of March, 1848 as though in a state of fever and expecting the great event at any moment. No one knew whether this event would be a firing barricade or a burning castle, a mobilization against France or an oath of German delegates. But men were prepared to be fervent, to sacrifice, to celebrate, or to march. "It is as though everyone had a fuse on his head and only awaited a match," wrote Kügelgen on March 5 to his brother.[83] The storm of events came more rapidly than prophets had conjectured. The concessions of the governments were soon no longer a gift, but at best installment payments which they had to throw to a public movement that on March 1 they could have easily inspired to their side. The penitence on the part of the governments was certainly general, but it came too late. The concessions contained something degrading because they were never sincere, and friend and enemy had the feeling that they would not be kept. Kügelgen was absolutely correct when he said, "to give a promise that I *cannot* honor makes me despicable."[84]

The best sign of a certain maturity in the German people as a political nation was the spontaneously parallel nature of events and perceptions in all parts of the land. It was like Paris during the feast of brotherhood. In the smallest provincial town there were illuminations, festive parades by the riflemen's associations, banquets of local notables, and embracing in the streets. Everywhere a joy, a satisfaction, a concord between the high and low predominated that left expectations of the maximum and a premonition of a significant turning point in time. A united fatherland, a common constitution, a Reich flag, a pan-German army, perhaps even a ruler "as powerful as the Hohenstaufen" seemed to approach palpably, and Frederick William IV, with every breath of his magnanimously sentimental effusions, corresponded to the emotional enthusiasm of the burghers. "Oh, what sort of spring this could be if the king took the new path with complete conviction and a really courageous heart!"[85] The overwhelming majority of idealistic adherents of the revolution absolutely agreed that the entire work of the new order must culminate in a monarchical pinnacle. "Only one can give the constitution, and what is more, only one, in whom psychological and moral powers are united. However, if nine hundred try to make it (as in the Frankfurt parliament), then without God's miracle nothing special will emerge."[86] This miracle, however, was to be accomplished by a new-born King of Prussia, and the enthusiasm of contemporaries fanatically overlooked his autocratic nature as well as the convulsion of his authority in the March Days. It was the great chance for the Prussian monarchy, which at that time, under the banner of unity and freedom, had to wed itself to the will of the people. The older generation, without a doubt, remained bewildered and dubious. The venerable Mayor

Smidt of Bremen wrote anxiously to his son, "Nationality-fever and the thought of unity are on everyone's mind. Otherwise moderate people say, the unity of Germany is not bought at too high a price with five years of anarchy and five years of despotism."[87] But no one listened anymore to the old sceptic of bygone particularism.

All the young men wanted to be soldiers. Even established burghers and court administrators were seized by the restlessness and had the feeling that they must join in, seize a rifle, and march off to battle somewhere. Not as though anyone had any clear idea of against whom the war would be directed. The news of a French invasion was most uncertain and, as we know today, exaggerated in panic. The mobilization of the Russian troops on leave was perhaps more threatening; however, the news did not produce too great a reaction in central and western Germany. But the opponent was not so important; he must only attack and offer an opportunity for action. We would misunderstand the enthusiasm for war of a man like Kügelgen if we tried to relate it to nationalistic plans of conquest or irredentist wishes. It was only a special form of mass excitation, which was available to a people that until then had only been moved to action by foreign rule and martial self-help, and except for the storm of 1813, actually had no common experience. What Kügelgen confessed applied to a hundred thousand German burghers. "Really I have no other desire than to put my musket on my shoulder and take part in a campaign. I am not alone; many feel this way, and thus little by little, in a growing current, a militant spirit is pouring over the entire population."[88] They wished to act at any cost and to participate in the responsibility; they wished to represent the nation by leaving everything behind; they wanted to do something together and did not know any other way than by becoming a soldier.

So forty year old men went off to maneuvers, fired their half-pound of powder in high spirits, applied for commissions in the citizen companies, and took part in defensive rendezvous. On the guard posts and in the popular restaurants of the militias forming everywhere, nobles and merchants mixed with chamberlains, lawyers, and cobblers in new harmony. They met with an unaccustomed citizenly respect; with a concerned civility and a tentative valuation not only of the personal worth but also of the political worth and popularity of individuals. As long as the mysterious wind of the revolutionary psychosis blew, signs of the conquest of historical barriers appeared everywhere, and a new hierarchy of men seemed nascent.

To be sure, even at the end of March the first voices of disappointment were heard. The impressions of the political emigrants streaming in from abroad showed this backlash clearly. It spread like a sudden wilt over the flowering of the revolution. When Stephan Born, the labor leader, came to Berlin a few days after the victorious breakthrough of the revolution, he was painfully surprised with the picture of the city. "In Paris I saw a happily excited population, who even in late March had lost none of its triumphant frame of mind. In Berlin just a few days after March 18 there was hardly a trace of the revolutionary intoxication that actually had taken hold of all of Germany. The excitement had rapidly vanished, the people looked serious as though they feared the future."[89] The sudden reaction to revolutionary enthusiasm was also noticeable in southern Germany, and not only the man in the street but also the politically initiated were touched. Already on April 13, David Friedrich Strauss wrote a friend from Heilbronn, "A nature like mine was more comfortable under the old police state, where one had tranquility in the streets and encountered no excited men, no newfangled floppy hats and beards."[90] The academic élite, even persons that only a month ago had enthusiastically expressed the *iuvat vivre* of the new times, turned back decisively and almost bitterly to Goethe and Metternich. "Yes, dear Rapp, let's not fool ourselves, the new times that have begun cannot be glad tidings for us at the beginning. The element no longer exists in which we used to prefer to move. . . . Because our element was really . . . theory, I mean free activity that was not directed toward goals and needs. This is hardly possible any more and soon will not even be respected. For the principle of equality is as much the enemy of spiritual preeminence as of material preeminence. It hates scholarship as it does possession. . . . Certainly until now things were not really good for us, but on the whole they will become even worse."[91] So wrote a man who had been dealt with rather harshly by the ecclesiastical and civil authorities, and who now appeared a likely candidate for the Frankfurt national assembly; a man moreover who felt within himself the march-step of the machine age, and one of the first who grasped the character of the railroad as the expression of the mass man. Neither a idyllist nor a reactionary, but an "epigone" of Goethe's educational ideal, as he described himself, and an independent man to whom the discharge of wisdom into every alley was completely repugnant. He would have liked best to study agriculture and emigrate to America, like so many whose basis of existence the revolution threatened to sweep away from under their feet. Hardly five weeks after the outbreak of the great crisis, the spiritual and parliamentary spokesmen of the bourgeois opposition seriously entertained the thought of conveying their individualism to safety in North America.

The more basic reason for the darkening of the mood may lie in the social ferment. The groups who were demanding attention as active revolutionaries in towns and villages, now that the bonds of established order had been loosened, did not belong to those who had for many years prepared the program of the revolution. But no one wanted to arrive too late, not the peasant nor day laborer, artisan nor worker. So they marched on the closest objective: the tax office, the castle, the custom house, the home of the factory owner, the machinery building, and in isolated cases the parsonage. But precisely this impelled the bourgeois constitutional and liberal movement into the arms of reaction.

VI

SOCIAL UNDERCURRENTS

From the history of the Great Revolution in France we know of a remarkable occurrence. While in Paris the Bastille was stormed, the national guard established, and the march on Versailles staged, the "Great Fear" spread through the provinces. It was no uniform event that took place in villages and country towns, on the borders, and deep in the most distant corners of the provinces, but if we wish to understand the character of the French Revolution it is more important to grasp the significance of this event of the "*Grande Peur*" than to study the oratorical achievements of the Constituent Assembly.[92] The French people trembled in gloomy fear of a counterblow by the deposed powers and expected any day the invasion of hostile foreigners. They hated the reaction and at the same time were apprehensive of plunderers from the large cities and the mob of their own movement. They dreaded tranquility and inactivity, the idea of having been left behind, passed over, by the revolution. They were frightened by their own audacity and mistrusted their closest friend. Old accounts were settled and violent acts perpetrated, because they would not be conspicuous in the general uncertainty. They ventured out with the intoxication that accompanies taking the law into their own hands, but they drew back just as quickly into the common herd. Men armed themselves in order to maintain order and robbed to produce justice.

The revolutionary panic in Germany never went so deep as in France during the summer of 1789. But a great deal of what the chroniclers reported is without a doubt similar to the wave of the "Great Fear" in France. The drive to arm oneself, to play

79

war, to march on the border, the fear of foreign invasions, the
citizen guards in villages and country towns, who wanted to protect
themselves more from extreme elements in their own ranks than
from the backlash of political reaction, the peasant rebellion, the
destruction of machines, the dangerously frantic ovations for the
monarch, the urge to be in the street all the time: all of these
were expressions of a panic which accompanied the experience
of the great hour.

In south-west Germany this state of tension intensified into the
so-called "French fright," an actual psychosis which certainly, like
everything that happened in 1848, showed a comical Philistine side
all too clearly. On March 23 at dusk, an itinerant journeyman
passed through Offenburg and cried out that pillagers were on
the march from Alsace, the mob was already surging toward the
town. The alarm bells were rung, riders galloped in all directions,
and the warning was transmitted from village to village. In Freiburg,
Rastatt, and Mannheim they already claimed to know the exact
size of the invading army. The undulation of terror rushed across
the Black Forest into Wurtemberg. Now it was 12,000 Frenchmen,
who were sweeping through Baden burning and laying waste. Bands
of armed townspeople marched toward the west to protect the
border. Women and children hid in the woods and buried their
silver. In the Pforzheim market place moving farewell scenes were
enacted as the men set out with rifles, pitch forks, and hoes to
protect home and hearth. Refugees arrived and recounted in deadly
earnest, "Where we live, we are at war." According to the news
in Stuttgart, which was brought by the official postillion in white
leather breeches to the ministries, it was already 40,000 Frenchmen
who were driving everything before them. Rottweil, Tübingen, Leon-
berg were supposedly already plundered and in flames. So passed
Annunciation day, the "French holiday," in anxious expectation
and excitement. Only in the course of March 26, as there was
still no sign of fire in the Rhine valley to be seen from the crest
of the Black Forest, and the bringers of bad news slowed down
and finally stopped coming, gradually the blind clamour ceased,
and a general abashment took its place. But the wave had passed
over upper Swabia and far into Bavaria.[93] Almost simultaneously
in the extreme northeast a similar panic was being acted out. In
Königsberg a popular commotion occurred before the post office,

because the suspicion had arisen that a Russian courier had gotten through transmitting a call for help to the Tsar to lead a reactionary army against Prussia.[94] It was as if the revolution thirsted for a bloody seal, as though men sought an internal or external arch-villain against whom they could finally draw the sword. But the German revolution was denied its villain, which may be the actual cause of its failure.

What the worker wanted most was an immediate target for his hate. Proletarians were in the front rows of the march on the House of Estates in Vienna's Herrengasse on March 13, and an eyewitness described one of the adventurous figures. "A gigantic man wearing a coat patched on all sides that certainly was not tailor made for him, a filthy cap boldly pulled down over one eye, his fists balled up, with a gleaming eye and looking ready for a fight, strode deliberately with giant steps down the middle of the street toward the House of Estates. In his rear pockets he must have carried a number of stones as munition, since his coat was tightly drawn down in the back, and you could see that he was making a great effort to avoid being pulled backwards by the burden of the pockets."[95] But only a small portion of the workers could answer the call of the students. The mass remained closed out before the gates and now descended upon the more obvious objects.[96] The unfettered crowd demolished the hated customs houses, destroyed machines, which they thought robbed them of their bread, threw a customs collector into the flames, and plundered the houses of hated employers. They ripped up gas lines and ignited the escaping gas, they set entire blocks of houses in flames, so that the city ring of Vienna was surrounded by a wall of fire. Only after days of battle with the army was peace restored. Many factories and workshops were so thoroughly destroyed, that a crisis of employment set in, and the new government could think of nothing else to do but increase contracts for excavation work on the Wien River and train the masses in the notorious national workshops for the idle.

In the rest of southern Germany it was more often the peasant village that turned to revolutionary popular justice. They rebelled against feudalism, burned documents and books, demanded the delivery of papers that were the basis for their wages and bonuses, death and market dues, withholding and emigration duties. Political demands were raised only seldom, the program points predominately concerned community law. The feudal lords should pay communal taxes like all other citizens; they should lose the nomination right in the election of mayors, and lease hunting and fishing rights for the good of the community exchequer. The peasants in the Duchy of Nassau certainly went farthest. Already from March 2 to 4 they streamed, stirred up by liberal agitators, into the residence city of Wiesbaden* and helped to raise the constitutional party there into the saddle. But how much did these 30,000 peasants from the Taunus and Westerwald really comprehend about freedom of the press, jury trial, and a German parliament? The only thing which was clear to them and awoke their jubilation was the demand that the princely domains should be declared property of the state. Many peasants had already appeared with moneybags at the government offices to bring their shared portion right home in hard Thalers. After March 4 the peasant revolution spread over the plains and there led initially to the removal of all village mayors and forest wardens. They no longer paid taxes, and proclaimed the universal freedom to hunt and the unlimited use of forests. Entire peasant communities armed with rusty flintlocks and muzzle loaders went on great battue hunts. Woods were cut down without plan and the lumber offered for sale in abundance. Finally, however, part of the village inhabitants themselves imposed an end to the offences against the forest laws and pointed out that they would still be needing a little wood a few years later.[97] Similarly mild and of purely local importance, the peasant disturbances in the other south and central German territories ran their course. On March 6 the subjects of Prince von Fürstenberg revolted in Donaueschingen. In the night of March 7 a mob ignited a great conflagration in the castle courtyard of Baron von Adelsheim, into which all the books of the lord's library were thrown that might contain their oaths of obligation.[98] Even the liberal Prince von Leiningen, who had long wished to end the privileged position of the mediatized lords, was challenged by his villages and community councils and incurred severe damages. In Wurtemberg it was the Count von Neipperg and especially Prince von Hohenlohe who were threatened.[99] In the district of Weinsberg a host 900 men strong drew

---

*WIESBADEN: capital of Dutchy of Nassau and site of Duke's residential palace.

up before the Weiler castle and demanded the delivery of documents and deeds. As the intimidated magistrate offered the key to the wine celler, he was informed, "We did not come to eat and to drink; we want nothing, absolutely nothing, except to burn the documents that reduce us to beggars, and then we want to go to the king and tell him of our need and poverty."[100] It was like the great Peasant War of the 16th century. Men sought help among the higher authorities against the lower authorities. They did not want to clash with forces of order, but merely to assist the victory of good old peasant rights. Men were loyal to the emperor and king and could raise a "vivat!" for the archduke, but they were determined to be unchained from feudal arbitrary power and burdens. The burdening land taxes were of course viewed as an evil right which they wished to set aside along with the encumbrances of the soil.

Naturally, during these peasant disturbances, isolated destruction and acts of violence also occurred. In the Riedesel Castle in Lauterbach (upper Hesse), the interior furnishings were despoiled, the women and children threatened as hostages. In Bavarian Franconia many noblemen fled before the insurgents to save their lives.[101] But the witch hunt of the upper Hessian and Franconian peasants was directed as much against the bourgeois capitalist money lender and Jewish merchant as against the noble lord of the manor. It appears that major action occurred only in the old districts of the Peasant War, in Prussia only where the legal work of peasant emancipation had come to a complete standstill, as in Silesia.[102] In all of north-west Germany, the flat lands never were turbulent at all.

Since the new governments, with the help of the old military, put down all these incidents, and restored order, during March, one can hardly speak of an independent phase of revolution. They were rural by-products which forced the acceleration of the last stage of peasant emancipation and fed on the well-spring of the peasants' sense of justice. This did not really introduce any new motifs into the ideological struggle of liberalism for the bourgeois state based on law. Heinrich von Gagern, the liberal minister in Darmstadt, tore up the declaration of renunciation by Count Erbach, which was forced from him by the peasants, before the eyes of the assembled chamber of deputies. The leaders of the constitutional movement did not wish to place themselves on the same level with acts of violence. Each insurrectional mob had to account for itself before a regular court of law within a few weeks.

The new central powers distanced themselves especially from the few urban riots committed by the masses in blind excitement and uncontrolled desire for action. The more popular the new men were, the more quietly and harmoniously everything proceeded. Robert Blum, for example, had almost the entire population of Leipzig united behind him and therefore could protect the city from all excesses. In Stuttgart during the tumults of April 10 and 11, it was the winegrowers, that is the poorest of the settled inhabitants, who most strongly fought the republican disturbers of the peace and restored the bourgeois order with their long sticks.[103] In Breslau and Magdeburg, in Vienna and Berlin, to be sure, isolated red cockades showed up beside the liberal black-red-gold Reich colors. In Solingen too, men attacking a factory carried a red flag. But only seldom did they speak in the slogans of the class struggle. The Prussian king on March 13 was handed a petition from workers that sought state protection against "capitalists and usurers," and demanded a ministry of labor after the French model. But this was a rare exception. What happened more often were local outbreaks of indignation against those who were stronger economically: against the factory which constricted home industry, against the machine that robbed them of bread, against the bureaucrat who created the hard conditions, against the merchant whose payment in goods brought him a double profit. Thus occurred in Schmalkalden the destruction of a factory building, in Salzungen a confrontation with the head of the salt works, and in Sonneberg a rising against the wholesale business. In Solingen the unemployed scissorsmiths reached such a fever pitch during a popular assembly on March 16, that they roamed by the thousands destroying the hated foundries in the area. These works had switched from the excellent hand wrought scissors to poor cast steel products, which were sold under the name of Solingen wares, thus decreasing sales in the export lands and damaging their good reputation. It was therefore really a struggle against dumping that the worker in the Berg region carried out in the street, as he set out to destroy the products of these businesses. It was more a struggle of quality goods against the mass-produced article, an insurrection of artisan-produced home industry against large-scale production. There was no evidence of a basic conflict with capital, of an assault against the bourgeois state or even the bourgeois social arrangement, even if the rumbling crowd cast angry glances in passing at the businesses which paid in goods instead of cash. The next morning, most of these merchants had large signs on the door proclaiming "No more payment in wares," and with this the matter was settled. After only two days, peace was restored in Solingen, and a sergeant with four men was enough to maintain public order.[104] Such outbreaks of popular passion were not really a part of the great march of historical events. Where the proletariat did play a historical role, it was as an ally of radical students and writers. The workers of the Borsig locomotive factory and the laborers of the Viennese textile mills performed as armed auxiliary troops to the bourgeoisie in the street battles of the capitals. They were called out, the way the peasants in Wiesbaden and Weimar were brought from the land, to intimidate the rulers. Some of these bourgeois radicals, to the extent that they belonged to the left wing of democracy, were influenced by the socialistic train of thought of the French February revolution. But these incidents hardly signified an emergence of the proletariat as a new class in the political and social character of Germany at this time. The workers themselves had a certain lack of independence, which indicated that they did not have a body of men backing them. The later much celebrated journeyman locksmith and barricade fighter Gustav Hesse, who stood among the fighters like a monument in a blue blouse with an iron bar in his hands, was only able to gain attention and some obedience among the raging crowd, when, leaning on his staff, he stepped to the edge of the barricade and harangued his fellow citizens with magic French words like "*Citoyens! Liberté!*" and a few other unintelligible fragments borrowed from the Parisian revolutionary vocabulary.[105] It cannot be denied, and the diplomat of the French Republic, Circourt, himself ridiculed the fact, that there was not a great deal of originality of form in this German revolution. The actual German qualities in all this were really moderation, aversion against excesses, easy tractability, and the ingenuous honesty of the revolutionaries. This was also evident in the timorous social undercurrents which accompanied the March events in Germany.

VII

THE APRIL REVOLUTION AND THE
CREATION OF POLITICAL PARTIES

Before the Revolution of 1848 the active parties in Germany consisted of only two groups: the camp of the government and the camp of the opposition. In the realm of the government, the conflicting forces of enlightened and romantic ideas gathered frequently: absolutist and feudalist, pietist and Hegelian, men of God's grace and adherents of enlightened welfare, believers in the Christian-Germanic idea and technicians of the police state. In the broad field of the opposition battled radicals and moderates, democrats and liberals, anarchists and anglophiles, and even some religious and upper-class conservatives who had some objections to the "officialdom" of the *ancien régime*, to official arbitrariness or state religion, to censorship or thought control, to disregard of the rights of individuals or of groups. In this camp of the government's adversaries stood individualists next to collectivists, adherents of a *habeas corpus* act beside students of Rousseau, republicans next to monarchists. During the first wave of the revolution, radicals and constitutionalists still worked hand in hand, and even many conservatives friendly to reform were infected by the idealism of the moment. On the other side, the champions of a monarchy based on the estates, whose struggle against the absolutism of the crown had acquired a popular reputation for them, in the face of the danger of complete downfall, drew closer to authority and the throne.

The outbreak of the revolution had worked as a catalyst and instituted new coalitions as well as divisions. While clarification in the camp of authority took place only during the course of the summer, the differences of opinion within the party of movement occurred in the days of April, 1848. The disintegration of the former opposition into a liberal and a democratic wing, into an anglophile and a francophile direction was certainly the most important result as the situation cleared up. In the two chambers, action groups then began to crystallize on the right and along confessional lines, which stepped forward with explicit, solidly outlined programs and created parties in the modern meaning of the word. The structure of relationships which the political parties constructed at this time were to last for almost a century.

The assumption of full governing powers appeared to be the most important task, above all among the liberal burghers of the south-west. This was very soon demonstrated by perceptive politicians like Ludwig Häusser in Heidelberg who realized that the recent conquests by the revolution were not merely to be defended against the forces and ideas of yesterday, which had been momentarily overshadowed, but also against the radical influences of tomorrow. The acceptance of political responsibility imposed much heavier obligations than had the complaints up to now against the encroachments of the government and the forms of state that were more or less intact. The politically uneducated bourgeoisie of the moderate center proved to be unequal to the responsibility. "Too long accustomed to opposition, liberalism only slowly and timidly became convinced of the necessity of using the entire energy of the party to hold on to recently and swiftly conquered freedom," remarked Ludwig Häusser with justice.[106] While in the north this defense of the new position had to be directed more against the automatic regression to the old authoritarian condition, in the south and especially in Baden, it had to reckon with a popular republican movement as opponent. In the Alemannian district, the extreme left, which in the rest of Germany was rejected by the "incalculable majority of the nation,"[107] had support in the broad peasant-petty bourgeois social stratum. With their help the honest, yet in part Jacobin-taught, democrats could hope to achieve by direct action those revolutionary goals they had sought in vain to attain at the meetings of parliamentarians held at Heidelberg and Frankfurt. The left was better prepared in its programs and especially in its tactics to take charge of the construction of a political community

87

than was the liberal middle, which limited itself to a demand for the inclusion of public opinion in all areas of political life, and then, after this goal was accomplished by freedom of the press, freedom to assemble, and trial by jury, had no concept of how to proceed further. Still, the republicans of the south-west possessed an energetic program, an unfailing will to fight, a popular momentum, and revolutionary vigor.

But audacious Hecker and his pale associate, Gustav Struve, the merchant Fickler in Constance, and the lawyer Brentano in Mannheim, immensely overrated the attraction of their ideas and were burdened by their abortive operations in the rebellion of south Baden with a curse of ridicule from which the left in Germany never recuperated.

Baden was the only state where they were working for a social republic as early as March and would not be satisfied with a reform of the monarchy. Fanatical newspapers and impetuous speakers using unequivocal Paris language called the archduke "Citizen Leopold Zähringen" and demanded the immediate abolition of all appanages and pensions. Instead of indirect taxes, a sharp income tax was suggested, amounting to 10% of income over 2,000 Gulden, which was tremendously high in the contemporary view. But humorous scenes lay close at hand. In Heidelberg a republican merchant's wife held a fiery speech with a cavalry sword in her hand by the fountain before the city hall. The armed country people who entered through the Karlstor brought large sacks in order to immediately relieve the city dwellers of their excessive prosperity. The serious-minded were shocked from the beginning at how much nonsense went on, how much ridiculous military play-acting raged among the citizens and students. It was not just a humorous, but a sad sight. Frau Henriette Feuerbach, the step-mother of the painter and one of the best correspondents of the century, wrote very discouraged reports at that time to her friend Emma Herwegh in Paris. By March 8 she was full of painful irony. "I confess candidly, that I am not at all capable as yet of exulting about freedom and fatherland; the authorities are persons who inspire in me so little respect . . . . Here's what I think: that we shall be absolutely, extraordinarily free, exactly as our liberal lord deputies order." And on April 30, as the rebellion in Baden also blazed over Freiburg and every day brought Jacobin-style arrests, executions, the arrival of partisans and disturbances, she wrote completely agitated by the travesty of freedom. "A beloved picture in my heart has a stain of absurdity that a thousand tears could not wash away."[109]

The liberal deputy Karl Mathy, who had risen to minister, clearly saw the danger of radicalization, and had the excitable popular leader Joseph Fickler of Constance arrested in the Karlsruhe train station. But the disturbances in the four electoral districts of Baden only increased with this, and Friedrich Hecker took advantage of the excitement. From Lake Constance he declared the government of Baden invalid, and passed through the towns along the lake with his partisans to gather armed reinforcements. He thought of himself half as a hero wrapped in ancient Germanic legends described by the chroniclers, and half as the standard-bearer of the German republic, who wanted to eradicate vestiges of the Middle Ages. A wonderful stylistic mixture of old Germanic fanaticism, Karl Moor-idealism,* and the French Revolution, the good-natured Hecker was a victim of his fervent belief in the goodness of human nature. He felt that he was supported by the willingness for sacrifice and the fervour of the Alemannian people when keepers of post houses where he stopped would not accept any payment from him! On April 20 near Kandern, exactly a week after the unleashing of the rebellion, his fate already overtook him. Regular troops of Baden and Hesse under the command of General Friedrich von Gagern scattered his forces. Hecker himself escaped to Basel. His followers, however, were only with great effort protected from the rage of the soldiers. A second group of insurgents under Struve was defeated at the exit of the Wiesental near Steinen. 5,000 men then easily conquered Freiburg, which was defended by members of gymnastic societies and an army of peasants. Finally, the Wurtembergers gave battle near Dossenbach to the militarily rather undisciplined and leaderless German Democratic Legion, which the poet Georg Herwegh had assembled in Paris and sent on foot to Alsace. One of the most irreproachable and bravest of the Baden revolutionaries, Theodor Mögling, the Swabian farmer from Holenheim, designated this legion curtly as "riffraff."[110] Herwegh also had to flee in an adventurous escape to Switzerland disguised as a day laborer with a pitchfork on his shoulder. The leader of

---

*character in Schiller's *Die Räuber*.

the rising himself, Friedrich Hecker, never returned to Germany. His application for amnesty was rejected by the Frankfurt national assembly. So in September, 1848, he emigrated via Strasburg to North America and there, like so many of his comrades in arms, served in a high military capacity during the American Civil War. His memory lived long among the people for many years. Its spirit is shown by the Hecker song, the only revolutionary battle song that was sung by the students and handworker apprentices in dead earnest:

> When in flames stand church, school and state,
> Casernes fall, then flourishes our crop.
> Yes, thirty-three years the slavery has lasted,
> Down with the dogs of reaction!

The memory of Hecker kept the radical-democratic movement alive in the south-west and thereby maintained enough strength to risk a second armed revolt in the spring of 1849. In Berlin, however, by the summer of 1848, the democratic-republican *élan* had faded to make room for a very north German, very Prussian, very sensible disenchantment. People would have been happy to see the disciplined troops of the Berlin garrison return and the entire uproar be over. A Swiss officer, who had come to Berlin at this time, perhaps with ambitious intentions, described quite instructively his impressions of conditions in the capital of the revolt after he had visited the popular assemblies and radical clubs for some time. [111] "The majority of the established citizenry is weary of the soldier games and would only oppose the entry of the soldiers if the working population dragged them along. The better part of this mass is rather weary with the phrases, the newspapers, and the tongue threshing of the rabblerousers. Evenings they visit the clubs, scream and yell; that is all . . . . There is no organization; a leader is lacking. There are lots of lovely speeches; practically nothing at all is prepared and acted upon." Certainly there were wild, revolutionary countenances among the participants at the popular assemblies. Secret committees existed, which assembled as committees of public safety and met to prepare for a revolutionary defense of Berlin. They gathered officers and non-commissioned officers, who volunteered to go over to the people; they sought to win over a commander in chief and to stockpile war material. But how naive and incompetent all this was! One of the consultants believed that they could procure cannon by boring a vent in the hollow cast iron columns which served as chain-holders before public buildings. They had neither money nor strategy, nor provisions, not even an intelligence link to the provinces. The few officers who volunteered were, in the estimation of the Swiss expert, "very inferior merchandise." The non-commissioned officers left no doubt that in an engagement between the army and civilians only a few troops would desert; even they themselves would have to shoot if the people fired first on the soldiers. Even in the Prussian capital they were as far removed as ever from any fraternization between workers and soldiers; there was absolutely no question of an incitement of the provinces. It remained a relatively small minority who vented their fury in the democratic clubs, and even they were basically tired of the revolution. The moment to strike for power had completely passed in spite of the remarkable victory of March 18.

An experienced observer like Georg Herwegh had already earlier censured this mistake and developed thereby a theory of revolution which despite its hidden cynicism is really illuminating. In a letter to German friends, he nailed down the cardinal mistake of the German revolution. "You had a few good days in Berlin, but, for all the heroism, genuine German days. You stopped fighting at the moment when the cry '*Au Château*' would have decided everything for you and for Germany; a republic has to be *created*; a dozen men are enough; and if they could only sustain it for a quarter of an hour, then it would be accepted by forty million for ages. The bourgeoisie resigns itself to everything."[112] It is a theory clearly derived from the Paris experiences, which defined the revolution without hesitation as *coup d'état*. One can "create," without a doubt, any form of government by a successful act of violence; the only question is how long it will last. Even in France the constitution of the February revolution only endured for a few months, then it was thoroughly transformed, because the newly-enfranchised millions did not want a parliamentary republic at all. Germany was even less prepared for the reception of this polity. Moreover, the German radicals could only be repulsed by the Paris scenes. Those who had witnessed the storming of the Tuileries

91

and seen how the new wielders of power allowed themselves to be served by the royal servants on the day after the overthrow, how the barricade fighters had to be bribed with booty and alcohol to withdraw from the king's castle,[113] wished no repetition of these scenes in Germany. Above all: if the takeover of power was not consummated in lawful form it could not convince the Germans, with their obsession for order, of its legality.

There was countless testimony for the triumph of the love of order in the German revolution. What Fritz Reuter humorously recounted in his "Flood-tide" really occurred in many princely and manorial residences. Before the rebellious peasants drew up before a castle to demand the delivery of the manor's documents, they brought along the district judge from the neighboring county seat, so that everything remained within the confines of law.[114] And when popular justice in Berlin burned the household goods of an enemy of the people in the open street, they placed a citizen guard over it so that no fire broke out in the neighboring buildings and so that nothing would be carried away.[115] We can despair at these attitudes and lose patience with these stubbornly patient Germans. But one must admit that a very deep instinct of law demanded this continuity in legal conditions. After all, it was not a minor matter that in the chaotic days and weeks of the victory, crime did not increase, rather declined, that property was almost never touched, and even in assaults on houses no personal enrichment occurred. The revolutionary movement in Germany lacked verve, but it was also unsoiled by all the atrocities that otherwise usually appear in mass action. The only ones committing acts of violence were actually the troops of the regular army. The few outrages perpetrated by the rabble encouraged the counter-revolution more than any other event. Far into the ranks of the democrats the murders in Vienna and Frankfurt destroyed the good conscience of the revolution and caused a paralysis from which the left never recovered. It can surprise no one that the German burgher drew back and was repulsed when he saw the wild faces of the revolutionary Poles, who gloatingly pointed out in passing the spots where Lichnowsky and Auerswald were slaughtered.[116]*

---

*Prince Felix Lichnowsky (1814-1848) and General Hans von Auerswald (1792-1848)—members of the right in the Frankfurt assembly, murdered by a Frankfurt

Perhaps we ought to specify still another reason for the laming of the revolutionary energy. The radical propaganda from the beginning had made concrete material promises to try to draw the people in the streets, in the workshops, and in the factories out of their political and economic lethargy. When a popular meeting was held in the Berg area in the first March days, the flowing discourse of the liberal speaker before a room full of workers was interrupted by the demand, "What does freedom of the press mean for us; freedom to eat is what we want."[117] In Vienna a popular emissary mounted the podium with a burning cigar. "I did not come without a reason with the cigar in my mouth. It is a fine Havana I'm smoking, and it is expensive . . . but in the future everyone should be able to smoke his Havana cigar."[118] Such promises and threats were hardly suited in content and form to win the politicized middle class for the ideal of the red republic. They wanted nothing to do with anything that slipped into crass materialism. The leaders of the extreme left in Germany also held back from the massive concerns of the working class and under no circumstances wished to raise slogans of the class struggle. The circles of the Hegelian radical left agreed that dialectical progress, through intense cultivation of the social contradiction between the bourgeoisie and the proletariat, was undoubtedly desirable in theory, but they concluded that this emphasis on contradictions was practically out of the question in Germany. Instead of announcing the harsh struggle of the workers against the bourgeois society, as dialectical doctrine demanded and as the Paris example (of course condemned to failure) suggested, even the left preached a reconciliation of both classes in the concept of "*citoyen.*" They wanted to educate the middle class and the proletariat not to seek their advantage and their welfare in isolation, but rather in the "community and common assistance," in a "system of association and common insurance."[119] From a historical point of view, this meant nothing less than that the second stage of the revolution, expected by socialistic theory, was cut off by the intellectuals themselves, and the historical plane of the Paris February revolution would definitely not be reached in Germany. The ideal of complete bourgeois democracy was at

mob during the riots resulting from the ratification of the Treaty of Malmö on September 16, 1848.

this moment almost a retarding force and undoubtedly contributed to the sudden end of the 1848 revolution. It paralyzed the proletariat, still hardly aware of its own existence, and could not in the least make the liberal bourgeoisie abandon its doctrine of state ruled by law. Every threat to this condition of the rule of law by subversive movements necessarily benefited the power of the authorities. Since they faced a divided opposition, they had a simple task not merely ideologically but also in terms of power politics.

Also, as soon as the old powers learned to handle the new political tactics and turned to founding great parties among the wide masses, it would necessarily obtain the ascendency. The shaping of a conservative and a clerical party, which until then had not actually existed, was an indirect consequence of the democratization of political life. Indirectly the modern form of mass control brought by the forty-eight revolution contributed not a little to the victory of the counter-revolution in Germany. The reaction first became a factor in public life through an appeal to public opinion. Since then the path to the reform state has been closed. Political life in Germany separated into the implacable conflict of left and right, between whom no non-partisan mediation based on a belief in evolution could exist. The tendency toward the class state, which in France was sketched out before the June slaughter and thwarted by the emperors, Cavaignac and Napoleon III, was not embarked upon in Germany. In its place ensued the development of the party state, that had to seek its integration on a difficult and untried path.

While the governments showed a changing character dependent on momentary power relationships, and the so-called March ministries almost completely adopted the character of the bureaucratic governments, the opinions of the governed broke down clearly into three groups (if we include the intermediate levels, it was five), which from then on constituted the political spectrum in Germany. The division had already begun in April, 1848, and can be most clearly illustrated in the creation of associations. We choose as example the provincial capital of Königsberg, because a cross section may be more easily shown here than in the large centers.[120]

On April 25, 1848, in Königsberg, perhaps the most important creation of the early wave of revolutionary enthusiasm, the "Constitutional Club," made its appearance. For the most part recruited from the members of the bourgeois "Ressource," that discussion club which in the *Vormärz* era had so courageously subscribed to the wishes and concerns of the East Prussian liberals, the club from its first beginnings assumed a mediating position. It disseminated instructively and on a remarkable oratorical level the advantages of a monarchical representative constitution and warned of demagoguery from the left as well as from the right. Every Wednesday evening its meetings took place, which often attracted women too. It enjoyed high regard beyond the city limits, joined ranks with sister associations for declarations and congresses, and sent letters of sympathy to German brothers in Vienna. Despite its competent leaders and its popularity in wide circles of the permanently passive middle class, the Constitutional Club only gained a solid membership of 400 adherents and quickly lost its power of attraction with the disappearance of the "political storm period." At the end of the period of revolt of the revolution, the drawing power shifted to the extreme wings: the "Workers' Society" on the far left and somewhat later the "Prussian Society" of the right, established at the beginning of August. The latter at the time of its foundation experienced severe resistance, but in the course of the autumn received such strong reinforcements that, with 6,000 enrolled members, it was by far the largest popular association in East Prussia. The opposition to further progress of the revolution and also against the absorption of Prussia into Germany unmistakably found a wide response. The attraction of the Prussian Society was so strong that its meetings had to be held simultaneously in different parts of the city. But also the Workers' Society, which under the leadership of the writer Dr. Dulk made its responsibility a basic discussion of political and social objects, possessed a tenacious vigor and even survived the political stagnation of the year 1849. All intermediate parties that were formed in the course of summer 1848, however, withered very quickly, even a right-center, so-called "Constitutional Society," that soon began to fraternize with the "Prussian Society," as likewise the "Democratic Club," which endeavored to organize the bourgeois left. What remained were the three characteristic "parties" of 1848: a bourgeois-liberal middle, which more and more withdrew into social life and aesthetic concerns (the Ressource), a very effective right, that only now developed the theory of old Prussia into dogma and propaganda (the Prussian Society), and the numerically small but tenacious and highly principled left, which sought to organize the sleeping political powers of the proletariat by bourgeois means (the Workers' Society). Out of these three intellectual-political columns and the intermediate transitional groups of bourgeois-progressive and liberal-conservative middle class levels, the working of German parties has gradually been constructed since April, 1848. Outside as within parliament we observe these same groups of opinion, which may vary somewhat according to the regional characteristics and the religious situations, but exist everywhere in their basic structure. In general, it is more instructive to study the political societies than to labor with the shadings of parties of the various chambers of deputies and the Frankfurt national assembly, which never extended to a real formation of factions and hardly emerged from the plane of elevated armchair politics.

Only the royalist party, in Prussia at least, had at its disposal a disciplined central leadership. After the epoch of bewilderment and perplexity, in which people were inclined to take the victory of the constitutional principle as a dispensation of Providence, they very quickly learned how to build, with democratic means, an almost invincible political fortress. As early as April of 1848, in the quarters of General von Gerlach in the "*Schwarzen Bären*" near Sanssouci, a small circle of men absolutely loyal to the king gathered to found the *Neue Preussische Zeitung*. Established under the sign of the iron cross, the newspaper, by its clear program, competent collaborators and skillful propaganda soon had a very great effect. The editorship was conferred upon a gifted young court assessor, Hermann Wagener, who was a special protégé of the controversial Chief Justice of the Magdeburg District Court, Ludwig von Gerlach, and from the beginning he underlined strongly the social components of the new Prussian monarchy. The circle of men who stood behind the new newspaper and acted partly as sponsors was characterized by the chamberlain of the queen, Herr von Bethmann-Hollweg, the pietistic friend of the king, Baron Senfft von Pilsach, Count Voss-Buch, the original Baron Hertefeldt, mostly people of individual and self-sufficient political opinions; neither in the question of Germany nor in Prussian domestic politics were they bound to an inflexible dogma. While the Prussian national assembly was in session, this group of the *Kreuzzeitung*

("Cross Newspaper") was joined by a more economically oriented interest representation of the east Elbian nobility, first in the form of the "Society for the Protection of the Interests of Landowners," then by the so-called "Junker parliament" in Berlin. While the relatively narrow objectives of these associations, relating only to the tax privileges of the landowners, were spread by the numerous district agricultural societies, the idea of a Christian monarchy found a wide echo in town and country in the new groups that sprang up from nowhere (Prussian Society, Fatherland Society, Society for King and Fatherland, Veterans' and Pastoral Societies). A sort of "political general staff" formed within the pietistically influenced Berlin Central, [122] in whose hands the threads of these multi-branched patriotic and religious societies came together. Besides the two Gerlachs, the Pomeranian Kleist-Retzow, Herr von Below, and his friend Bismarck-Schönhausen belonged to this inner circle. They considered mobilizing an armed force following the example of the Vendée in Pomerania and the Mark. They aroused a storm of petitions and put pressure on the king and the ministry with them. They supported venal agents to obtain information from the camp of the democrats. Hermann Wagener recounted that the *Kreuzzeitung* was better informed than the government and police in all the activities of their opponents, because they had not spared money in finding individuals on the other side who at "ten o'clock in the evening, when the drink took effect, used to take off their secret-concealing coats and hang them up without watching them." [123] In the ranks of the *Kreuzzeitung* party they operated with very unscrupulous methods of slander, flag-waving, and dirty personal insinuations. But it also brought extraordinary success and with entirely modern mass tactical means bred a following that in 1848 no other party had at its disposal, with perhaps the exception of the Catholic collective movement (*Sammelbewegung*). In the midst of a stormy period for the Prussian monarchy when so many old Privy Councillors sighed, "One would only too gladly blow with the wind if one only knew which direction it blew," here emerged a focus of political willpower. Religiously determined by the circle of Pomeranian pietists, led by the court camarilla and exploited by the Junkers for their purposes, but still supported by a deep patriarchal general mood in the rural north German population, perhaps it would not necessarily have to flow into rigid

97

reaction, but still had the possibility of winning an advantage over the bourgeois progressives by a partnership of the crown with the social question, like the modern Tory Party in England under the leadership of Disraeli. We are not seldom surprised by the political perspective and lack of social prejudice, by an understanding of problems of leadership and the openness to social responsibilities that was found in the circle of the *Berliner Revue*, in the *Kreuzzeitung*, in the *Volksblatt* of Halle, or among individual conservatives like Viktor Aimé Huber or Rodbertus. For the most part the attempts foundered in the economic concerns of the agrarians and the blind crusade against democracy. But did this completely exclude the possibility that Germany might also construct a two-party system with a conservative and a liberal mass party as in England? Even on the right, quite popular leaders existed who came from the tiny middle class and could replace the old ruling caste, people like the cobbler Panse, who led the Artisans' Society in Berlin and was sketched in a splendid portrait by Hermann Wagener, "A man, wise and clever, energetic and careful, at the same time upright and dependable, a born parliamentarian, equally skilled in presiding and in debate, in short, a man that in a republic like America would have the stuff of a president; his talent was so outstanding and superior that he was recognized freely and readily by his peers as leader and authority."[124] The death of Panse was intensely regretted in the camp of the conservatives. His admirers in the *Kreuzzeitung* party obviously did everything to deny him constitutionally the chance of having a career as an American sort of president. But still, they had discovered and honored the new sort of parliamentarian and thereby shown that they were not rigidly hardened in absolutist theory of state, but wished to ascend to a new plane of political struggle and activity.

Even earlier and with greater results than the right, Catholicism had started a movement among the masses and, using democratic methods, created an instrument of power. The beginnings of clerical publicity work using the methods of an educational press and political societies go back as far as 1846. At that time the popular preacher and "agitator" (as he called himself) Franz Joseph Buss, from Freiburg im Breisgau, instituted a mass Catholic petition which the Baden chamber was able to thwart. Buss, who himself was a man of the people and knew how to speak with his Black Forest peasants, had already drawn up a plan on the basis of his experiences in Baden, going into specifics for the organization of a propaganda crusade including founding small local newspapers and regional societies, using an over-all organization and central press guidance, with attractive speakers and political-religious enlightenment work, to draw in a membership of a million. But only after the March events and with the victory of the freedom of association and the press did the movement extend to all of Germany, and for the sprouting Catholic societies offered an object worthy of their zeal in the electoral campaigns for Reich and state assemblies. The church question definitely stood in the foreground of the agitation. With liberal arguments they pursued a clerical objective. By freedom of conscience, opinion, and association they understood in the first¡and almost only sense the independence of the Catholic church from the state, the freedom to establish religious orders, the abolition of the ruler's consent for a bishop's edicts, the abolition of patronage, and freedom of instruction conducted by the church. In influential circles they believed, and even Buss himself agreed, that this division of church and state only became necessary when the state abandoned its orthodox basis. But during this transitional time of troubles, even if it should last for centuries, clericalism and liberalism had to go hand in hand, not in what pertained to goals, but in methods. The alliance with liberalism directed itself as much against the old police state as against the atheistic radicalism of the revolution, which strove toward a new and much more effective monopoly of power by the state. The pronouncement of Archbishop Geissel of Cologne is proof that the ruling circles agreed on a secret reservation dividing the liberal and clerical movements: "We will not say freedom of instruction for all, rather freedom of instruction for the church."

The heart of the new party formation was the Mainz Pius Society, which was founded on March 23, 1848 by Hessian clergymen and spread over west and south Germany through the organization of a wide net of subordinate foundations. Central societies in the larger cities, local societies in the rural districts led the layman in the thinking of the clergy. The social Vincentius Society, the Borromäus Society devoted to adult education, the journeymen's movement of Kolping, and the Catholic press society provided additional support. Catholic daily newspapers were founded in

Cologne, Mainz, and Salzburg, and the *Rheinische Volkshalle*, the *Mainzer Journal*, and the *Süddeutsche Zeitung* acquired importance beyond their provinces. An imposing demonstration of the Catholic people took place in the first Catholic congress at Mainz of October, 1848 where, with the restless circuit rider Joseph Buss presiding, representatives of all the Pius Societies gathered to show how much support the idea of religious freedom had in the wide masses. On this occasion the "Catholic Society of Germany" was founded to adopt as its principle goal the struggle against social abuses, and Buss, Ketteler, and August Reichensperger adopted a tone which led to hopes for a successful alliance with the worker movement. They energetically demanded an efficacious protection of emigrants, reform of factories, the pursuit of occupations for the unemployed, savings banks, welfare institutes, public libraries. They even advocated workers' sharing in company profits, while at the same time clinging to the moral postulate of the return to a patriarchal relationship at work. Ketteler consciously sought to shut out the state from these social goals and to transfer them entirely to a new movement of the people directed by the clergy, to a new Christian charity, and a religious duty of property ownership. Even though, especially for Buss, foreign models were detectable, and decisive inspiration came from Owen, Saint-Simon, and Fourier, from Blanqui, Buchez, and Montalembert,[125] still in Kolping and Ketteler, men appeared who recognized the stroke of the hour in world history, who drew from the German experience in artisan circles and found extensive support in the church apparatus for their practical social work. Although the princes of the church themselves, after November, 1848, went over openly to the camp of the governments and approached the standpoint of the *Kreuzzeitung*, still, in the Catholic lay movement and the activities of its societies, there remained the social element at work that made it possible for the Catholic church to maintain its contact with the wide substratum of the people even in the age of industrialism.

The left likewise took advantage of early summer in the revolutionary year to spread their ideas by forming societies and extending their journalistic activity. They also accepted the contemporary demands of French socialism. The principal connections were to the existing gymnastic societies and workers' associations, to petty bourgeois reading societies which were politically activated, or to the newly founded "people's societies." The cooperation reached as far as the communist wing of the worker movement, that rallied in Cologne around the *Neue Rheinische Zeitung*. But even in reactionary Pomerania, district congresses of democrats were called. Frankfurt saw at Whitsuntide a "Congress of German Democratic Republicans," attended by more than 200 delegates representing 89 associations. A "Central Committee of German Democrats" from Berlin was supposed to hold together a net of district and local societies and to make agitational preparations for the immediately impending struggle for a German central government. Almost by chance, Julius Fröbel was placed at the head of the organization, who as a publisher in Zürich had acquired Swiss citizenship and possessed some facility with business. But the mutual mistrust and suspicions, the jealousy and thirst for power among the leading personalities, a certain naive lack of premonition and fantasy prevented the construction of a really powerful apparatus.[126] The left, in the sphere outside of parliament, just like the intellectual representatives of liberalism, lacked a gospel for the masses and thus the disposition over material powers which alone might have supported a new governing power. Bismarck in his judgment of the year 1848 underlined heavily this failure to create a following; as Karl Marx likewise said, the revolution had only officers and non-coms but no soldiers.

There were, of course, on the extreme left wing, radical men of the people like Robert Blum, Arnold Ruge, Friedrich Hecker, Stephan Born, who attempted to correct this evil in their midst. But how doctrinairily even most of these radical party leaders seized this problem. Arnold Ruge, for example, the son of a leaseholder from Rügen, whose ancestors had lived on the island for generations as peasants and craftsmen, was certainly a passionate and successful mass speaker, who in Leipzig, Breslau, and Berlin attracted assemblies reportedly numbering up to 30,000 people. His popularity was largely due to his keen attacks on bourgeois intellectuals and the "distinguished society of St. Paul's Church." "Be wary of bureaucrats, they cannot wish to be free. Be wary of the professors, . . . they have put slavery into a system. Be wary of the lawyers, they are accustomed to defend even the devil. Be wary of the clergy, their kingdom is not of this world. Elect all men of the people, but not too old!"[127] And yet this youthful radical leader of the people was himself the prototype of the doctrinaire. He had acquired his system of "unlimited reason," which now was to replace the epoch of the unlimited monarchy, as a student of Hegel and worshiper of the Greeks, as a frustrated academic teacher and philosophical writer. It was not difficult for the satire of his opponents to ridicule this renegade professor, who spoke of himself proudly as the "cavalry general of Hegelianism." A cartoon showed him as the "Minister of the Most Foreign" (*Äussersten*), striding ahead toward the Ministry of the Future with a night watchman's lantern in his hand, wearing a night shirt, with all pockets bursting with manuscripts. But still, Ruge was one of the most absolute and strident apostles of direct action. Even on October 31, immediately before the backlash in Vienna and Berlin, he led a mob with red flags to the theater where the Prussian national assembly was meeting. At one moment he felt like Pericles before the Athenians: an hour later the leadership had completely slipped through his hands. In reality the "terrorist of reason" was only strong when he could command ideas and failed at mastering human masses.

This is how it happened everywhere. When the insurrectionary throng grouped itself together, it was without a leader. Where constitutions were discussed, they were without a popular basis. There were plenty of martyrs left behind; in Baden alone court actions were brought against 3,500 persons and gruesome sentences imposed; but no one stepped forth to carry them out. There seemed no other way left to attain a new state than a wise arrangement between the governments and the Frankfurt national parliament. But even this was not left to the option of the participants, but rather depended on the constellation of the European powers.

VIII

GERMANY AND
THE EUROPEAN POWERS

Since 1830 in Europe a bloc of conservative powers, consisting of Russia, Austria, and Prussia, confronted an *entente cordiale* of west European states, which was based on the ideological and tactical cooperation of English and French liberalism. The overthrow of the bourgeois monarchy in France recalled the memory of this solidarity, after Guizot and his threatened regime, in its last years, had increasingly sought support in the system of the Holy Alliance, and in 1846 even came forward in company with Metternich against Swiss radicalism. The outbreak of the revolution in France immediately enhanced the feeling of unity with the recognized protector of political progress in Europe. The leading English statesman, Lord Palmerston, admittedly did not announce immediate official recognition of the republican government in Paris, any more than the other cabinets. But it was obvious that his sympathy did not lie on the side of the powers that were considering an armed intervention against apostate France, and that he was only waiting for the moment when the new government in France seemed stable and permanent enough that one could regard it as the legal expression of public opinion. Since Palmerston patronized the revolutionary endeavours in Italy which were directed against the foreign domination of Austria, the radiance emitted by the Paris revolution over Europe was a useful factor in foreign policy that he could assess and appreciate. The resurrection of the Polish independence movement would absorb Russia, the encroachment of the wave of freedom on southern Germany and Hungary would put pressure on

103

Austria, and hope existed that the iron bloc of the eastern powers would be entirely blown asunder by the process. England would certainly not take part actively even on the side of the revolution in this continental controversy; the anxiety that an expansion of France would be in the direction of Antwerp was too intense in English consciousness for that. The island state would rather fall back on its trade and ocean interests and remain in close consultation with the related royal house in Belgium so that no surprises occurred on the channel coast. Under this powerful English protection, Belgium actually was able to completely seclude itself from the European wave of republicanism, and expelled its communist guests from the land. England was determined to send over neither subsidies nor troops to the continent in order to restore the monarchy in France, as had once been the case in a similar situation during the first French Revolution. But likewise it was also interested in seeing a strong political barrier developed on the Scheldt and the Mosel.

The state that believed it was responsible for the maintenance of existing conditions in Europe, besides making its own practical considerations in keeping with its leadership claim, was Russia. What Tsar Nicholas I feared above all was that Prussia might use the opportunity to shake off Russian tutelage. The jealousy of independent political transactions by Frederick William IV and his Foreign Minister Count Canitz caused almost more apprehension in St. Petersburg than the revolutionary wave itself, and Russian policy left no means untried to keep a very tight rein on the efficient military power between the Rhine and the Vistula. We know of the political correspondence that the Russian Ambassador at the Berlin court, Baron Peter von Meyendorff, carried on with his superior minister Count Nesselrode[128] and can draw from it the arrogant superciliousness with which the Russian ruling class, who actually were mostly Baltic German or Swedish in origin, looked down on the Prussian vassals. One would perhaps need the sharpest sword of the continent if it came to the great European struggle of principles. Therefore they could not offend Prussia and let it feel deserted. But one also should not give such a schemer as Frederick William the illusion that he could choose freely between the world political fronts. One could not allow them to negotiate independently, otherwise they could link themselves to German nationalism and drastically deviate from Russian guidance. In February, 1848, they were just negotiating about the high tariff wall on the Polish border, long an item of Prussian complaint. Meyendorff used this discussion as a means of appeasement, but proceeded in the political question that much more dictatorially. "I was very gentle so long as it was only a question of tariffs and cartels, but I could become extremely unpleasant when they were making signs of undertaking the slightest matter without us and Austria. . . . The people here cannot be permitted to make any decisions in major policy for themselves, because they understand absolutely nothing about it."[129]

One should not wonder that German patriots, in remembering 1792, reckoned with the same danger that the Russians and even the English considered a serious political possibility. If it came to a war on the Rhine border, this time it would not merely be a war of principles between revolution and authority, rather it would necessarily be a war of peoples between the French and the Germans. Even the possibility of a military entanglement probably became a justification for the feeling of a great number of persons, who for a considerable time already had recognized a federal reform and above all a military reform as the central problem of German political life. Who was going to meet a national danger if it suddenly arose? Who would confront a war of revolution in Germany's name? Who would expound the claim for an independent political line *vis-à-vis* the arrogant Russians? The Diet could not do it, Austria would not do it, so only Prussia remained as the bearer of a military and political freedom of negotiation. Frederick William IV saw his German mission very clearly after autumn 1847, but he did not want to take the path from below, using the opinion of the people and fashionable ideas. No federal parliament was to be called and no demagogic national consciousness awakened. From above, rather, the 38 sovereigns of the German Confederation ought to conclude a new treaty in holy concord, reconcile currency and weights and measures, post and railways, criminal law and commercial law, standardize armed forces and place them under central inspections, comply with a federal judiciary, and recognize a common leadership from Vienna and Berlin. Prussia as federal military commander and Austria as emperor should stand at the pinnacle of the union: so read the reform plan that Major General Joseph von Radowitz worked out in November, 1847 and to which Frederick William IV returned just now on February 21, 1848.

Some advisors to the Prussian crown had already gone further. Even before the inspiring phenomenon of the Paris February revolution occurred, on February 22, Commissary General Count Redern laid before the king a memorandum in which he urged him to snatch the emperor's crown from the powerless hands in which it rested. Austria's preoccupation with its provinces of alien nations made it incapable of fulfilling its German mission. Foreign states would and could not intervene if Prussia decided to act. Now was the moment to sweep the other sovereigns to unity under Prussian leadership. The king, the next day already, gave a strong refusal. "Your warm feeling has deluded you about the shape you wish for Germany. You see, it would then be a statue without a head. Austria is Germany's head (*Haupt*), even when this head will not exercise the functions of a head."[130] Frederick William was even then in the course of sending his confidant to Vienna to win Metternich's state for a conference of ministers which should put Radowitz's design into practice. They agreed to meet on March 25 in Dresden. In the meantime, however, the bourgeois monarchy collapsed, and Metternich fled from Vienna. Count Dönhoff, the Prussian representative at the Diet in Frankfurt, advised taking a public oath in favor of the constitutional system to show the leaderless nation the way to a constitution. The Interior Minister von Bodelschwingh thereupon pressed for a transformation of the United Landtag into a representation of the people, and step by step drew concrete promises from the king. The Ambassador in Paris, Heinrich von Arnim, who returned through Belgium and the Rhineland and on March 29 became foreign minister, went even further. The King of Prussia, as the provisional German ruler, should invite all princes and all state assemblies, whether organized by estates or constitutionally, to Berlin and discuss the question of unity with them. Frederick William gave in to the pressures, but did not consistently focus his actions on these German goals in the critical days.[131] In the proclamation which he sent to the printers on the morning of March 18 and which was edited by Bodelschwingh and the Lord Lieutenant of the Rhine Province Eichmann, he promised in general terms to set himself at the apex of the German movement. King Leopold of Belgium and the Prince Consort Albert of England wrote very clearly emphasizing the mission of Prussia toward the liberal unification of Germany and the protection of Europe against a French encroachment. If France should invade on the Rhine, so assured the Coburg prince expressly on March 6, "the enthusiasm of the Germans in repelling such an attack would awaken a like enthusiasm in us (the English) and restore most resplendently the fine old league of 1814 in the souls of all our warriors."[132] The English alliance instead of ominous Russian help perhaps was available to the Prussian monarchy. But Frederick William, apparently on the same day or at the latest on March 7, at any rate before the arrival of the princely advice from London, preferred to request Tsar Nicholas in a private letter to draw up Russian troops on the Prussian border,[133] and to seek his salvation in a quarter where his German plans certainly would confront unceremonious rejection.

In France the consequence of the revolution was not, as feared, Thiers and nationalism, rather Lamartine and the party of peace as head of the government. Lamartine's proclamation to Europe, while full of a lyric tempo and peaceful gestures, certainly still made an ambiguous impression with its political contents. It indeed emphatically renounced war as a method of propaganda, but yet demanded at the same time the dissolving of all bonds on France that fettered its dignity and the resurrection of its rank as European Great Power. The foreign policy of the revolutionary government refused to recognize the legality of the 1814 and 1815 treaties, but it allowed existing territorial conditions to prevail as facts and wished to regard them as the basis for relations to neighboring states. Lamartine appealed to a love of peace of a reasonable and fair-thinking Europe and declared in the name of the French that a revolution like theirs did not want to set the world on fire, rather only to be its guiding star. But obviously a policy of revisionism was announced whose limits no one knew.

The German Confederation consequently prepared itself defensively. The federal defenses were not in an admirable state. Rastatt could have been taken by surprise in three days, and Mainz's new works were not armed. The Prussian posts were maintained better, but one could not be certain if the Prussian militia (*Landwehr*) would be trustworthy in a war against a citizen republic. Austria, which was obliged to post 100,000 men on the western front, hardly had enough troops to hold out in northern Italy, and, even if it supplied a federal corps, it could only resist a French invasion at the earliest near Ulm. If Prussia had set herself at the forefront of liberal endeavours, and at the same time let it be clearly understood that it would not tamper with the borders of the German Confederation on the west, it would have had public opinion entirely on its side. Certainly such a decision would have assumed not merely a break with Frederick William IV's autocratic-privileged conception of rule, but also with the Hohenzollern state's traditions of foreign policy. Because for German national consciousness the eastern borders were also inviolable, and the idea of Frederick William IV to concentrate a Russian auxiliary corps on the Rhine or on the Elbe for protection against the revolution encountered an indignant abhorrence far into the ranks of the moderate bourgeoisie. To be sure, a Prussian leadership in Germany also had the implication of the sacrifice of Habsburg interests in Lombardy and a break with the power of the emperor, since the brother monarchy in its exertions in northern Italy so obviously was inciting the counter-revolution in this matter. Whether Prussia was capable of carrying out a German-liberal policy without the support of both eastern powers, perhaps even in armed operations against them, was the fateful question of foreign policy for the revolution. The Prussian initiative was crippled, because the state of Frederick the Great was caught in the political fields of tension between western and eastern Europe and could not move without one power complex or the other making a threat to its very existence.

The only feasible step open for Prussian policy was in a south-north direction. Even then, in the spring of 1848, a combination was afforded that in an almost incomprehensible manner was passed over time and again in the last century and a half of German history. The combination with Italy and England would have required a clear decision for bourgeois liberalism and the English ideal of constitutional government, and probably it would have drawn in its wake certain sacrifices benefiting the nationality principle in Italy and Poland. Lombardy and Venetia, perhaps also south Tyrol, would have to be renounced, and they would have to be willing to discuss Posen, if this line were pursued. But if one contemplates what would have been gained under the flag of a national

unified state and in the name of the idea of freedom according
to the English model, then perhaps no sacrifice would have been
too heavy that would have been necessary on the far side of the
Alps and the Vistula, perhaps even on the Eider border and the
Vosges mountains. It was a strange tragedy of the history of the
year 1848 that the movement for unity and freedom, in its first
and nearest goal of Schleswig-Holstein, immediately had to collide
with the suspicion and vigilance of England. It was certainly asking
a great deal, that a revolutionary movement should begin with
a number of renunciations, with the abandonment of Posen, of
Alsace, of Lombardy, and of Schleswig. But if one keeps in mind
how the British Empire in the course of its history has taken in
stride, out of a desire for higher unity, sacrifice after sacrifice to
historical positions of power, one would wish that the budding
German national state had shown the wisdom of statesmanship
to insure the only support in foreign policy that was available
for the peaceful evolution to a constitutional system: England.

In regard to the posture of Britain toward German unification
and the German revolution, we shall have to distinguish among
three groups of opinions. Distinctly friendly toward Germany was
the court, Queen Victoria, and the Prince Consort Albert, who
were under the influence of German liberal nobles such as Frederick
von Stockmar, who as Albert's tutor possessed a great deal of
influence, and his cousin, Prince Carl von Leiningen, who through
an English marriage of his mother had become a relative of Queen
Victoria. This "Coburg circle" sought from the beginning to en-
courage Frederick William IV to give the awakening German nationality a political focus for its consciousness and its activity, and
to create a progressive, active federal central government in Berlin.
The language of the second group, the responsible parliamentary
cabinet members, whose primary goal was the maintenance of peace
in Europe, was more careful and restrained. The Prime Minister
Lord John Russell, Foreign Secretary Lord Palmerston, his future
successor Lord Clarendon, and the still influential Sir Robert Peel
found themselves relatively unanimous on the line which Palmerston, as Secretary of State for Foreign Affairs, outlined. In a dispatch
to the British ambassador in Berlin on March 17, 1848 Palmerston
put a damper on the all too optimistic estimation of English policy
made by Baron von Bunsen, the distinguished and learned Prussian

ambassador in London. He stressed that while admittedly a certain protection for the Rhineland and Lombardy was inherent in the fact that their present ownership formed an essential part of the Paris peace treaties over which England must watch; however, he emphasized that a guarantee for these territories and their possession by Prussia and Austria had never been made explicitly; only for the Prussian province of Saxony and for the neutrality of Belgium and Switzerland had England accepted such a guarantee at the Congress of Vienna. England had therefore only the *right* to support Prussia, or Austria, against an attack on its foreign districts, but it had no *commitment* to do it.[134] The future relationship of the English government towards German developments would be based upon political conditions and certainly in the first line upon German proceedings in the Elbe Duchies, where on March 24 a provisional, that is revolutionary, government was formed, which was protected from Berlin.

The third group of attentive English observers sat on the benches of the opposition in the lower house and were led by the most important individual of the rejuvenated Tory Party, the forty-four year old Benjamin Disraeli. It was outspokenly friendly toward Denmark and stigmatized the crossing of the Eider frontier by the Prussian troops which was, after all, provoked as a flagrant violation of international law, which England ought not to countenance without censure, completely apart from the fact that it did not lie in England's interest that a new sea power should arise between the North and the East Seas, threatening the "Dardanelles of the Baltic Sea." The appeal to the Germans of "that dreamy and dangerous nonsense called German nationality" made absolutely no impression on the conservative speaker: that was only the ideas of "starry-eyed professors and mad students." If Prussia and Germany continued on this path, it would logically throw down the gauntlet to France and bring Alsace under her sovereign authority. It then would have to occupy the Baltic provinces and weigh its strength with Russia. In his famous lower house speech of April 19 Disraeli left no doubt about this: if one would preserve peace in Europe, then one had to resist the first beginnings of national liberation policy by the Germans and not even allow the dogma to appear that a German state must reach as far as the German language was spoken.[135]

Although the letters to the editor of the *Times* often expressed similarly threatening language, Palmerston remained nonpartisan and persisted in his point of view that one ought to place no obstacle in the way of a voluntary union of the inhabitants of Schleswig with one or the other political pole, with the German Confederation or with Denmark, as long as it was of their own accord and without the use of force. He too demanded, in a protest note of April 12, the withdrawal of Prussian troops from Danish soil, but he offered himself at the same time as mediator to clarify the question of the legal succession to the throne of both the Elbe Duchies. The German Diet and the Prussian Foreign Minister also did not ask for the complete separation of Schleswig from Denmark at that time, but just a constitutional autonomy for the German subjects of the Danish crown. It was, then, a very aggravating arbitrariness by the German national assembly when it resolved the inclusion of the delegates from Schleswig into their midst and with this revolutionary act annexed a district belonging by legal right to a foreign state. But in May, 1848 perhaps an English suggestion of mediation could still have led to a peaceful solution of the entire question. According to the English plan, both duchies, under an Augustenburg ruler, should be allowed to join the German Confederation after the succession materialized; in return, however, north Schleswig, on the basis of language statistics, would fall to Denmark without a plebiscite. Herr von Arnim, the Prussian Foreign Minister, declared his acquiescence to these proposals from Palmerston, but the provisional government of the Elbe Duchies in Kiel and the Danish March ministry in Copenhagen made difficulties. The German patriots no longer wanted to give up the Danish-speaking areas, and the liberal nationalists in Denmark wished absolutely no compromise. They were strengthened in their obstinacy by the attitude of English public opinion. The Germans by their incursion had placed themselves in the wrong in the eyes of the entire world, and General Wrangel and the Holstein volunteers received a deserved chastisement when they had to withdraw from Jutland in July before the pressure of the Russians and Swedes.

For the young German revolution it was a most bitter disappointment to find themselves in conflict with world opinion even at the point where they most passionately opposed legitimistic thinking. That the massive power interests of Russia moved against an establishment of the Germans on the Sund and Belt was understandable. That the statesmen of the reaction, Count Nesselrode and Disraeli as later Manteuffel and Prince Schwarzenberg, failed to recognize the existing "national need" in this corner of the world as they did everywhere else, and designated the liberation of the Schleswig German without hesitation as "swindle,"[136] one must accept. But also that the hearts of European liberalism were closed to this pious concern and turned away from the lawbreaker, that the cabinets of the three non-German Great Powers withdrew, in a seldom witnessed unity, to a guarantee for Denmark dating back to 1720, this was a painful defeat that the German revolution never overcame.

It was a heavy burden for German matters that Prussia, by its patriotically motivated but rash step of April 10 and its military incursion into Schleswig, had alienated the sympathies of the great mass of Englishmen. Once again a weaker neighbor had been assaulted, the peace of Europe broken, a general crisis conjured up, and a irremediable situation created. The nuisance for the world was less the matter itself than the method by which the German revolution proceeded, and this allowed even the very questionable legal title of the Danish nationalists to appear as a property of European civilization that must be protected in common. When Prussia, intimidated by the reports from Petersburg and London, in August, 1848 concluded the armistice of Malmö with its Danish opponent and thereby belatedly submitted to the English mediation, it was then too late to recoup the loss in moral prestige. The effect on England exhausted itself in poorly concealed, gloating enjoyment of Germany's discomfiture, while the effect on the Frankfurt assembly was almost disastrous. A wild flare-up of chauvinism, above all on the far left, was the answer to the retreat of Prussian reason of state. The handling of the question of Schleswig-Holstein in the St. Paul's Church showed that the ecstasy of nationalism was not carried by the moderate middle and the kings, rather that it proceeded from the bourgeois radicals, who had already accustomed themselves to thinking in millions and to reckoning with the passion of millions. The most ardent expression of German indignation and the German standpoint of honor in the Schleswig-Holstein affair was reserved for the Silesian democrat Heinrich Simon from Breslau, who throughout mastered the tone of the mass demagogy of the twentieth century: "Let Russia, let France, let England dare to interfere in our just affairs. We shall answer them with one and a half million armed men. I tell you, not Russia, not France, and not England shall dare it, and I will tell you why. . . . For the reason that they are intelligent, because they realize that when they undertake an unjust attack on Germany this will motivate a German national uprising which perhaps has not yet been seen in the history of the world."[127]

The unleashing of the German national feeling and its conflict with the world of European states could have possibly been avoided if Prussia had relied from the beginning on the light touch of England and diplomatic logic in the Schleswig-Holstein affair and had not aimed for national popularity. England probably would have been prepared to become the godfather of the emerging German national state through its mediating role in the German-Danish border question. Naturally they were a little jealous and suspicious on the island towards the concentration of power of a people of forty million that sooner or later also could build a fleet. The thought of the possible consequences of a comprehensive policy of protective tariffs by a centrally led German federal state certainly might cause sleepless nights for the English merchants. But if this emerging German Reich and its Prussian spokesmen avoided throwing a stone into the European pond, the influential circles in Great Britain were benevolently prepared to support the formation of a German state, especially since Gagern's plan offered the possibility of embracing merely the more narrow concept of Germany and avoiding a Reich of seventy million (with the inclusion of the Austro-Hungarian Monarchy). Also from a European standpoint, at any rate in the eyes of English liberalism, the *kleindeutsch* (small German) solution was more welcome than a greater Austrian.[138] It was always a secondary matter for the English whether it was managed from Berlin or whether a new political center was created in Frankfurt (possibly with a Baron von Stockmar as the Reich's Foreign Minister!). They did not fear even Prussia's military might. Into the winter, the Whigs and the Tories still found it thoroughly in order that Frederick William IV brought the Prussian national assembly, which had been terrorized from the streets, under the protection of his battalions and restored his authority in Berlin with the help of Wrangel's troops. For England the preservation of the monarchy was a demand equally as self-evident as the parliamentary system of selection of ministers, which must respect the will of the majority. If the Germans had not contradicted the basic principles of peace and freedom in the employment of political means, then, led by Prussia, they could have achieved all goals that one reasonably might have expected: a central executive, a constitution, a German military sovereignty, and an efficacious economic unity, all without fear of military protest or a diplomatic obstruction from England. The only condition was certainly: Hands off the borders! An arbitrary change in the state of territorial possessions was, in the eyes of the English, just as reprehensible as a radical democracy and demagogic nationalism. It was a threat to European balance and thus contrary to civilization. England expected, as an article in the *Times* on March 13 had declared, that Germany would undertake the "principal defense of order and authority on the continent."[139] It could naturally only play this European role if it did not break asunder the existence of European political society.[140] As justified as the German complaints over the evil intentions of the Danish centralists may have been, how foolish and juvenile was the assertion of its own power in the moment when everything depended on reconciling the world to an interior strengthening of a German national state. The premature swordplay deprived Prussia and Germany of the auspicious chance to play a European role as the leading power of liberal reform supported and desired by England, and to create a healthy mean between the French revolution and Russian autocracy. If the German isolating bloc preserved peace between the conflicting principles of barricade and cossack, then the organic strengthening of a German Reich answered European interests as well as the natural and justified wishes of the German middle class. The peculiarly tractable and moderate character of the German upheaval was then more an advantage than a weakness. The orderly, legally authorized transfer to the liberal constitutional form could only make the German national state more appropriate in the eyes of England to play its role as the "main defender of order." In alliance with the English policy and in step with the Italian national movement, supported by a European mission and aligned in a wide ideological front, the events of 1848 undoubtedly would have led to success. The problem of Germany's unity might then have been

solved at a point in time and in a form when it could have been
completed in harmony and not in conflict with the spirit of the
times.

Austria was at this moment as far away as China. Neither the
European cabinets nor the German governments seriously considered it, and the old German question of Prussian-Austrian dualism had practically vanished in the spring of 1848. The anxious
princes in south and central Germany all had the feeling that the
only choice left for them was between a republic and Prussian
control. They were prepared, together with their moderate March
ministries, to subordinate themselves to an active Berlin course
if it held to a bourgeois-constitutional line. The obstructions lay
on the whole in Berlin, where they only reluctantly grasped the
great chance and were internally divided at every stage. A great
liberal statesman never emerged, impotent principal ministers from
Bodelschwingh to Auerswald were insufficient to overcome determined old Prussians, who agreed with their partisan friends of
St. Petersburg that things could not improve unless the masses
were fired upon. Between them stood Radowitz and the king with
their romantic plan of a greater German (*grossdeutsch*) dualism
and Herr von Arnim with his unfortunate idea that one must earn
the trust of the nation by an active offensive in Schleswig-Holstein.

So the great chance was missed, and the line carelessly cast
from English policy never seized. Recently an attempt has been
made to exculpate this failure in terms of foreign policy and to
trace the failure of the revolution and of a German national state
generally to fateful conditions.[141] The great danger with regard
to foreign policy for the growth of a narrower German Confederation led by either Berlin or Frankfurt lay, in fact, in coordinated
action by the flanking powers in the west and east against the
aspiring nucleus of power in their midst. Between France and Russia,
of course, there existed profound ideological, political, and sociological conflicts. Could they have been bridged by a common anti-
German interest? Did the possibility exist for an alliance between
the republic and the Tsar if German unity grew seriously strong
(and in addition perhaps with the will and knowledge of England)?
Each of the two powers was, individually regarded, certainly an
opponent of German unity, no matter in what form it was consummated. Count Nesselrode expressed this quite openly to the English

ambassador as late as the end of July; he said that the division of Germany into individual states was preferable to a Reich which was capable of meeting a French or Russian attack under its own power.[142] And in France it was not merely the journalism of Capefigue, but also the official exchange of correspondence by the diplomats which betrayed a general aversion for German unity.[143] However, so long as this indisposition was limited to diplomatic speculation, it offered no historical obstacle. France as much as Russia could only consider a military action if cooperation based on an alliance of both powers was assured.

International relations in the summer of 1848 have been thoroughly studied and in fact the traces of a French-Russian conspiracy found in meetings of Lamartine and of his successor Cavaignac, a man of a completely different nature. We know of the diplomatic discussions between the Paris revolutionary government and the Tsar's court rather completely through an article by the Bolshevik historian Pokrovsky, who in this question certainly has to be considered nonpartisan.[144] Pokrovsky based his study on the letters of the Russian ambassador in Paris, Kiselev, and the Paris reports of the Russian secret police agent, Jacov Tolstoy, from the spring and summer of 1848, which were preserved in the Moscow central archive. What do these communications signify? They prove that Lamartine made zealous advances to the Russian government and in his most verbose and vague language even offered them an "alliance." This happened in the first conversation with the Russian ambassador on March 25, long before the formal recognition of the new Paris government could have been considered and while Kiselev had no orderly courier and information link with St. Petersburg. The purpose of this offer of friendship was apparently only to prevent the Russians from becoming the enemy of the republic from the beginning and to sweeten for them the bitter fact that the government of Lamartine had just allowed the Polish emigrants to return to their homeland without hindrance. It was no alliance against Germany, but rather more an attempt at an agreement over the troublesome Polish question which divided the two Great Powers so antagonistically. Lamartine wished to recruit trust among the old powers in order to gain support through a diplomatic *détente* for his weak domestic position. No more. Only in St. Petersburg and only a month later did Nesselrode discover that the combination sought by Lamartine out of pure anxiety might offer an advantage in foreign policy that Russia could not afford to overlook during the upheaval in European conditions. If Austria were eliminated as a solid Great Power and the German Confederation should be replaced by "a unitary democratic power" of the German Reich, a situation might result in which the "immediate danger for us no longer threatens from France," rather possibly from the new German Central Power—certainly only as far as it "was capable and also willing to offer us earnest difficulties." Therefore, only in the case of an aggressive posture by the German revolution, or if the German democrats should give themselves airs as the proponents of Polish unity, was a situation conceivable where France "could serve as a counter-weight against the hostile intentions of our neighbors." Everything remained on the plane of diplomatic conjecture; nowhere is it possible to discover the proven fact of an anti-German coalition of the flanking powers. Nicholas I emphasized expressly that the French, in an aggressive war on the Rhine, in no case could count on Russian help. All the same, on both sides a train of thought developed which glossed over differences of principles and concluded that in an area of pure policy a community of interests could exist even between France and Russia.

A quarter of a year later, on July 13, after the victory of Cavaignac over the workers' revolution was settled and the domestic political gulf between the French and Russian systems of government had perceptibly diminished, the St. Petersburg cabinet returned to the question of balance. The advance of Prussian troops against Jutland gave occasion for Nesselrode to speak again to the French of his anxiety about a change in central Europe and make them aware of "the creation of a strong, compact power not envisioned in the existing treaties, in a nation of 45 million people all of which harken to a central will." As soon as the danger of a Prussian occupation of Kattegat was removed by the withdrawal of the troops and the armistice with Denmark, the Tsar lost interest in the balance of political power in the west, and Russian diplomacy limited itself again to promoting its point of view in France by seeking to aid Cavaignac to victory against his radical and Bonapartist rivals. Only at the most sensitive points of the political game, the Polish question and the Schleswig problem, did the

Russian-French alliance become acute, and very massive acts of harassment from the side of Germany would have been necessary for them to arrive at a military cooperation. France on the whole remained passive in this interplay of forces, and in Russia too there was a great loathing of war and especially of any aspiration for a war. A flexible and restrained foreign policy by the liberal unitary state in Germany, from all that we know, would not have brought the two flanking powers together. Russia was happy if the Germans and the Poles did not get together in their drive for freedom. But even this was hardly to be feared after the local struggles between Polish insurgents and German citizens in Posen noticeably dampened the German friendship for Poland, especially in north Germany. After the division of the province of Posen into a German and an independent zone, Russia could hope to occupy this free zone without striking a blow, and this must have decisively calmed Russian policy.

Thus, however one looks at it, the foreign powers in the year 1848 certainly would have observed the formation of a Germany with mistrust, however, they never would have prevented it if it had taken place within the framework of a small German state (*Kleindeutschland*), without disturbing its borders. England would have seen with pleasure even the separation of German Austria from the complex of Habsburg lands, because thereby the world power Austria would have been weakened as the partner of Russia on the chessboard of European policy, and the new Prussian-led Germany would have emerged as the liberal partner of England in continental policy. The conditions with regard to foreign policy were therefore favorable for a moderate German constitutional state, and if this German national state was not born, we shall not find the causes in the hostile European preconditions, rather we have to seek them in the midst of the revolution itself.

118

IX

THE WORK OF
THE PAUL'S CHURCH ASSEMBLY

To expect a revolutionary *Assemblée Nationale* from the "German Constituent National Assembly" which met in St. Paul's Church in Frankfurt on May 18 would be measuring it with a false standard. The great chance to construct a revolutionary executive power and a German committee of public safety had already been missed by the pre-parliament, for good reasons. The national assembly from its very beginning had more the character of a coordinating convention (*Vereinbarungskörperschaft*), similar to the Prussian national assembly and the south German chambers of deputies, rather than a revolutionary tribunal. They worked with a legal fiction (that certainly corresponded to reality in the south German federal states), that a constitution already existed and the common parliament merely had to occupy the limited and long vacant position in this constitution, that is to say, a legitimate popular representation for the entire federal territory of Germany. As the legislative chamber of the German people, they wanted to confront the aggregate of the federal governments and accordingly did not challenge the legitimacy of the Diet as the organ of these governments. Actually the Reich parliament March 30 and April 7 was even legitimatized by the old Diet in its German task; the voting law which was used for its formation was legally prescribed by each government specifically for its own country.

These election laws were totally different in the various German states. The candidates for Frankfurt were nominated and elected in Germany, Austria, and German Bohemia from largely out of date lists of voters and completely different forms; sometimes the delegates were chosen directly, sometimes indirectly, using electors, in one district without any census for the exercise of the voting right, in other areas (and preponderantly) excluding dependent occupations, servants, and day laborers. In the Austrian Alpine districts, interest was slight and probably clerical resistance also great; in half of the electoral divisions there the voting was not even carried out. The Czechs in Bohemia abruptly rejected participation in the Frankfurt parliament, and also deputies from the other mixed ethnic portions of the Habsburg monarchy belonging within the borders of the confederation frequently only arrived during the winter. In their place, East and West Prussia, Schleswig, and the western portion of the province of Posen were included from the beginning in the proposed German federal territory. Already during the elections, therefore, a significant hint was given of the future national state's probable borders. Austria withdrew, Prussia pressed forward, the irredentist zone was exclusively the north mark. In the remaining ethnically mixed border territories of the old Reich a strongly centrifugal movement was at work, strongest in Poland and weakest in the south-eastern regions, that were still dreaming of a Slavic kingdom. The only politically active area in the German border lands, except for Schleswig, was the Sudetenland, where the "Society of the Germans of Bohemia, Moravia, and Silesia for the maintenance of their Nationality" first came into existence in defense against the proclamation of a "Bohemian political law," and against the Czech theory of the historical homogeneity of all the lands of Wenceslas' crown.

In spite of the great differences in the manner of election, in the political maturity and responsiveness of the citizens, in the social and economic structure of the German territories and provinces, the composition of the national assembly was surprisingly uniform—a proof that in all parts of Germany a bourgeois social stratum with its own political claims existed and was recognized as the spokesman of the nation. This new social layer, which emerged with the trust of the people in city and country to take over the political responsibility in common with the dynasties, was the academic middle class, which in the Frankfurt St. Paul's Church included fully two-thirds of around 800 deputies. Practically speaking, at no time were all 800 seats filled. At the beginning the number of members amounted to around 500, later the attendance rose to over 600, and in the last months it again fell to fewer than 500. Among these men of Frankfurt were included, all together, at most 140 names from the business world, 60 landowners, something over 50 merchants and industrialists, a few artisans, a single farmer, and no workers at all. Instead there sat on the benches 160 judges, 70 lawyers, 120 civil servants, 20 mayors, in addition 40 writers, 30 clergymen, 20 doctors, around 50 professors, and 60 teachers of secondary schools.[145] The Frankfurt St. Paul's Church was thus a jurists' parliament or an officials' parliament rather than a professors' parliament, if we take note of the professional composition. Sociologically it was the meeting place of that educated middle class which had been appealed to and acclaimed already in the Prussian-German rising by men like Gneisenau and Humboldt as the true representatives of public opinion, as the quintessence of the nation. The independent landowner, whom Stein had once wished to make the pillar of the commonwealth, surprisingly stepped back. Even the nobility who were represented in St. Paul's were recruited more from the learned professions than from among the land-holding class. The assembly had an intrinsic right to elect an outstanding former student association leader, Heinrich von Gagern, as its first president and to call the old, already decrepit Ernst Moritz Arndt as its patron.

Very few of the members of this orators' parliament had political experience, so the outer structure turned out to be complicated, awkward, and childishly loquacious. Even in appearance and bearing the great abundance of brilliant and extravagant, eccentric and imposing personalities presented a confusing picture.[146] Furthermore, in parliamentary experience and practical transactions, the enthusiastic and helpless company of St. Paul's looked half-touching, half-comical. Even in January, 1849, after working for eight months, in which time the parliamentary speakers' mood of burning impatience could certainly cool down, ninety-four delegates came forward to take the floor on the principal question.[147] Gustav Rümelin wrote vividly in letters to his young wife how these eager but inexperienced representatives of the nation exerted themselves. January 11, 1849: "There was an immense tumult during the registration; various secretaries drew up the lists; on one roster I was the fifth; this was later declared invalid; on the valid list I am

around the sixtieth, and so many did not even get on it . . ."
January 20, 1849: "I was unable to talk this week; but now next
Monday I shall be the third or fourth . . . It is outrageous that
one must be prepared for a week to speak and still is not allowed
to and does not know when it will happen."[148]

But it was also the special enchantment of the Frankfurt St.
Paul's Church that the political work did not yet have any routine.
Actual factions did not exist, just as no party apparatus had conducted the electoral campaign. The grouping into a right, a left,
and a center nevertheless had been carried out in the first weeks.
Of course, within the groups there immediately arose more schisms,
splinter parties, closer alliances, and the building of bridges to one
or the other side. There were many isolated individuals, who absolutely refused to join any association whatsoever. Among them
were famous names including Arndt, Beseler, Döllinger, the Gagern
brothers, Moritz Mohl, Uhland, and Soiron. On the other hand,
there were also consultations and understandings between the various clubs and many shifting tactical coalitions. The associations
and coalitions all took their names from the Frankfurt inns and
restaurants where their informal meetings were held. There existed
a continuous fluctuation, dispersion, groping and self-examination.
In the "Steinernes Haus" at first all of those gathered who desired
no attack on the executive and did not want to touch the sovereignty
of the individual federal states; finally it consisted of only the Bavarian and Austrian clergymen, while the north German conservatives gathered around Radowitz and Georg von Vincke in the "Cafe
Milani." The parliamentary center soon split into a right- and a
left-center, and the most important incision in domestic politics
doubtlessly followed this line through the moderate middle. The
right-center dominated the "Kasino," the most numerous and most
intellectual club, in which the representatives of the liberal reform
movement gathered under the leadership of the north German historians Dahlmann, Droysen, Waitz, Giesebrecht, Duncker, and
Hugo, and also in which the liberals of Baden and the Rhineland
felt understood, men like Welcker and Mevissen and Hegelian
enlighteners like Rudolf Haym. Progressive Prussian officials and
Austrian bureaucrats with a black-red-gold approach strengthened
the front of these moderate constitutionalists. Not the elimination
of the old, rather the continuation of historical evolution, not the

method of revolution and the idea of the sovereignty of the people, rather agreements with the government and the dualistic construction of a German federal state were the objectives they had in mind. Nowhere else was the path of an organic constitution for Germany to be seen so clearly, but also no one else was as aware of the difficulties that stood in the way of its execution. These considerations and restraints, this knowledge and calculation without a doubt gave a greater momentum to the opposing left-center. Here they unconditionally believed in the right of the assembly to proceed as a constituent. They agreed unequivocally with the theory of the sovereignty of the people, even if the parliamentary monarch and not the parliamentary republic was agreed upon as sovereign for Germany. The aspiration toward unity was stronger here, the mistrust of hegemony by Prussia was stronger, the south German element predominated, and the popular tendency of the German movement was more strongly developed than in the professors' party of the "Kasino." However, the cliquishness was more intense, and the concentration into a large party was more hopeless than anywhere else. The "Landsberg," "Augsburger Hof," the "Württemberger Hof," the "Westendhalle," and for a while also the "Nürnberger Hof" embraced circles and groups of this inclination. They were called "the Left in dress coat" by their opponents. As a result of this fragmentation they never actually played the role that their numbers would suggest. Their center of gravity lay in the "Württemberger Hof" and above all in the "Augsburger Hof," where the south German particularists gathered, Gfrörer from Freiburg, Rümelin from Nürtingen, Arneth from Vienna, and where they also sought contact with the Reich ministry and the Imperial Vicar, and thought a great deal of Heinrich von Gagern. Next on the left, in a not too abrupt transition, was the "Deutscher Hof," which was primarily under the influence of Robert Blum, the only representative who had something approaching a mass following. A real man of the people and agitator, this independent book-seller had jeopardized his entire bourgeois existence, and as paterfamilias was forced to maintain his family in Leipzig on small loans while he dedicated himself to his responsible office as Frankfurt delegate. From the beginning, a shadow of pessimism lay over the countenance of this devoted politician, whose real popularity was only attained by his martyred death. The "Donnersberg," finally, with its 47 deputies forming the far left, was also completely bourgeois in its structure, but a resolute proponent of democratic action, filled with the idea of a united German republic, which was to be achieved through a daring parliamentary iniative and a collection of military powers, perhaps with assistance from France. Arnold Ruge, Julius Fröbel, and Wilhelm Zimmermann, along with Ludwig Simon of Trier and Brentano from Mannheim were the leading figures on this wing; Prussian names were in the minority. The men of the Donnersberg alone, except for the party of the hereditary emperor, possessed something like a firm program for a constitution before the meeting at St. Paul's. But they also lacked a man like the legal-minded Dahlmann, who had drafted a sketch already for the committee of seventeen of the Diet, which we must designate as the most impressive constitutional plan of the German revolution. Although Dahlmann's outline was never laid before the plenum of St. Paul's, it contained the framework for its discussions and the quintessence of what the German revolution was striving for. A constitution which conformed to the ideal of personality of the philosophers of Königsberg and Jena, which fulfilled the yearning of the student associations, must above all contain the following basic elements: an hereditary emperor at the pinnacle, a house of states in which the reigning princes should also sit, a house of commons chosen in general elections, a Reich court as the last instance of legal authority, extensive unitary competence for the authority of the Reich, and inalienable basic rights for individuals.

Such a bill of rights was therefore the most important item of debate before the assembly during long weeks and months. It lost much precious time with discussions about problems of a liberal world view. But the ridicule attached to this political self-confession of the German theoreticians is not entirely fair. The "Bill of Rights of the German People" was meant as a vigorous blow against German particularism, as a strong obliterating stroke through the German territorial absolutism of the past.[149] They did not merely intend to testify that the feudal state with its gradations in rights and duties, with its peculiar privileges and exceptions had come to an end, and that from now on every citizen of the state expected equal rights and equal duties, rather they underlined with this that the maxims of unity must also prevail against any sort of local arbitrary power. They accumulated a catalog of demands which were supposed to be valid in each of the 38 state constitutions. The bill of rights was an avowal of the principle that "Reich law breaks state law." The epoch of civic equality that was now to dawn for Germany compelled the suppression of all socially discriminating prerogatives and the supersession of all feudal encumbrances on the soil insofar as they still existed. The claim of the German people for a public life presumed the abolition of the dogma of the limited mentality of inferiors. This objective was served by the long desired rights of freedom: freedom of association, freedom of political assembly, freedom of the press, academic freedom for teaching and research. The idea of the constitutional state was also to be anchored in the bill of rights in every federal territory. The administration of justice must be completely independent of the executive and administrative organs of the state. Thereby the independence of a learned and unremovable corps of judges was as important as the introduction of publicly transacted jury trials. There were, to a certain extent, two guarantees of justice which should, in the future, make impossible a misuse or bending of the law: the scholarship of jurisprudence and the administration of law in public view. Erudition and public disclosure were the constitutive articles of faith in the bourgeois confession.

On these basic principles, perhaps, a constitution might now have successfully been concluded, if the presupposition at St. Paul had been correct, that Germany already was a national state like France had been and remained throughout all its revolutions. But Germany was anything but a national state. If we observe its borders alone, what irrational complexity, what entangled circumstances! Alemannic Alsace in France; Luxemburg as a grand duchy belonging to the German Confederation but tied in a personal union with the crown of the Netherlands; Limburg, a dependent province of Holland, and yet since 1839 member of the German Confederation; the "perpetually indivisible" Elbe Duchies divided by the Eider so that Holstein belonged to the confederation, Schleswig however did not; the Prussian Vistula territories and East Prussia were still outside of the union of the Reich as they had been since 1525; the hinterland of Cracow, Moravia, and all of Bohemia were component parts of the confederation; south Tyrol as far as Lake Garda was already a hotly disputed irredentist district of the Italian

125

national movement; Trieste was a carefully cherished access to the Mediterranean; Istria with its Italian-Yugoslavian population was an independent district. Toward all four points of the compass, question piled upon question, insoluble by the idea of nationalism, but also insoluble by the basic principles of historical political law. Everywhere the fact was apparent that Germany was no national state and could never be a national state without bringing either to German or to foreign minorities the most painful hardships. And as long as no clear German borders existed, no German state could be formed.

A similarly insoluble dilemma presented itself domestically as the St. Paul's Church proceeded to create a central executive (*Zentralgewalt*). They wanted to combine such a central authority with the surviving states. Heinrich von Gagern had expressly proclaimed, "To procure the cooperation with the state administrations is part of the mission of this assembly." Also the constitutional committee of the national assembly, which in turn met as the committee of seventeen under Dahlmann's leadership, concurred with this path. They suggested forming a tripartite committee composed of an Austrian, a Prussian, and a Bavarian prince. The result could only have been a resurrection of the Diet with a lower house at its side. Then the confidence of the revolution awoke in the President of St. Paul's Church. With a "daring trick" he insisted that the representation of the sovereign nation had the complete power within itself to create a central authority. With incendiary language, he drew up the Dahlmann group behind him, and on June 29 the Archduke Johann of Austria, the youngest and most popular brother of Emperor Francis, was chosen as the Imperial Vicar and head of a provisional central authority by the grace of Frankfurt. He formed a Reich ministry under Prince Leiningen and occupied the departments with liberal men of the Kasino party like Schmerling, Mohl, and Beckerath. But already with its first appearance, the Reich government showed that it had no firm ground under its feet. As the new central authority, to which the old Diet had transferred all its authority in due form on July 12, requested a display of allegiance by the federal troops and intended to derive from this a military executive organ, not only Austria and Prussia refused, but also Hanover and Bavaria. And when the Imperial Vicar sent his own diplomatic representatives to the European cabinets, no one anywhere cared to recognize them, in many places not even as a matter of form. For Europe, Prussia and Austria were still the power-political representatives of the strength of the German people, and when in August, 1848, the conclusion of the armistice with Denmark unleashed a rising of the people, calling for a national convention and a Jacobin popular war, the distinguished society of the St. Paul's Church including its Reich commander could not even defend itself. Prussian and Austrian troops from the Mainz fortress garrison had to rush to protect the new Schmerling ministry from the fate of Prince Lichnowsky and General Auerswald, who were brutally murdered by a mob in a garden north of the Friedberger Gate.

After the victory of the forces of counter-revolution in Vienna and Berlin in October and November, 1848, the two German Great Powers confronted the national assembly with restored self-confidence. It appeared more and more clearly that the work on the constitution until then had been built on a self-deception in assuming the existence of a national state. On the plane of reality a possibility still existed that a revolution in Prague and Milan in harmony with the central concerns of Germany might be unhinged by the Serbo-Croatian regiments. The constitutional committee had shared a general belief that a political rebirth could be found within a purely German framework. It had therefore, in its constitutional draft, excluded all non-German crowns and had drawn a line through the Habsburg Empire that was supposed to divide the Reich from Eastern European portions of Austria. "§1. The German Reich consists of the area of the former German Confederation. §2. No part of the German Reich may be united to non-German territory in a state. §3. If any German state has the same chief of state as a non-German state, then the relationship between the two states is to be arranged according to the principles of a purely personal union." German-Austria, according to this plan, was destined to be brought into a merely formal connection to the remaining Habsburg territory, similar to the relationship between Hanover and England before 1837 or as Luxemburg was then joined with the Dutch crown. When this draft came before the Frankfurt plenum, still prior to the events of October 31, it experienced very little opposition. Even the majority of the Austrian delegates, insofar as they did not belong to the right, accepted the precept of personal

127

union. Only a small black-yellow minority, together with the conservative wing of the south and west German Catholics, spoke for the annexation of the entire Habsburg state into a future German federation. If the national assembly had been free to decide, then the future Reich would thus have been greater Germany (*grossdeutsch*) but not greater Austria. It is true that the authors of paragraphs 2 and 3 of the constitutional draft did not really believe in their paper solution, because men like Dahlmann and Droysen, as historians, had too high a conception of the internal coherence of the Habsburg monarchy. But it is incomprehensible that one therefore, in the same breath, accuse them of a "cold hearted scepticism," a complete contempt for emotional values, a treason to Arndt's dreams of a great German state, while at the same time complaining that they had not mustered "even then the least understanding for the tendencies incarnated in the historical character of greater Austria any more than for the political unity of the German Austrian."[150] In reality these supposedly cold-hearted sceptics had inwardly renounced their greater-German national state for the very reason that they mustered such a great understanding for the power of inertia in the historical qualities of the Austro-Hungarian state. It may be that they wished, with their notorious two paragraphs, to pose a question to Austria, so to speak, an ultimatum on the idea of the Habsburg's Danube zone. But they did this, (as is disclosed above all in a speech by Waitz) certainly not out of malice, because they finally saw before them an open track for a *kleindeutsch* or even Prussian goal, but rather because they knew that the decision lay on the Danube and in the Alpine regions. The German Austrians had to choose whether their German consciousness or their state consciousness predominated, whether they wished to belong to the German Reich *or* to the Danube monarchy.

The disposition within the districts of German ancestry in the Habsburg state was divided. They were emotionally *grossdeutsch*, but without ever realizing the political consequences or even associating clear legal conceptions with this feeling. The Tyrolese, Styrians, and upper Austrians hoped for the restoration of the German imperial magnificence of their dynasty; they wanted annexation to a German customs union and a union of the "united power of the German nation" with its focus in Vienna, without racking their brains about the Bohemian, Polish, Hungarian, Illyrian, and the Lombardo-Venetian questions. For their black-red-gold enthusiasm these problems seemed not even to exist. Another group, especially the Viennese bourgeoisie and the academic legion, who had fought through a civil war in the capital, saw only the domestic battle front, not the conflict of the nationalities. They welcomed the struggle of the Hungarians and the Italians against Metternich's oppression and adopted as axiomatic, in their doctrinaire optimism, that the common freedom would reconcile all the nations of the monarchy peacefully and would lead to a greater Austrian federal state of peoples. What would happen to Germany did not interest them in detail; it was enough that freedom be achieved everywhere. With this frame of mind no revolutionary constitution could be constructed for Germany. The one enthusiasm was as useless and as far from reality as the other. The two groups agreed only that they did not seriously consider being separated voluntarily from the non-German portions of the Reich which had grown together with them for centuries. However, the German Austrians thereby entangled themselves in an insoluble inconsistency. They sang Arndt's song "What is the German Fatherland," but they wrapped their patriotic feelings with a deep lack of awareness. Friedrich Hebbel characterized them aptly as he wrote in April, 1848, "The dear Austrians are now musing upon how they can be united with Germany, without uniting themselves with Germany. It will be difficult to carry this out, as difficult as if two people who want to kiss wish to do so standing back to back."

In this case the men who saved the Austrian state for the Austrian temperament were really more logical. Windischgrätz and Jellachich consistently opposed the *grossdeutsch* enthusiasm. On the contrary, they worked for a complete separation of the German Austrians from the fate of the confederation so that Austria might form a new black-yellow Habsburg Reich, which would develop into a largely federal Austrian-Slavic-Magyar triumvirate under a German ruling house. If the new Prime Minister, Prince Schwarzenberg, did not continue this line and did not distance himself from German matters, this was only because he could not bear any competition near him, because he would not allow any powerful German national state to emerge next to his great Austria. Out of this, then, the plan of a Reich of seventy million was born. To call this plan "*grossdeutsch*" is a delusion, since Schwarzenberg's plan of a middle

European Reich would have stamped the area of the German people (*without* the north-east) as an appendage to the Habsburg monarchy. It was a greater Austrian project, that was conceived no less from historical-political ideas than the intention of many greater Prussian politicians who wished to make Germany as far as the Main or beyond into an appendix of a state dominated by Prussia.

Not a single Austrian was willing to pay the price of a *grossdeutsch* unification: the sacrifice of the Austrian state's existence; and yet exactly this unreasonable expectation had to be imposed on the Germans in the east mark if they wanted to build a great German state. Whoever wanted to become a citizen of the German Reich had to give up his citizenship in the Austrian Reich. This unreasonable demand, however, was rejected by the delegates from the Alpine regions in October, 1848, with few exceptions. "The German Austrians will be friends of Germany and keep in step with it, will be Germans as long as they do not demand that we can no longer be Austrians," declared the delegate Beidtel in the name of his countrymen on October 24, 1848 in the national assembly.[151] One can sympathize with emotions evoked by history and blood, with the feelings and interests which united the majority of the Austrian families to their multinational state and its great traditions. However, if Austria wanted to preserve its unitary state and east-middle European function as an entity, then only a political separation was possible, since Germany was determined to finally become something complete. Georg Waitz and especially Dahlmann, in their October speeches in St. Paul's Church, discussed seriously and with the strongest inward sympathy the fate of their German brothers beyond the Raab. The highest goal of the Frankfurt architects could only be to build a united and circumscribed construction without exceptive paragraphs, without incessant considerations for a federal state gravitating towards a foreign center. If German Austria entered the proposed Reich completely and without reservations, all of the wishes of the Germans would be fulfilled. If it could not do it because Austria-Hungary was determined to remain together, the national wishes must recede and the political necessity be observed. Then only an international legal tie would exist between a united Germany and a powerful Habsburg state. The hope of a later reunification of the divided brothers was never ruled out. For when the building of the German national state was completed, and if the process of national decomposition in the Danube Monarchy progressed further, then the millions of Germans west of the Leitha themselves might someday wish to move into the finished house of the German Reich.

That was the draft of St. Paul's Church for the solution of the German question. It was so little *kleindeutsch* in its most intimate striving that, on the contrary, it laid the entire decision of Germany's future in the hands of the Austrians. Could it have done more? If the Moravian delegate Giskra, who was ready to tear up the Pragmatic Sanction like a scrap of invalid paper and was prepared to concede every nationality complex its own constitutional body, had prevailed upon his Austrian countrymen then perhaps like would have attracted like. If the Viennese revolution in alliance with the Hungarian and Italian revolts had finally been successful, then a chance would have existed for a state including all Germans. The German Confederation would probably have included the Kingdom of Bohemia and thereby have given shelter to a strong center of danger for the future. But the question of a monarch for the nascent national state would have then been easy to solve. In the competition for the throne of this liberal united Germany the house of Habsburg (perhaps in the form of a collateral line) would have had justifiable prospects for the first position; because the *grossdeutsch* sentiment still predominated in Frankfurt, and in most other parts of the Reich, in October 1848. And Frederick William IV certainly would have done his part to make the imperial dignity hereditary in the Austrian house. He was already carrying on a correspondence with the Imperial Vicar Johann on this matter.

All of these dreams certainly ended when Schwarzenberg declared on November 27, 1848: Austria's continuance as a political unity is a German and a European necessity. Now a clear difference of opinion was unavoidable. Now the glib Baron Schmerling, who obscured hard reality, was replaced by a clear proponent of a national state in the presidency of the Reich cabinet. Schwarzenberg's manifesto was a declaration of war by the new centralized double monarchy against the unification work of St. Paul's Church. And soon there developed out of this the desire for the entrance of the entire absolutist Habsburg unitary state with all of its non-German territories into the future German constitution. This meant a predominance of 38 million Austrians compared to the 32 million remaining Germans; also in a house of states the 38 imperial votes would stand against 32 "others." This would have amounted to an intensified reversion to the old confederation and a surrender of all the accomplishments of the March revolution. St. Paul's Church was now thrown back on itself, and it had to prove who among the representatives of the people was still prepared and capable of protecting the idea of the national state.

Since Schwarzenberg had made it clear that Austria would never allow itself to be split apart without a show of force, in reality only two parties remained in Frankfurt: the greater Austrian and the hereditary imperial. Between them swung a richly nuanced group of unionists, that is, of plan makers who still hoped to draw both power nuclei in middle Europe together on a basis of equality in some sort of looser form of confederation and to avoid the alternatives between a national state and the historical Danube Reich. For instance, the *grossdeutsch* constitutional project of February 15, 1849 was such a unionist program, which envisioned for Austria a solution similar to that for Holland and Denmark: in the German Austrian provinces, which henceforth, as previously, would alone continue to belong to the confederation, a purely German regency should be established; in addition, the confederation would be led by a directory, in which the imperial executive dignity would alternate between the Austrian Emperor and the King of Prussia. It was perhaps a usable suggestion for a compromise to find the way out of a tactical bottleneck, but it was hardly the original political construction the revolutionary situation surely demanded. The only serious antagonist for Schwarzenberg's constitutional plan arose in Heinrich von Gagern. Against the perceptive tactics of the Viennese statesman and the general mistrust of the Prussian government's intentions, against the hesitant behavior of the Berlin authorities and the strong *grossdeutsch* inclination of the nation, Gagern only slowly won support for his plan of a hereditary emperor from the house of Hohenzollern and the alliance of the narrower and the wider union. In November, during a trip to Berlin, he sought to win the King of Prussia for his plans, but only after mid-January found a narrow majority in St. Paul's Church and some understanding at the court of Frederick William IV. The Prussian plenipotentiary at the Frankfurt central authority, Ludolf Camphausen, had made scanty preparation of the groundwork, but the successful counter-revolution in Berlin and the dictation of a separate constitution in December, the growing emphasis on the unique nature of the Prussian state in public opinion and the cooperation of the Brandenburg-Manteuffel ministry with the reactionary imperial court in Vienna laid new impediments in the way of the *kleindeutsch* plans. The decision again, and more clearly than ever, had to come from Austria's side. Schwarzenberg on March 4, 1849 dissolved the constituent Reichstag in Kremsier and issued a constitution for the entire Austrian state which was completely tuned to an absolutist bureaucratic apparatus. On March 8 he placed his own draft concerning the question of an executive before Frankfurt, which provided for a directory of seven and a chief Reich executive which should rotate every three years between Austria and Prussia. On March 11 the news was finally verified in St. Paul's that Schwarzenberg demanded the entrance of the new unified Austrian state in its entirety into the German Confederation and required a majority in the future house of states. Now the *grossdeutsch* party, which had hitherto been kept alive by all kinds of illusions and had been struggling with double and triple solutions, had to collapse. Schwarzenberg himself, by his demands, forced the federalists into the camp of the hereditary emperor. The idea of the national state was still living in the hearts of the *Kleindeutschers*, and even freedom seemed better guaranteed by a Prussian imperial ruler than by the young Emperor Franz Joseph, who had already bluntly rejected a hereditary crown of Germany around the end of the year.

On March 12, 1849, the conversion of the freedom fighter of Baden, Welcker, into the camp of the *Kleindeutsch* gave the signal for a new coalition of parties in St. Paul's Church. Heinrich von Gagern, to insure himself a majority, opened communications with the left of the house and made generous, democratic concessions in the new Reich constitution, which won above all the members of the "Westendhalle." Universal suffrage in its freest form without electors, without census, and without any other limitations was conferred on all reputable Germans over the age of 25. The Emperor was limited to a suspensive veto over the measures of the *Reichstag*. Half of the house of states would be nominated by the governments, the remainder delegated by the popular assemblies of the states. It was neither an assembly of princes nor a hereditary house of peers, and like the popular house, had the right to propose laws and to indict the ministers. If both houses voted three times in the same sense, such a measure of the *Reichstag* would become law even without the approval of the hereditary emperor. After such protection of the parliamentary governmental form in the Reich constitution, on March 27, 1849, the inherited nature of the emperor's office was approved by a slight majority, the constitution accepted on its second reading, and on the following day with 290 votes against 248 abstentions, King Frederick William IV was elected as sovereign. Prussia and 27 individual governments had already consented in February to the constitutional plan of the hereditary emperor, and there is no reason to suggest that this constitution did not correspond to the will of the German people.[152] It suited not merely the majority of the nation's representatives, but also the circumstances of political power and showed how the revolution could be spiritually overcome and a bond between the monarchy and the popular movement could be re-established in the German question.[153] No one had a better solution to suggest than a political union in a narrow *kleindeutsch* circle, and a broader connection, perhaps constitutionally based, with greater Austria, if this disdainful state could exist in the midst of the unleashed national passions. Finally then, only those who rejected the *kleindeutsch* way from pure negation were prepared to completely capitulate to Schwarzenberg's demand of absolute hegemony. Not because they associated any political expectations with Vienna's generous universal state intentions, or because they had in mind an explicit picture of a particular form of state, but only because Prussia still terrorized them like the bogey man, did the west German Catholics, the Bavarian particularists, and the Swabian democrats in the St. Paul's Church draw together to form a very unbalanced anti-Prussian team, that hardly deserved any more the name "*grossdeutsch.*" The true *grossdeutsch* party was carried to the grave on October 31, 1848 with the victory of the Yugoslav regiments over the German bourgeoisie in Vienna. Since then groups certainly existed in Germany who would have been happiest if the triumphal sweep of Prince Windischgrätz had continued in a march on to Berlin. The ebullient Privy Councillor Buss in Freiburg once expressed it, "Only when our Radetzky stands in Berlin will the fortress of Protestantism be taken." But no one would call this *grossdeutsch.*

The attacks against the north German Great Power could not, however, disguise the fact that the German constitution in a bourgeois-liberal, constitutional sense could only be administered by Prussia. The central problem of the revolution was not republic or monarchy, not federal state or unitary state, and not even *kleindeutsch* or *grossdeutsch*, but rather: Prussia and the Reich. It was still the same problem in 1871 which encumbered Bismarck's creation, and had not settled down even in the Weimar Republic. It is highly possible that in the year 1848 under the jurisdiction of liberal doctrines it would have been more easily soluble than later under the hand of the Mark Junker, who disdained development through ideas. To a great extent the German people are indebted to the romantic conceptions and the personality of Frederick William IV for the fact that a satisfactory solution of the Prussian-German question did not occur in 1848-1849. The autocratic reverie and fantasy of the mentally ill king was thereby almost as pernicious for our national development as the romantic armament delusion of William II and the romantic racial dogma of Adolf Hitler. The Prussian King, who after all had promised to set himself at the pinnacle of Germany and to bring honor to the black-red-gold banner, even deprived the bogged-down German Revolution of its fruits and squandered the little that could have been saved by the forbearance of princely sovereignty and the approbation of foreign states. That Frederick William denied the law of the hour, not from frivolousness, but rather from an inner urgency of conscience, does not lessen the fatefulness of his conduct. He not only destroyed the German constitution, but also dug the grave of German unity. He had not merely refused to participate in the revolution with contempt for a crown, "by the grace of bakers and butchers," out of animosity toward the sovereignty of parliament and universal suffrage, but rather from a profound aversion to the illegal act in itself. Usurpation from below as from above seemed to him the root of all evil, and an attack on the holy structure of the old Reich hierarchy seemed to him a criminal blow against the validity of law itself. As the romantic admirer of the Holy Roman Empire of the German Nation, he was moreover of the opinion that "Germany without Trieste, Tyrol, and the glorious grand duchies would be worse than a face without a nose." So in the hour of 1848 a true respect for the basis of all law and an exaggerated dream of the old imperial glory combined to rob the Germans of the reward for their endeavours. Even in the days of Baron vom Stein, perhaps an idealized glance backward at the middle ages, that combined the true conservatism of Stein with fantastic ideals to capture a historical outward trapping for its character, hindered any clear aspiration toward goals and stable constitutional construction in the political reconstruction of Germany.

The constructive spirit of the constitutional drafts of St. Paul's Church had originally considered another path. An hereditary or elected emperor for the proposed Reich of the Germans would be transplanted to Frankfurt. He would not be vested with his own house regiment, rather merely with a civil list. Without a political apparatus, in order for this sovereign to exist, both Great Powers, Austria and Prussia, and the more than 30 other sovereign Princes would have had to renounce voluntarily their authority over the army, foreign policy, patent rights, the courts, and customs matters. Such an emperor without a country could have only established himself and played his part if the princes and kings were deposed by the revolution or if the states were dissolved. And in fact close attention was paid at least to the dissolution of Prussia as the presupposition for the Frankfurt imperial dignity. Only a portion, so they reflected, not the entirety of the Prussian state could be absorbed into a German unitary state. This Max von Gagern had already recognized on his tour, and all sorts of pamphlets and newspaper articles had developed this train of thought. But the states' sovereignty itself gained new support from the constitutional developments. From the time that not merely the lesser states, but also both of the large states possessed their own legislature, their own parliamentary apparatus, and their own revolutionary memories, the division or the dissolution of states was out of the question. The Berlin national assembly was correctly perceived by the Frankfurt St. Paul's Church as its most dangerous opponent. The recognition that only an emperor ruling the Reich with his own palace guard could prevail against the other states was therefore thrown into the debate at an early stage by realists like Droysen and Heinrich von Gagern, as probably had always been intended by Dahlmann in his drafts. Therein lay not a disguised Prussian power egotism, but statesmanly insight and prudent resignation in face of political necessity.

Also the suggestions coming from abroad made by the English-Belgian-Coburg circle began with the assumption that a German state able to survive could only be created if Prussia took its place at the top of the liberal structure, making a distinction between the Hohenzollern possessions in the Reich and the other territories. Prussia would then have to forego its own constitution and be ruled under the Reich constitution. At most, the Prussian provincial legislatures could be allowed to remain beside the Reich parliament. The other federal states might retain their chambers. These would have already declined in importance to the level of provincial assemblies if the King of Prussia ruled over the whole with a Reich cabinet and a two-chamber *Reichstag*, and was invested with authority over the army, foreign policy, the courts, and tariff and commercial matters. Austria would be free then to remain a unitary state outside the new borders, or to allow its German portions, Bohemia, and the Erzlande to be absorbed into the Prussian-German Reich. "Under no circumstances can it rule Germany." This sentence was an established fact for the Coburg advisors as much as for the *kleindeutsch* liberals. Prince Consort Albert of England, his uncle King Leopold of Belgium, Archduke Ernst of Saxe-Coburg-Gotha, and his worldly wise and perceptive counsellor Baron von Stockmar had assailed the King of Prussia since the end of March, 1848 with memoranda and letters. Under the influence of Stockmar, they intensified their opinion that Frederick William must set himself, in the form of the Prussian hereditary emperor, at the summit of the bourgeois revolution in Germany. He should be on intimate terms with Austria as a support in their internal crisis; in Germany he should be liberal and work with that coupling of Prussia and Reich which would allow the King-Kaiser to reign more monarchically with a *Reichstag* and an upper house of princes than with a democratic Prussian legislature.[155] It was indeed an almost Bismarckian solution of the German constitutional problem, only without black-and-white reservations and without the pride of an individual state. At that time a Prussian government, by proceeding energetically, perhaps could have shaped the iron of German unity in the cooling fire of the revolution to hammer out the form of a constitution by which Prussia commanded matters and simultaneously merged into Germany. There was talk of an offer from the Frankfurt authorities that Prussia should occupy the posts of prime minister, foreign minister, and minister of defense in a Reich ministry, and at one time Stockmar and Bunsen, besides the officeholding General Peucker, were mentioned as candidates.[156]

But in Berlin the wind was already blowing from a completely different direction. Since the resignation of Heinrich von Arnim in June, 1848, no one really had a heart for Prussia's German policy, least of all the king himself. The answer that Frederick William IV imparted in August, 1848 to his liberal advisors was full of absurd superciliousness. The quick-tempered king, in long marginal comments, answered the suggestions that his ambassador in London and his Coburg friend had submitted to him. The national assembly in Frankfurt was for him only a "meeting of 600 subjects of various princes and cities," who hopefully would never possess the effrontery to lay before "a prince of over 16 million people" the ultimatum of whether or not he wanted to lead them. The King of Prussia still thought of himself, in spite of his speeches of a bourgeois king on March 18 and 19, as the absolute master, who commanded a magnificently disciplined 400,000 man army. He feared that he as emperor would not even have "command" of his five Reich ministers. Instead, the body corporate of the people would control the actual command of the Prussian armed forces. A Reich minister of defense responsible to parliament would wrench disposition over the troops from the hand of the king. The Prussian military monarchy could thus only lose if it submitted to a Reich constitution. Only Germany, not Prussia, according to the curious conception of Frederick William, had undergone a revolution, and the Prussian crown would be very foolish if it let itself be fettered by a Reich ministry which was responsible to the people. It would retain its character as a military monarchy only if it remained apart and did not allow its sovereignty to be encroached upon. As for the desirable shape of Germany, Frederick William now as ever had his brocaded conceptions that related to the imperial magnificence of 1806 and even to the Christian world monarchy. The king "wished in his own land, as in the entire German land, delineation of what actually exists, the thousand-year-old arrangement, which has made our German people, consciously and unconsciously, . . . on this side and across the ocean, into the leading people of the world (since the decline of the Romans)."[157] This "thousand-year-old arrangement" demanded that the Emperor of Austria, with his 20 million non-German subjects, remain the "greatest lord of Germany." Even if the empire had fallen into decay, which there was no denying, one should not forget that the throes of the Ottoman Empire lasted more than a thousand years. The Roman Empire of the German Nation must be allowed at least this much time, and in the meanwhile be treated with due honor. Frederick William IV openly admitted that Austria, perhaps spontaneously and under its own volition, would withdraw completely from the Reich association. He realized "that Germany would allow no troops for the conquest of Hungary, Croatia, Galicia, or Italy, yea not even arrange for unauthorized volunteers." Nevertheless, he was so dominated by his historical conceptions and his unfortunate notion of the thousand year Reich of the past, that he could only see the relationship between Prussia and Austria as it had been dogmatized by Radowitz. Moreover this division of roles was really only thirty, at most one-hundred-fifty years old, and had nothing to do with the "thousand-year arrangement" of the old German Reich. It is almost unbearable to witness how for a precious irretrievable year the monomania of Frederick William IV stifled every political innovation. The ideals of political romanticism could hardly offend against German life more than they did by the ultra-divine right of kings and the Reich ideology of the absolute soldier king. The king had himself acclaimed by his faithful as the oracle and mouthpiece of the deity while German matters wasted away.

Also in the autumn and winter 1848-49, Frederick William held rigidly to his refusal. Neither Gagern's compromise, which would have drawn Austria back in the form of a wider union, nor Palmerston's encouraging hint that offered the prospect of England's recognition for a federal state under Prussia's guidance,[158] could elicit from the Prussian king any other response than a dismayed rejection of the Frankfurt constitutional plans, as he was filled with aversion which was intensified by his own sinful behavior during the March days. The emperor's crown, which lay at his feet unclaimed for many months, was to him "carrion," a devilment "baked from dung and dirt," since he had again purified his own royal crown in the fire of counter-revolution. When in April, 1849 a delegation from the Frankfurt St. Paul's Church under Edward Simson transmitted to him the offer of the imperial dignity, Frederick William scorned this "dog collar, with which they want to chain me to the revolution of 1848."

Historians have tried to apologize for the decision of the king.

Not legitimist thought, rather foreign clouds and the fear of a seven years' war were supposed to have held the king back; his denial was, seen realistically, correct. Now certainly Austria and Russia were allied and jealous of Prussia's enhanced power. But they were tied down in Hungary. On the other hand, Louis Napoleon was prepared to abandon the smaller German states, and the English foreign secretary had expressed himself relatively clearly in favor of a *kleindeutsch* Reich. It is therefore absolutely uncertain, even extremely doubtful, whether Frederick William IV would have been compelled to fight for his emperor's crown. Perhaps he might have been forced to give the rising Caesar in the Tuileries some compensation, but Bismarck later reckoned with this too; even the intelligent Cavour had to pay this price. Frederick William need not have been either a great military commander nor even a great statesman. A modicum of political usefulness and common sense would have been sufficient, and a Frederick the Great on the throne was absolutely not necessary. Probably a simple Coburg prince on the throne and a capable ministry in Berlin would have sufficed to procure a solution to the German question.

Even in May, 1849 the sturdy proponents of a hereditary emperor had not given up all hope. They had taken into account a retreat by the romantic king.[159] But in spite of the nervous excitement which also went through the Prussian monarchy, in spite of the insurrection in favor of the Reich constitution which flared up in Saxony, Baden and the Palatinate, in spite of the approval that the plan of the Prussian-German state found even among the people of lower Saxony, the work of St. Paul's Church had miscarried. The national assembly was obliged to witness how it crumbled away progressively, first through the recall of the Austrian, then of the Prussian delegates, and how without the protection of the Prussian power-state it was impotent. There was no choice for the representatives of the people who had to persevere in Frankfurt but to pass their days playing dominos, until they were completely scattered in Stuttgart by the Wurtemberg cavalry.

Nevertheless one should not throw stones at the men of St. Paul's Church. Karl Marx, in a malicious pamphlet, called them "an assembly of old wives" and thereby set the tone for really wounding criticism.[160] The Frankfurt national assembly was no "mere debater's club made up of a number of gullible simpletons."[161] The tragedy of German idealism, which sought and could not find the path from conception to reality, at that time acted out an especially vivid part which gripped the heart. That Swabian delegate had really characterized correctly the essence of the Frankfurt parliament when he defended the unfortunate assembly in a letter to his Nürtingen and Kirchheim constituents: "The equitable and impartial critics of the contemporary and future world will say that it was incapable of overcoming the weaknesses of the German character; however, it was not lacking in the finest and the best characteristics of our people, and a nation cannot demand of its representatives that they be better than it is itself as a whole." [162]

X

THE VICTORY OF THE COUNTER-REVOLUTION IN VIENNA AND BERLIN

It is not entirely accurate to say that the German revolution was subdued by the Slavs because a Bohemian magnate and a Croatian officer closed the ring on Vienna. It is even less true that only the entry of Tsar Nicholas I into Hungary directed the counter-revolution to victory. It is even doubtful that the Magyars' insurrection would not have been finally overpowered, without any Russian help, by the Viennese emperor's innate strength after Austria crushed the Italian freedom movement. Above all, neither the alliance with the Tsar nor the alliance with the Croatian Ban was a surrender of the Danube monarchy to Slavism. Vienna was not conquered in the name of Czech or Yugoslavian political power, but rather because of the Habsburg's imperial ideal, whose dynastic-military idea of state still possessed an indestructible power over the nation in the Danube area; for this reason, the revolution in the western half of the double monarchy collapsed. Also this imperial state of the black and yellow flag, although it proceeded from the beginning against the Frankfurt St. Paul's Church, acted in the name of Teutonism and believed that German influence in the Habsburg's aggregate monarchy, in the remote regions of Bohemia, Galicia, Hungary, Serbia, and Lombardy, still prevailed by right. The Teutonic ideal in this context, to be sure, had no nationalistic undertone. The imperial state was German, not because its *objective* was to Germanize the south-east, but rather because by its *nature* the German element predominated in the military and bureaucracy, at the court and in the judicial system. On the other hand, one expected that a Habsburg emperor master as many as possible of the several languages spoken by his eleven distinct peoples. This tradition of the black-yellow Danube state could also still completely fulfil and intoxicate the urban masses of Vienna. Black-red-gold, the flag which fluttered from March until into October from the tower of St. Stephan's cathedral, was in Vienna actually only a domestic political banner, the sign that the Viennese bourgeoisie demanded a constitution after the model of the French and Belgians. Black-yellow, on the contrary, were the colors of foreign policy, the flag of the state, of the Catholic faith, of tradition, and of a powerful history. One needed only to show it clearly to awaken the devotion to all of these values among the Austrian people. The revolution of 1848 was smashed on the hard reality that one cannot destroy historical political fabric and historical symbols, proud memories and hereditary continuity through resolutions of a victorious party. These can only be extinguished from the memory of man when they have lost their vital inner force.

It was not merely a surprise for the revolutionary, but also for the counter-revolutionary, and above all for the cabinets of London, Paris, and St. Petersburg as they witnessed the astounding energy of the Habsburg Reich, that after a generation of pacifist, almost cowardly, policy, it now suddenly tightened in the fire of the revolution to a martial rigor that no one would have ever expected of this ponderous and old-fashioned colossus.

The March revolution had set Metternich's state into dissolution. The Czechs and the Poles conspired, the Hungarians and the Italians stood in revolt, Croatia and Slovenia set their own objectives. The emperor fled to Innsbruck, and in the capital the main lecture hall of the students and the national guard of the burghers dominated things almost as earlier in revolutionary Paris. The alliance of radical students, especially from the technical schools, and the workers from the suburbs was nowhere as intimate as in Vienna. The Calabrian hat and the student's cocked hat, romantic figures with knotty cudgels and pistol-decorated belts dominated the street scene of the elegant city. The greater part of the aristocratic society and the flood of foreign diplomats had disappeared. Beside the ardent revolutionary enthusiasm and the bloody barricade spirit, there flourished a cheerful sense of the *gemütlich* Viennese. Any day could bring the proclamation of a republic from the side of extremists, but any day a victorious general also might march from Prague, Verona, or Zagreb and dictate a new order with bayonets and cannons.[163] The eighty-two year old Field Marshal Radetzky had scattered the army of Charles Albert of Piedmont, partially with Hungarian and Yugoslavian troops. The forty year old Margrave of Croatia, Slavonia, and Dalmatia, Joseph Baron von Jelachich, stood ready in Zagreb. With his bald forehead, his muscular stature and fine hands, the black dragoon officer was an almost Napoleonic figure, all in all the expression of unusual vigor and wild love of life, who already enjoyed in the circle of his regimental comrades an almost passionate affection. The Commander of the City of Prague was Prince Windischgrätz, a large landed proprietor in Bohemia and a capable general, whose beloved wife had just been shot in his city palace by the rebels. He had become the "guardian angel" of the German inhabitants in Bohemia and was included by clergymen in their pulpit prayers every Sunday. A consummate gentleman, he remained as military commander without any feeling of personal revenge, imperturbable, powerful, self-assured, so that even the Czech burghers of Prague finally began to admire him almost fanatically.

The only thing which might have caused the collapse of the Habsburg monarchy in the summer of 1848 would have been an invasion by France in northern Italy. If Field Marshal Radetzky, who had just triumphantly entered Milan and had assembled the Habsburg's Reich aristocrats in his officer corps, had the victory wrested out of his hands by the French army, it would have been the end of the empire. Then in Vienna the republic would have been proclaimed, Italy been annexed to France, Hungary and perhaps the Czechs would have gone their separate ways, and the historical political unit of the double monarchy have been dissolved. The Frankfurt central government and its Austrian members had already followed this idea to its final consequences. Above all it was Schmerling who, in his trusted circle, discussed the division of the Danube monarchy: Hungary to the Archduke Stephan, Bohemia and Moravia for the heir to the throne Franz Joseph, Poland and Lombardy independent as payment on account to England, France, and Piedmont, German-Austria to provide house regiments for the Imperial Vicar, Archduke Johann. But actually only a military defeat on a great scale on the battlefields of the Lombardy plains, the old chessboard of the Reich's history, could have brought this result. And Cavaignac, the dictator of France, wanted no foreign conflicts.

Meanwhile chaotic conditions spread in Vienna. The elected Reichstag conferred day and night and honestly supported the ministry, which was forced to install the regular army, in addition to the burghers' national guard, to maintain control over new putsch attempts by student extremists. A strong gift for statesmanship was even more rare among the Viennese bourgeoisie than among the Frankfurt delegates and the Berlin opposition leaders. The young, slender, hardly thirty year old Finance Minister Bach was really an outstanding, courageous, and independent technical official, but as such, naturally rather an enlightened absolutist than a parliamentary party leader, and was no match for the waves of such a complicated domestic struggle, in which religious, national, and ideological fronts cut across one another in confusion. Slavic and Reich German, bourgeois and socialist agitators criss-crossed each other in their radical propaganda. Palacky, Fröbel, Hecker, and even Karl Marx were personally in Vienna during this summer, spoke in the clubs, and each hoped to win the decisive battle for his cause on this fervid soil of Vienna. And how far their concrete objectives were from one another! As is well known, Marx had always emphasized that Bohemia was part of a future German cultural sphere of influence, even though the Czechs might retain their own language for "a few more decades." Palacky, however, the important Czech popular leader and historian, wanted to transform Austria into a federal Slavic Reich, that would be obliged to annex a great portion of eastern Germany; "Dresden and Leipzig are Slavic cities, in which the Germans have established themselves."[164] Julius Fröbel had expressed the fear even then, in his pamphlet, "Vienna and Europe," that if it was not possible to create the democratic union of the United States of Middle Europe from the hub of Vienna, then the Russian border would be extended to the Austrian capital.

Who could make order out of the domestic and external confusion? Who was the man able to prevail against the multiplicity of revolutionary powers, groups, persons, and tendencies, which

145

already in August and September governed in confusion? The quarrel in the Reichstag over the abolition of enforced labor without compensation (*Fron*), the dispute between the unemployed and the ministry about wages for public works, the enlistment for the Italian army, and the national war of the Serbo-Croatians against the Magyars offered occasion for deep divisions. Neither the Reichstag, the national guard, nor the student committee was holding the reins, and the Bach-Latour ministry opened secret ties to Radetzky, Windischgrätz, and Jelachich. On October 6 all bonds broke. On the occasion of the departure for Hungary of a grenadier battalion that was supposed to come to the aid of the reactionary Ban of Croatia, the German regiments, who refused to allow themselves to be misused in this civil war, mutinied. The street people and countrymen united with them. Armed peasants were approaching from Marchfeld. The Minister of War, Latour, to whom was attributed the primary responsibility for the bloodshed of this morning, was discovered in the attic of his ministry and brutally murdered. This lynch justice was signal for a wild civil war between civilians and military, in which the "March heroes" played a very inglorious role, and the regular revolutionary power was no longer able to direct the masses. The armory was evacuated by the government's troops under orders of the Reichstag after a battle lasting hours. The court withdrew for a second time under military cover to Olmütz, and executive power was transferred to a quickly formed committee of public safety, then later almost completely to the Viennese city council. The bourgeoisie trembled before the newly formed mobile guard with red cockades, before the student committee flushed with victory, and before the terror of the worker battalions. A central committee from the democratic societies sought to play the role of the Jacobin Club and to gain control of the reins of government. Even the man who finally was appointed by the remaining members of the Reichstag and the committee of public safety as the commander in chief of revolutionary Vienna, Wenzel Messenhauser, was no political leader. Son of a drum major, who nevertheless advanced in the imperial army from common soldier to lieutenant, he appeared to be more a man of letters than a strategist. He was a friend of the worker and had written a social drama whose production he was discussing with the municipal theater on the day before his execution. But he was much too soft to play the part of a revolutionary dictator. The Polish General Bem, an ingenious farm laborer who had taken part already in the Napoleonic wars and enjoyed great prestige, from his iron-hard soldier's nature, was supposed to defend the walls of the rebellious city against the approaching northern army. But funds were granted by a finance minister faithful to the constitution, who was ruling in the name of the emperor and naturally could only half-heartedly arm for defense against the imperial officers. In addition, on October 17 a delegation from the Frankfurt leftist parties arrived, headed by Robert Blum and Julius Fröbel, to underline the world revolutionary meaning of the Viennese struggle. They were received with jubilation, girded with swords, and named honorary members of the academic legion. The fanatical Robert Blum got carried away in his passionate speeches and went completely over to the side of the rebels. He declared that another 200 men must be "Latourized" before freedom was secure.

It was no longer German liberalism which was fighting in Vienna, but an unclear democratic-socialistic Internationale, its political objectives hardly really conscious yet, which wanted to form an alliance of the Germans, Poles, Hungarians, and Italians against everything that smelled of the old state and the old faith. It was the struggle of the permanent revolution against the status quo, against society, against the existing forms in general. This united red front encountered now, however, not merely the historical imperial state and the reaction, not just the hesitating mistrust of the peasants of upper and lower Austria that refused to muster for a general levy,[165] but also the instinct of the Viennese petty bourgeois, to the extent that he did not belong to the politicized proletariat. All observers agree that the Viennese population, for the most part, was disposed toward the black-yellow, and the triumphant entry of the troops of Generals Windischgrätz and Jelachich received an unparalleled outburst of enthusiasm, even though these soldiers entering Vienna were a bloody military regiment. They knew precisely that the wild Croatians in red coats and fez had drawn their naked daggers only shortly before in the field camp and remarked with a grin, "For the students!" In this liberation very little pardon could be expected for the host of the rebellious Viennese youth, for the remaining loyal members of the Reichstag and the revolutionary city council. Nevertheless the blood-red regi-

147

ments of reaction were cheered. Among the foreign diplomats, who at the time watched the unequal struggle from the sidelines, the sudden change in atmosphere of the masses awoke a deep mistrust for the inconstancy of public opinion. "The good Viennese have shown themselves in their absolute baseness. Yesterday, hardly had Prince Jablonowski stormed the outer city gate and taken the municipal and paradise gardens than the troops were greeted with joy, and in the open market the national guard, which a few minutes before had fired on them, greeted and embraced them as liberators. The exultation with which the Ban was received today in the entire city, the unending cheers which greet the Croatian heros, are new proof of the lack of character of this population. . . . The city council crawled on its knees to thank Prince Windischgrätz for the deliverance of the city, for the restoration of order and true freedom, and for the leniency and consideration which His Serene Highness deigned to display in this. And a week ago the Field Marshal, in a proclamation of this very same city council, was called Mr. Windischgrätz, who, like a new Brennus, was trampling under foot natural rights and international law."[166]

Perhaps the disdain of the Saxon diplomat whom we have to thank for this report would have been less bitter if he had realized that the uneasiness of the Viennese population had actually lasted for several months, and had only been suppressed by the revolutionary terror. Disregarding the fact that real power usually makes an enthusiastic impression on most people, and the power and success lay clearly with the regular troops, the capture of Vienna freed hundreds of thousands from an agonizing conflict of deciding which side was right and who was really protecting whom from whom. For an instant, indeed, the decision seemed to hang from a thread, when on October 30 the Hungarians under Kossuth crossed the Leitha behind Windischgrätz's army to relieve Vienna, which had already unconditionally capitulated. But the hope was deceptive; even a breach of the capitulation forced by the partisan leaders could not alter the fate of the capital. The Hungarian general levy was thrown back, and on the following day the besieging army, after a bitter week-long struggle in the heart of the city, advanced to Stephansplatz. After the victory the field marshal, arrogantly and severely but neither brutally nor vindictively, cleared out the "snot-nose establishment," as he called them contemptuously. The Reichstag, to make it independent of the capital's influence, was transferred to the small Moravian town Kremsier, where it could hammer out constitutional plans for a few more months without any disturbances. The court martial in the meantime worked unobtrusively but without any consideration for the rest of the world. Even the execution of Robert Blum no longer made any special sensation in stupefied Vienna. His companion Julius Fröbel was pardoned, because in his pamphlets he had extolled Vienna as the center of the German-European federative system. While the Frankfurt national assembly duly resolved the dissolution of the imperial state, Prince Felix Schwarzenberg stepped onto the historical stage as the new prime minister. The Danube monarchy suddenly was on the map again as an international eminence of the first order and also intended to demonstrate its character as a Great Power. The wielder of power in France, General Cavaignac, congratulated Windischgrätz that his glorious deed had proved of "the greatest benefit for Germany and Austria, and had also provided an outstanding service for France and all of Europe." The Russian Tsar sent the Great Cross of his two highest orders in diamonds, and in Vienna for days and weeks the "liberators" were given one ovation after another at banquets and in the theater. Even in moderate circles they were relieved that the Habsburgs had recovered their authority under their own power, because they feared that otherwise the knout of the white Tsar might restore the Danube Reich to a legitimate order from the outside. Now however, the Germans were spared this disgrace by the imperial army, and their dynastic patriotism was satisfied.

The law of the radicalization of extreme groups operated in the German revolution to the benefit of the reaction. Just as in April, 1848 the outbreak of social disturbances and rebellion, that had little to do with the political ideal of the constitutionalization of Germany, drove the entire middle class into the arms of the old powers of order and divided liberalism, the Viennese October revolt was more than adequate to provide an efficacious slogan to the counter-revolution. The chaotic regiments of students and workers, of barricade fighters and democratic clubs proved correct those who said: we have only the choice between military despotism and anarchy, between the reign of terror from above and the reign of terror from below. Windischgrätz, whose intelligent moderation

149

and scrupulousness is not to be denied, had the advantage that he incarnated dictatorship and legitimacy in one person, that he was at the same time imperial officer and a victorious Cavaignac. And this combination made him irresistible. The revolution had exposed itself as chaos and demoralization, as powerless frenzy and social upheaval. Let the Frankfurt professors continue to believe in the constitutional reconciliation of opposites, in Vienna they had undergone certain experiences and were happy to enter the safe harbor of enlightened reaction.

In Berlin they were about to go the same path and even without the test of strength of a rebellious commune, merely with the help of expansion of military power by the monarchy and on the basis of a certain psychological conformity with law.

In what we call reaction, the outward occurrence of a more or less violent restoration of the old regime and the internal event of a shift in mood and a backlash of public opinion may be clearly differentiated. The mental response of the masses to the events of revolution was quite complex. Exhaustion, indifference, and disappointment combine with a heightened greed for sensations and the desire for ever-something-new. In the soberness, self-consciousness, and cooling off usually lay some shame for one's own extravagances and a sceptical shrug of the shoulder, because in the tangible matters in life nothing had really changed, and the political disturbances had only made economic life and the working day difficult. Among the moderates and fellow travelers of a revolution this shift in mood found an especially rich soil. One became afraid of the ever increasing speed of the rolling wheel, of the social consequences, the effects on business, the disadvantages for commercial policy: above all, there was fear of the sinister downfall of the gods, that even threatened to carry away images that one did not wish to dispense with. Among those who at first were enthusiastic about the ideals of the revolution and then in the name of "education and civilization" very quickly imposed a check belonged not merely the unprincipled opportunists and those obedient to power, but also men like Alexander von Humboldt or David Friedrich Strauss, who were completely relieved when the confused hotheads on both extremes were again tamed. Among those who applauded the reaction numbered not only the family fathers, who were attached to house and profession and wanted to risk nothing, but also the high school teachers and the school rectors, who had had to assemble their students voluntarily or involuntarily at memorial services for the fallen barricade heroes, yet now were relieved that they could again commemorate the old heroes of the fatherland. Also the artisan master and the small shopowner had found a hair in the soup; tired of the obstinacy of their journeymen and apprentices, they were pleased with the arrival of a new disciplinarian. Even the man on the street had enough of the hubbub and found a solid authority to his taste. All who did not welcome a civil war and did not wish to be swept along by a radical ideology to the next abstract step of the revolution instinctively moved to the right and were thus the natural support for the reaction. Only the revolutions of the 20th century have found the means to cut off this law of the reversion of mood. Late in the year 1848 it was in full validity, and it would be false to try to make only the "Camarilla" and a saber-rattling clique of military, just the "court party" and the noble politicians of self-interest responsible for the recoil of events. Certainly there existed in Potsdam even more distinctly than in Schönbrunn an inwardly untouched group of ultra-royalists, who in every stage of the revolution only spoke of it with deep aversion and considered it incompatible with their honor to hold any conviction in common with it. When a Herr von Holtzendorff-Jagow heard that his son had fallen on the barricade, he answered in a cutting tone, "If that is true, then he is no longer my son!" And only as it emerged that his son had not been killed as a rebel, but rather by mistake, did he give way to mourning and pain.[167] Out of this group of unconditionals, to whom at the Berlin court the brothers Gerlach, General Rauch, Count Alvensleben, and Edwin von Manteuffel belonged, the dealings of the reaction originated. But they could only succeed because the people were already prepared in Austria to raise the black-yellow flag as in Prussia the black-and-white, in order to prevent one day only the red color's remaining in the black-red-gold banner.

The actuating event in Prussia was especially significant. It was again a question, as on March 18, of the king's absolute right of command. The Prussian national assembly had resolved on August 9, 1848 that the Ministry of War should give an order to the army warning the officers against reactionary endeavours. Those persons who could not become accustomed to the new constitutional legal state should feel it an obligation of honor to voluntarily resign from the army. The government hesitated in carrying out the chamber's order; finally the Minister of War on September 4 declared point-blank that he would not enforce the resolution. A proposal of deputy Stein in the national assembly renewed the demand to the royal government and was greeted in the assembly and in the streets with stormy approval. Berlin seemed to be on the verge of a new revolution. But the party of the king, alerted by letters of the Tsar and spurred on by the royalist rural population, this time had prepared matters better. Forty to fifty thousand men were distributed around the capital in a wide arc under the orders of the commander of all the troops in the Mark. Father Wrangel, in his rustic and affectedly populist manner, made all sorts of utterances which partially delighted and partially terrified the Berliners. Thus he complained that their beautiful city in the few months of the rule of the people had so declined that grass was growing in the streets. Then he held a parade of the troops in Berlin itself and praised the sharply honed tool of the army. The conciliatory ministry of Pfuel-Eichmann-Bonin-Dönhoff, that honestly wished to come to an agreement on a constitution with the popular assembly, was not strong enough to carry its point against the more strident strain of the secret advisors to the crown. Step by step the constitutional ministers gave way before the sharp will of the king, who had already begun to fall back more on his commanding generals than his legal representatives. The Commander of the Sixth Army Corps in Breslau, Count Brandenburg, had earlier, on his own responsibility, used threatening language about the "inflammatory goings-on" of his provincial capital. Since the end of September Frederick William had developed a conception of his royal mission which agreed neither with the spirit nor with the letter of a constitution. He received a congratulatory delegation of the national assembly in Potsdam with pathetic obstinacy and notions about the basis of the monarchy that were simply against the law. He attempted to sweep along the ministry with the proven means of sentimental appeals. "The die is cast! Your King, gentlemen, goes forward. He will truly not give way. If you forsake him—which God forbid—he will still stand in the breach! Frederick William."[168]

That was the frank program of the counter-revolution. The contrasts deepened as the demonstrators in the streets propagandized tumultuously for support of besieged Vienna with torches, speaking choirs, and a surge of questionable figures. The masses visibly slipped from the grasp of the leftist parliamentary leaders. When the radical delegate Berends, a very famous speaker in the assembly and until then the darling of the working class, stepped from the besieged meeting hall of the national assembly and urged moderation, a burning torch was thrust in his face and an angry howl arose. A few riots, during which first two workers and later a constable were shot during the night, gave the burghers a new occasion to entertain grave fears for their safety. The revolutionaries had not had a large following for a long time. The democratic congress in October ran its weak and helpless course; the intellectual leader of the Berlin left, Franz Benedikt Waldeck, had not taken part at all. So Frederick William IV could risk imitating the step of his distinguished cousin in Vienna and naming a man of military action as prime minister. The king this time entered the domestic political conflict with an excessive self-confidence, that would no longer allow the divine right of royalty to be questioned in great nor in minor matters. Count Brandenburg, who already as the commander in Breslau had adopted a cutting tone *vis-à-vis* civilians, relocated the national assembly into the province and informed it that it could deliberate in a more dignified manner there than before about the formula "by the grace of God," over the right of the king to confer orders, over the abolition of capital punishment and the suppression of the nobility. Wrangel's soldiers scattered their meetings in Berlin, and pursued the delegates wherever they found them, first in the theater, then in the *Hôtel de Russie*, then in the shooting gallery, in the municipal commissioners' hall, and finally in the Mielentz Meeting Hall. The final convulsions of the revolution lacked any support from the strength and courage of the Berlin people. Even the worker failed to give expected aid as comrade in arms to the persecuted parliament, and the slogan of refusal to pay taxes, which the exalted assembly passed around, no longer swept the people off its feet to participate. Since November 12 people accepted the martial law without resistance and even praised the mildness with which Wrangel made use of his mandatory powers.

It was characteristic for the calamitous personal role of Frederick

William IV that even the highly conservative men of his inner circle were far more conciliatory in their thinking than the king himself. The Pomeranian Junker, Senfft von Pilsach, whose opinion the king was accustomed to respect because of religious motives, implored the monarch at the end of November not to abandon the path of his royal promises. Even Leopold von Gerlach found a dissolution of the constituent assembly risky, and Edwin Manteuffel still held firmly to an "arrangement" with a better disposed chamber, that either would be chosen by an exclusive electoral law or by splintering off the opposition so that a sort of conservative rump parliament would remain. But all of these suggestions were too moderate and too indulgent for the dogmatic and self-complacent monarch. Since November he had been wanting "to settle matters and to triumphantly over-turn the March ministry." He was determined neither to confer a Belgian constitution, nor to agree upon a constitution drafted by Camphausen, nor to allow a new chamber to be elected. His intentions were tantamount to a dissolution of the assembly by force, imprisonment of the leaders, and then reversion to the United Landtag and its program of representation based on estates. The guard troops had to return to their garrisons in Berlin and resume the old sentinel duty in the royal palace.[169] If only the outward power and the undisputed command of the army were again in the hands of the monarchy, then the king could confer any constitutional form which appealed to him, even one based on provincial estates, in the manner of a gift given by grace.

On the plane of Prussia's German policy the same pronounced contrast dominated between the harsh king and his conservative advisors. The prime minister of reaction, Count Brandenburg, himself attempted to prepare the king for taking over the *kleindeutsch* imperial dignity and responded reassuringly to the approaches of the Frankfurt delegate F. D. Bassermann. Count Brandenburg understood that he would then have to promulgate a progressive constitution for the Prussian people. And a charter of the "most liberal sort" was therefore also in the anticipated plans of the November government from the beginning, although they also intended to subject this liberal constitution to a revision immediately with the help of a new chamber. But the stubborn old princely pride of Frederick William failed to concur with such a combination of imperial question and constitutional question. His autocratic interest after the victory was concentrated on the ceremonial of the order chapter of the black eagle, in which he would celebrate with a really un-Prussian pomp, in velvet and ermine, the re-birth of the Prussian spirit. Not merely toward the representatives of the people, but also in relations with his freely chosen ministers, the manner of Frederick William IV gave deep justification to the famous words of the Königsberger representative Jacoby, "That's just the problem with kings—they don't want to hear the truth!" The constitution which the king granted on December 5 was, however, copied from the Belgian example. It contained the basic rights of free citizens and combined the exercise of the monarchical powers of government with the cooperation of responsible ministers, divided the legislation between chamber and government, and ceded the representatives of the people surveillance over the state budget. The transition to limited monarchy in Prussia was completed by this constitution, even if the theoretical doctrine that all powers originated in the people was not included and a special right of emergency decree significantly strengthened the royal position. The basically dualistic structure of the constitution was also not called into question in the final form of the Prussian instrument of state that was passed on January 31, 1850 after more than a year of revisionary deliberations. But the tendency of these revisions that were suggested by the government and approved by a conservative majority in the chamber already showed the path which the administration of the constitution would take. The first attack was perhaps the most profound. By the decree of May 30, 1849 the universal equal and secret suffrage that Frederick William IV had publicly granted in March and in December, 1848 was dictatorily abolished in favor of an electoral system which prescribed voting in public and divided each electoral ward into three classes according to payment of taxes. This new suffrage law that gave, above all, the landed estate owners in the country a legal predominance, while the propertied bourgeoisie in Berlin were forced in part to vote in the second and third classes, was designed to insure a conservative party majority in the second chamber. While the democrats spread the word to abstain from the election and thereby possibly made themselves politically mute all too soon, the newly created chamber fulfilled all the expectations that were entertained for it. It subsequently approved the election decree, dissolved the citizen guard, and subordinated the freedom of the press to certain controls; it dismissed completely the administering of an oath to the constitution for the army, and converted the first chamber from an elected body into a house of peers.

Thus originated the revised constitution of January 31, 1850, under which the Prussian state was essentially ruled until 1918. On paper it was still a constitutional monarchy, in substance the mystical-military kingdom gave up none of its dignity. Ministerial responsibility was interpreted so that it diametrically contradicted the Belgian model. The state ministry chosen by the king was not responsible to both houses of the *Landtag* nor to the people or public opinion, but exclusively to the king, as an indignant Frederick William IV demanded in a marginal note already in autumn 1848. In countless conflicts the sovereign treated his ministers not much better than his servants, and there could be no question under these conditions of a steady political course. Thus the cherished work of the Prussian national assembly crumbled piece by piece. The king maliciously called the carefully deliberated constitution which the parliamentary committee already had prepared in July, 1848 the "Charte Waldeck," but the government itself had recognized the excellent work in it when they accepted its basic thoughts in the dictated constitutional document of December 5. Soon enough, however, the *Kreuzzeitung* party revealed its destructive intentions, when on May 16, 1849 it opened the notorious denunciation trial against the framer of the Prussian basic law, the supreme court justice (*Obertribunalrat*) Benedikt Waldeck. With the most reprehensible means, through forged letters, paid informers, a poorly played detective story, and an ugly straw figure from the radical camp, the Jewish shop clerk Ohm, the reactionary clique were able to entangle the most respected man of the left, the rigorously legal and sincerely monarchical proponent of a Prussian *habeas-corpus* act, the popular Westphalian peasant king, and chairman of the constitutional committee, in a most dangerous trial for high treason.[170] The Berlin jury granted the courageous man of the opposition a splendid vindication, and Waldeck received an award not only from the democratic People's Society, but also from the proletarian Society of Engineers: a silver citizen's crown, which perhaps depicts the purest symbol of the forty-eight revolution. But the martial law, against which Waldeck had protested with the utmost strength of conviction, was not raised. The three basic rights that he had fought for with untiring energy, the right of a fully free press, the right of free political and social association, and the right to be allowed representation by secret ballot for a voice in the government, were not restored. Even the great laws for the reform of communal and county administration, for the abolition of the hunting law and manorial justice, for the redemption of peasant's hereditary payments, where they still existed, were either no longer pursued, rescinded, or interpreted unfairly. Only in the decade of reaction was the constitutional thinking completely displaced and replaced by the romantic-patrimonial political theory of Friedrich Julius Stahl. Only since 1850 has the conflict between democracy and monarchy evolved into a life and death struggle of principles. Also in the Austrian imperial state, after the death of Schwarzenberg, the clerical and reactionary powers prevailed and repelled the Josephist enlightened tendencies which were originally supposed to be combined with the revocation of the constitution by Schwarzenberg's New Year Edict of 1851. Since then both leading German powers shifted just as much toward one another in their domestic conditions as they were endeavoring to cooperate in the questions of foreign policy since the Warsaw and Olmütz discussions (November, 1850).

In the small world of the German princely states matters took the same turn after the year 1850. Chambers and suffrage laws were rescinded and replaced by the arrangements of the *Vormärz* era; domains reverted to the princely families as private property, and the reform laws of the years 1848-1850 were cancelled by manorial regulations. In many cases it was only the resolutions of the restored Diet which made possible or forced the revision of the constitution. In other countries the example of the Prussian November *coup d'état* had already induced a change of system. The order of the day was popularized in Berlin by a rhyme that quickly made the round of Germany, "*Gegen Demokraten helfen nur Soldaten* (Against democrats only soldiers help)." Grand Duke George of Mecklenburg-Strelitz in a letter to the King of Prussia of January 26, 1849 gave the princely commentary to this principle of reaction, ". . . the best verse which has been made in recent times in Berlin and, I must say, in the entire world . . . Goethe has written nothing

157

that I like better."[171] History has not confirmed this all too simple guiding principle in spite of the astounding accomplishments of the soldier state in the next generation. Bruno Bauer, the brilliant sociologist of the Hegelian school, had already laid out the reason for this in 1849. Out of the historical relationship of masses, bourgeoisie, and army, he predicted the failure of the attempted counterrevolution, which he otherwise seemed not to deny a significant course. "The conquest of the dissolved masses," so ended his considerations of the bourgeois revolution in Germany, "its violent overthrow and transformation by the army is impossible. The army in its old organization is no longer conquering, the aristocracy of its leadership is no longer an advancing historical force; only those can conquer who know their prey better than it knows itself, and can subordinate it by virtue of this superiority of training and knowledge."[172] Who were these stirred up masses, who would no longer allow themselves to be intimidated by historical powers? Was it the bourgeoisie or the working class, the educated social stratum or the proletariat? Or was it a middle class of which we, because of our one-sided training, have no clear conception, that, however, obviously formed the problematic nucleus of the German body politic in the next decades and was evidently without leadership?

XI

THE MARCH REVOLUTION AND
THE GERMAN LABOR MOVEMENT

In the year 1848 there was no class-conscious
proletariat in Germany, but there was certain-
ly a working class, although it was numerically far smaller than
the peasant and artisan classes. Sociologically this newly formed
fourth estate combined different elements: *déclassé* artisan masters
who were no longer able to maintain their economic independence,
journeymen who had married and were no longer hired by the
guild craftsmen, factory employees who were already working in
manufacturing establishments at the end of the 18th century, hacks
and day laborers for whom the rise from apprentice and journeyman
to artisan master was closed, and finally those whom Karl Marx
called the "*Lumpenproletariat*": the unfortunate, the rejected, vaga-
bonds, the neglected, the weak-minded, the asocial elements. Among
the most important discoveries of the later revisionist worker movement was its understanding of the fact that in this proletarian
class actually three separate classes were hidden, whose paths would
necessarily part in the subsequent historical process, if this were
allowed to run its course. Besides the "fourth estate" of the established skilled worker emerged a "fifth estate" of the unskilled
worker, who gathered in masses wherever there was a possibility
of employment, and a "sixth estate" of the jail birds and the poor
devils who, to be sure, had proved themselves extraordinarily useful
among the barricade fighters, but in the restored order were really
troublesome and embarrassing. Actually these deep-seated social
differences excluded the idea of a dictatorship of the proletariat.
For who was supposed to really dictate: the established factory

159

employees or the surging mass of unskilled wage earners, or the street? It was predictable that in the wake of a victory of the fourth estate new social struggles would immediately arise, and the idea of the classless society, which Karl Marx prophesied, was obviously a utopia, which set a very arbitrary end to the dynamic process of history.

But also toward the other end of the social ladder the transitions were absolutely fluid. Reality revolted against the principle of an irreconcilable class struggle between the bourgeoisie and the proletariat. There existed in Germany, strictly speaking, neither a powerful bourgeoisie nor a powerful fourth estate, rather only a commercial lower middle class, which began to discharge certain groups upwards and downwards. The revolution of forty-eight fell in an important point of intersection in the development of the artisan class.[173] After seventy years of slow upward movement, in whose course the artisan estate as a whole first completely seized control of its bourgeois level and had grown into the *"Tiers Etat,"* this III-b-estate (so one may call it) began to dissolve on the upper and lower edges. A growing number of craftsmen and journeymen fell downward to the factory, and thereby devolved to the newly forming worker estate. The artisan journeymen and skilled young workers who held together socially through societies and fraternities, through common travel customs and political enlightenment, defended themselves with remarkable energy against being simply lumped with the factory people. In many places their sense of honor still demanded places of work and special conditions of work separate from the wage workers. But their detachment from the commercial middle class could already be foreseen, and they would melt into the proletariat during the next generation.

Since the 1830s, in Germany too the factory entrepreneurs were upwardly mobile out of the artisan class. With Manchesterian calculation, they made profit the single guiding precept of their operation. Favored by easy credit possibilities, stimulated by mass consumption, and supported by the state commercial policy and improvements in transportation, the alert craftsman raised himself out of his century-old stagnant situation. What we encounter among the successful entrepreneurs in Germany around 1848 were mainly talented artisans, who through mercantile prudence and skill in advertising, through fortunate speculation on real estate, or loans on good terms, had understood how to transform their businesses to large scale operations, ordered machinery from England, and besides journeymen, also hired "helpers," that is workers. Often they still worked actively with their hands in the businesses, maintained a patriarchal character in their work, and continued to sit in shirt sleeves at a common lunch table, as is told of the rich Hamburg cane manufacturer Meyer, the famous "Stockmeyer." They were naturally politically liberal and adherents of complete industrial freedom, not without a feeling for local self-government, but firstly businessmen and only secondarily politicians. In common with the older social stratum of merchant and liberal middle class, they possessed a strong bourgeois instinct for property and a pronounced desire for security. They had in common with the social order from which they originated an intense urge for social mobility, which also inspired those discontented journeymen who were wedged in between craft and factory and could no longer go forward or backward. These offspring of small business too, source of social unrest and candidates for emigration in the *Vormärz* era, wished to rise in the world, to own a house, open their own businesses, and to achieve financial progress, just as they would try to do in America, when they had saved the money for a ship ticket to succeed in escaping the destitute conditions of the Old World.

The poor journeyman, who could no longer open his own workshop and was forced to drift into the factory, and the nouveau riche factory owner, who was conquering the German market or even the world market, originated in the same historical class of the petty bourgeoisie and were products of the same crisis of the artisan class. Was it so astonishing that no real class struggle could originate between them, at least as long as the one was still not an actual bourgeois and the other was not yet completely a proletarian? One must observe in the United States of America how the failed and the successful artisan, that is the worker and manufacturer, in spite of the flagrant divergence between poor and rich, professed the same economic principle,[174] in order to grasp that the idea of class struggle in the year 1848 was enormously alien and premature, that even the revolutionary leaders of the journeymen did not really understand it, and only through extended systematic propagandistic operations among the fifth estate could it gradually become popular in Germany. Certainly the problem of the journeymen cried for a solution. The exit backward to the guild conditions was blocked by the growing numbers of the population and development of technology, however alive and genuine the powers of the German middle class still were. One was thus compelled to seek a path forward in the line of industrialization, as discerning political economists like the statistician Hoffmann had suggested already around the turn of the 18th century.[175] But was it not very likely that developments in Germany would take the same path as in North America, that the ascending social question would be smothered in a giant wave of prosperity? The prerequisite for this of course would probably be a clear political victory of the bourgeois revolution and a throughgoing democratization of public life. In this case the socialistic agitation in Germany might possibly have come to the same standstill as in North America, where the originally energetic beginnings from the Chartist movement of English origins, the secret societies of the Fourierists and the Owenists, the branches of German communism under Kriege and Weitling succumbed completely around the year 1850 and at most continued to exist as a hidden nuance within the Democratic Party.[176]

However one judges this possibility, doubtlessly the idea of the class struggle never grew from the actual sociological conditions in Germany. It was brought in by intellectuals, who were raised in the abstract philosophy of the Young Hegelians, and generalized their great historical-philosophical conceptions from conditions in England and from the events of the French Revolution. In the Germany of the forty-eight period they found entrance only with difficulty and for a long time were almost without a following. The champions of the older German communism, the schismatic journeyman tailor Wilhelm Weitling and the uncouth terrorist Karl Heinzen did not know where to begin with it, and where the lofty Marxist dialectic found an echo, there were practically no workers. The Cologne Communist League, the most important center for the distribution of Marxist ideas, certainly included physicians, discharged officers, journalists, and teachers, but among its three dozen members were very few proletarians. The only worker leader who managed to create a strong organization in Germany during 1848, Stephan Born, in practical work very quickly distanced himself from orthodox theories, although in Paris and Brussels he had belonged among the closest associates of Marx and Engels. In his illuminating memoirs he admits candidly that he was pressured by the force of circumstances to dissociate himself from the speculation that until then had consumed him, and had to make the best of a great deal that the masters noted as an evil descent from the ideal. "They would have laughed in my face or pitied me if I had presented myself as a communist. I was no longer one. What did I care about the distant centuries when every hour presented urgent tasks and work in abundance."[177] He could not even approach the alert Berlin worker with the *Communist Manifesto* and the doctrine of class struggle; the typesetter Stephan Born, who had himself worked in a Berlin printing shop, knew this better than the brilliant scholar at his desk in Brussels or the elegant manufacturer's son from Barmen, who had offended the German workers in Paris by his upper middle class life style and, during his agitation in his homeland, never found the bridge to the thoughts of the simple man. Even so, Cologne and Berlin were still the most promising places for the Marxist agitation controlled from London. In the other German cities the interested constituency was even smaller, the preparedness for world revolution and proletarian class consciousness much more restricted. The well informed police director designated to the minister of interior only two activists from Stuttgart, who might possibly be initiated into the endeavours of the London Central Committee of the Communist League: a journeyman cobbler Birk and a journeyman locksmith Mannes.[178] We can appreciate from this example how grotesquely exaggerated were the fears of the German governments, and even the March governments, of the international organization of the Communist League.

This did not hinder an actual secret net of revolutionary intrigues being spun from the London central. The covert organization was systematically constructed on "communities" and "directing circles," that is local groups and provinces, and was constantly monitored and held together by "emissaries," who were sent from England or Switzerland to Germany. These confidential messengers and inspectors not only had to maintain cohesion among the individual members, but also check for trustworthiness and carry out purges. It was highly indicative of the character of the March revolution that this surreptitious agitation within the worker societies before

1848 and after 1850 functioned more reliably than during the two revolutionary years themselves, when the Germans had so much to do with their liberal concerns as citizens, that even the worker no longer cared to devote any attention to the communists' objectives. In the summer of 1849 agitation also succumbed completely for other reasons. Only after autumn 1849 were the threads carefully brought together again and the "directing circles" and the "communities" received from the London Internationale renewed instructions to report in their systematic letters what was being done to win influence among the existing worker societies, gymnastic societies, and organizations of rural day laborers. The strongholds of the underground Marxist organization are known. Cologne, Hamburg, Breslau, and Nuremberg appeared as the most important "circles." In Mecklenburg they had approached the rural workers; in Schleswig-Holstein they had even formed a connection to the army. In addition Frankfurt, Hanau, Mainz, Wiesbaden, Berlin, Leipzig, Liegnitz, Glogau, Munich, Bamberg, Würzburg, Stuttgart, Mannheim, and Göttingen were indicated as locations of the league. In Wurtemberg, Baden, Hanover, and East Prussia no district leadership developed. The costs for the agents' journeys had for years already been defrayed by the London circle. It was preparing undeviatingly, on an international basis, for the world revolution. In France, in Hungary, in England itself Marx was awaiting a new crisis in the immediate future and sending out instructions for it. Some circulars of the Central Committee in London to the Communist League in Germany fell into the hands of the Leipzig police and were transmitted by the Foreign Ministry of Saxony to friendly governments as a warning.[179] What emerges from these documents is that there really were secret wire-pullers outside of the country, although their influence was infinitely restricted and really limited to a few dozen initiates in all of Germany. After the collapse of the February revolution the league resolved in all the states not just to exploit new bloody events, but to precipitate them by all means possible. "Far from opposing the so-called excesses in instances of popular revenge on hated individuals or public buildings associated with hated memories, one must not only acquiesce in these matters, but take over leadership of them ourselves." So began the secret directive for the preparation of acts of terror in Germany, which was edited in London in March, 1850, and pursued the objective of declaring the permanent revolution. The circular noted expressly that the proletarian movement must arm itself even more against the petty bourgeois democrats than against the reaction for the next exchange of fire. The actual secret of the Internationale was its system of selection, its hierarchical structure, and the strict guidance of the association through a secret central. "The emissary . . . everywhere accepted only the most reliable people to the league. . . . It shall depend on local conditions whether the various revolutionary persons can be brought directly into the league. Where this is not possible, those individuals who are revolutionarily useful and reliable, but who do not yet understand the communistic consequences of the present movement must form a second class of league members. This second class, to whom the association is presented as merely local or provincial, must constantly remain under the direction of the actual league members and the league authorities." Even among the selected activists, therefore, one must still conclude that a majority of the workers under no circumstances were prepared to take the "communist consequences."

The doubt of the reliability of even this select revolutionary group shows how weak the echo of the London communication of scientific socialism still was among the German workers' world. The trustworthy Marxists, according to this representation, could not have exceeded even a hundred men. The great, the overwhelming majority of those in the working class organized into societies felt that even the teaching of the French socialists, a St. Simon, Proudhon, Cabet, and Fourier were exaggerated and dangerous. The German student of the French utopianists, Wilhelm Weitling, who had enjoyed a certain standing among the German craft journeymen in France, Switzerland, and some German states, no longer possessed a strong attraction by 1848 and had no following in the year of the revolution. When Weitling came to Berlin in the early summer of 1848 his suggestions to the Berlin workers' congress were rejected almost indignantly, although his program of a "league of liberation" was not so unreasonable and consciously avoided an abrupt challenge to the bourgeoisie and an attack on private property. But even his idea of state socialism, which would have transformed the worker into a sort of insured state civil servant with a right of pension and retirement income, went far beyond what the commercial class in Germany expected as the blessings of the revolution. Weitling's newspaper organ, *Der Urwähler*, attracted hardly 150 subscribers in Berlin and environs and folded after a few issues.[180]

A young socialist agitator, the student Gustav Adolf Schlöffel, had better prospects for a mass following. Son of a progressive manufacturer in Silesia, the passionate barricade fighter and popular speaker was certainly more strongly interested politically than any other workers' leader of the period. Welcomed with great expectation as a German Camille Desmoulins, he perhaps could have been the founder of a German mountain party, if he were able to create a true social democratic party by an ebullient combination of economic and political demands. But even Schlöffel was left in the lurch because of the basic desire for order and conservative instincts of the Berlin working class. When he attempted to force the right of direct election with a gigantic rally before the castle, the expected multitude stayed away, and soon he was hidden from sight by a prison sentence. As an upright fighter for freedom he then fought in Hungary and lost his life in the Baden revolt.[181] Another note of political tactic and mass psychology was struck by Friedrich Wilhelm Held, which for a short time found an unusual echo in wide layers of the Berlin lower middle class. Former Prussian lieutenant, actor, and man of letters, he suddenly discovered his demagogic talent immediately on release from prison and swept along on the wave of the revolution. Through a mixture of wit, mockery, bitterness and drastic threats, found very engaging by Berliners, which recalls a very modern example of mass influence,* he had at his disposal a quickly growing following in the "tents," and a hard core in the Society of Machine Engineers, for whom he edited a newspaper, *Die Lokomotive.* The idea of a direct alliance between the mass movement and monarchical power, between the rule of the military and street socialism, anticipated a great many of the domestic political slogans of Napoleon III and was not without some originality. But as it became known that the popular speaker had held a secret discussion with Herr von Katte, the President of the "Prussian Society," in the residence of a noble lady, the working masses felt themselves betrayed to the counter-revolution, and all of his distortions, excuses, and theatricality no longer helped the agitator to regain a leading role.[182]

*Joseph Goebbels

Finally only Stephan Born remained of the Berlin worker leaders. One may see in him an earlier characteristic representative of the trade unionist, who sought to win an influence on the course of the revolution by way of job associations and wage cartels. Although he received stimulation from the Communist League, Born kept his organization independent of the London Internationale. This organizer, born in Lissa, Posen under the name of Simon Buttermilch, found his most important support among the Berlin printers, who recognized him as one of them and elected him as the head of their union. As such he led the first struggle for a wage increase in Berlin that made use of the age-old, but only recently legal means of the threat of a solidarity strike. Since a Berlin typesetter earned an average of only three and a half talers a week for working seventeen hours a day, while in France the wage for years had been twice that for a ten-hour day, higher pay and a shorter working day were certainly overdue demands, which were carried through without a great deal of effort against the laments of the publishers. The successful wage struggle brought the printers even closer together; the new pay scale spread to all of Germany, and in a short time the labor union was organized that Born had worked for, the German Printers' Society. The cigar workers and other trades took a similar path.

More important was Born's plan to lead the workers as a whole into a unified political organization. What sort of economic objectives the labor party should seek was not yet decided. Born himself inclined toward the idea of producer cooperatives created with state support which should open their own profitable establishments. His model for this was as much Louis Blanc as the village bakeries, dairy cooperatives, and community cheese factories which he had seen in Switzerland. Born went promptly to work. In April already a Berlin workers' meeting was called, a central committee formed, Born and the goldsmith Bisky elected as the presidents, and preparations completed for a general German worker congress.[183] The utopian-tinged direction of Weitling and Lüchow as well as the popular society of the "Rehberger" (those unemployed workers set to work at excavation on the Rehberg under the direction of the student Schlöffel) acted in the background. Born declared proudly in the name of the proletariat, "We are taking our affairs into our own hands, and no one shall wrench them away from us." In practical behavior, the Berlin worker movement under Born's direction did not follow any radical proletarian course, rather was affected with surprisingly strong guild conceptions, in accordance also with the sociological make-up of these "worker societies," in which the small craftsman and journeyman absolutely predominated.

The economic and social-political program of the Berlin central committee has been preserved.[184] In 25 points it contains demands which lay not merely in the interests of the worker, but also in the interest of the artisans and even the manufacturers. The state should facilitate exports, it should stimulate the economy by export premiums and the tariff-free entry of raw materials, it should reorganize credit matters through its state banks and create a clear patent law, whereby the inventor and the industries would be protected from unfair competition. State orders to smaller concerns and public loans for the acquisition of machinery ought to preserve the competitive capability of craftsmen. In place of the hated excise duties on various consumer items, a progressive income tax should be established. Free education for the youth in all schools, public libraries, and adult education should make possible the rise of the workers and lower middle class. The state should guarantee freedom of movement, first and foremost for the itinerant artisan journeymen seeking further training. Finally the requests for invalid pensions and the creation of work came together in the general statement that the community had a duty to insure a "proper existence" as man and citizen to even the poorest. The wage struggles between employers and employees ought to be settled by a mixed commission which regulated the hours of work as well as the minimum compensation, whereby the workers obviously had to be able to retain the right of collective organization as a weapon in the wage struggle. Also the number of apprentices that a master might retain would be set by a common commission in which the "help" and the master were represented equally.

This program clearly showed the outlines of a moderate social policy, which had incorporated a few elements of the French worker movement, but mainly was concerned with the interests of craftsmen and the younger generation, and would allow no conflict to arise between the industrial middle class and the factory working class. The right to education and the right to work were strongly highlighted, and one would not err if he saw in this the French example and French doctrines. However, the private economic structures of factory and workshop were nowhere touched; the state's interference was limited to the encouragement of industry through customs policies, and the question of salaries was left to a mixed court of arbitration. The distance from the communistic program of revolution is not to be denied. Their program, in 17 points, had previously been sent to Germans at the beginning of the March revolution by the Paris committee. Indivisible republic, arming of the worker, transformation of feudal estates into property of the state, and radical limitations on the right of inheritance, supersession of all private banks by a single state bank, levelling of the wages of officials, and gradation not according to rank but exclusively according to marital status: these were some of the characteristic demands of communist agitation, which however were not taken up by the German worker movement.[185]

The social program of the Berlin committee was foreseen as a resolution for a congress of craftsmen and workers. In various places such meetings had taken place since July, 1848. In Hamburg, Berlin, and Frankfurt they were impressive demonstrations of German manual workers. In a unique countermovement, the political breakthrough of liberalism was accompanied by a social-economic movement of the middle class, which perceived in the principle of free competition and the industry-oriented state policy the main cause of the decline and the misery of the artisan class. They were united in protest against freedom of trade and wished to alleviate their own suffering half through state social and half by guild means. This anti-liberal position of the lower middle class may not have been very perceptive and far sighted in terms of political economy, but socio-politically the revolt of the middle class against proletarization was one of the most significant phenomena of the forty-eight revolution. If the craftsmen in all parts of Germany, no matter under what trade law they stood locally, almost unanimously advocated a return to the restrictions of the past and spurned the "French" principle of unleashing a free economy, they were not expressing a reactionary, half-feudal, and medieval outlook, but a desperate protest against the degradation and loss of social status of the small business class, who did not intend to be surrendered to the same fate as their English and French compeers.

Also the young journeymen of the enlightened artisan and gymnastic societies, in whom we may glimpse a supporting element for the political left and which supplied the most steadfast fighters on all barricades, subscribed sweepingly to the socio-economic outlook of the middle class movement and did not allow themselves to be separated from the masters in spite of many internal points of dispute. As they could not obtain in due course seats and votes at the Frankfurt craftsman congress, they assembled on July 20, 1848 in an independent congress of journeymen, which met beside the masters in Frankfurt. In their circle the thought of the solidarity of all craftsmen was absolutely vital; they demanded in addition the formation of a "worker and journeyman's association" in every town to send a delegate to Frankfurt. To be sure, with this plan they now were anticipated by the Berlin central committee, and the Frankfurt journeymen's meeting, which drew out until September 20 and finally adopted the name "General German Worker Congress," was in a difficult position, since it did not appear to be regularly authorized and in the labyrinth of social policy evidently did not see a way out within its own powers. Nevertheless here perhaps a concealed central point of the German revolution can be sought. The social uncertainties of the year 1848 are nowhere so readily available for study as in the arduous and fruitless discussions of these weeks and months, which, in the language of the times, wanted to establish "federalism" and sought a way between liberalism and communism through a systematic "organization of work," that might end the monopoly-hegemony of capital and the heedless struggle of all against all. The peculiar combination of socialist and guild motives, whose formulation may largely be traced back to the leading role of a Cassel trade instructor, Karl Georg Winkelblech, called Marlo, did not originate in this case from professorial confusion, rather, it was an exact expression of the economic and spiritual transitional situation of society in Germany.[186]

Fundamentally this same junction of misunderstood proletarian and instinctive guild concerns also dominated at the Berlin worker congress, which assembled under more favorable auspices with Stephan Born's urging on August 23, 1848 in the Prussian capital to deliberate on a "Charter of the People." The objective was to outline a constitutional instrument for the commercial economy and its special human rights. From all parts of Prussia and Saxony, from Munich and Hamburg the worker associations had sent emissaries; also the Frankfurt journeymen's meeting had delegated representatives. Although certainly not several millions, as the congress boasted, but probably only 12,000 organized workers stood behind this deputation,[187] still, here met for the first time in the history of the revolution a recognized central channel of the workers, speaking for all of Germany. Represented were 25 cities and 31 associations; the number of deputies was around 40. In many respects the Berlin congress seemed like the executor of the concerns of the journeymen assembled in Frankfurt. As the Frankfurt group had directed a resolution to the national assembly, so also the Berlin assembly transmitted a motion to the St. Paul's Church to call a social chamber in addition to the political parliament where all social estates and occupational groups could be represented by a special means of selection, in order to discuss with expertise the economic and social legislation and then to submit their conclusions to the national assembly.

The most important result was the erection of a centrally directed organization covering all of Germany comprehensively, the "brotherhood," which had its seat in Leipzig. Stephan Born was elected as the first president, and he was also assigned the editorship of the group's publication.[188] The plan was to set up district committees in the 27 German large cities, from Hamburg and Kiel to Vienna, Prague, and Brünn (Brno), without regard for state borders and political tensions, and to assign to these local committees, in which should assemble the working class from the various factories and which should step in during wage negotiations between employers and employees. The resolutions of the Berlin congress, that were passed in ten days of consultations, went to the extent of directing that the local committee should be empowered with the direction of unions, to receive the payment of wages, and to retain seven to ten percent for an association account, which should acquire land with these funds for worker dwellings and establish loan associations for those desiring to build.[189] The resolutions moreover assembled a series of demands that were directed toward the state and took up some things from the socialist theories of various tendencies and mixed them with the basic demands of democracy. Besides the ten-hour day and the selection of foremen "with the assent" of the workers, they demanded the abolition of indirect taxes, the lowering of the voting age, the partition of large estates,

171

and free public education. Time and again the specific worries of the craftsmen penetrated. Thus the number of apprentices was to be fixed by a mixed commission and the competition of prison work limited. The petty bourgeois character of the movement was even clearer when we pass from the center into the provinces. In a few cases "purchasing societies" were founded and the cooperative idea developed. There were instances of the common buying of raw materials for fabrication in individual workshops. In Berlin the "brotherhood" founded its own disability insurance fund that eventually could command the respectable membership of 20,000 persons. But in the overwhelming majority of cases the district associations contented themselves with delivery of their monthly dues, subscriptions to the association publication, a relief fund for traveling journeymen, and demands on their district legislatures and governments. Above all in southern Germany the purposes of the organization quickly narrowed to the erection of job placement agencies and provident funds for traveling journeymen, a clear indication that the worker societies stepped in where the guilds had failed.

The density of the net of district and local associations ought not to be represented as all too great. Saxony and the Prussian cities remained the hub of the movement. In Bavaria in the course of time 35 associations were founded; in Wurtemberg, where the conditions are especially well documented by the confiscation of books of minutes, at the height of the development perhaps as many as twenty associations existed.[190] The administrative center here was first Ulm, later Göppingen, and the connection with the democratic popular associations particularly strong. Their own daily newspaper in Stuttgart, the *Deutsche Volkswehr*, served as orientation in the ideas and successes of French socialism, "as far as it shows practical use for Germany." Frequently the journalists of the left-tending middle class newspapers exerted a leading influence. Here and there talented laborers also entered politics by this path. Thus the Jewish metal turner August Hochberger, who for some time had edited the well-known *Neckardampfschiff* in Heilbronn, as the director of the Esslingen worker association became one of the most active personalities in the south German worker movement.

The artisan element conducted itself passively, but predominated absolutely. In Esslingen, among the 71 members, only 15 were registered as machine factory workers. In Ulm, among the 400 members who were listed over the course of time, except for two intellectuals, a legal adviser and a private tutor, two democratic merchants and two innkeepers, there were only settled and immigrated craftsmen: cobbler, furrier, tinsmith, tanner, and turner. Their horizon was limited to apprentice and journeyman concerns, their demands extremely unpretentious. At a general assembly of Wurtemberg worker societies in Reutlingen in September, 1849, they expressly declared that complaints about the conduct of the police toward itinerant journeymen were unfounded! The meeting wished to hear nothing of a prohibition of Sunday work. What the resolutions and petitions incessantly returned to was the request for Sunday schools and the possibilities for advanced commercial education. Where the state failed, self help was substituted, and many societies' self-characterization as workers' educational societies was not just camouflage, but their true essence. The instructional program extended almost more to scientific than to political matters. In Ludwigsburg the city's dean held lectures on themes of religion and morals. In another locality the lawyer Gwinner taught a course on the French Revolution in a popular society. It was debated in the Ulm worker society whether a globe should be acquired for geography lectures in order to secure better attendance in classes. In Stuttgart the typesetter Hirsch gave lectures about List's system of political economy, and for this reason in the spring of 1852 was banned from the city.

These details indicate the circumference of worker education. No explicit social program can be detected in the "brotherhood's" effort to enlighten. Gottfried Kinkel's pamphlet "Craftsman save yourself" appeared beside List's *grossdeutsch* tariff union plans and reports of the Paris national workshops as text material. In Nuremberg, at a revolutionary celebration the hall was decorated with busts of Blum and Hecker, of Franklin and Washington, but also of Louis Blanc and Professor Winkelblech.[191] A political alignment of the association members was increasingly foregone. Basically every member was left free to belong to his chosen political grouping.

After the events of the summer of 1849 and the suppression of the May risings, the labor movement was also on the decline everywhere. In a letter of October 5, 1849, to the central committee of the brotherhood in Leipzig, Secretary Engel from Göppingen complained in the name of the Swabian associations, "that unfortunately here in Wurtemberg too an indifference is coming into the open," that is "explained well enough by the defeat of our party in Saxony and the Palatinate, in the Rhineland and in Baden." The participation of workers and journeymen in the popular risings of this year gave the triumphant governments everywhere occasion to watch over the associations more closely, and the new political atmosphere robbed the people of the courage to burden themselves with membership in a suspected group. The worker associations shrank quickly. The Ulm society fell from 400 to 62 members. The magazine *Verbrüderung* ("Brotherhood") in the autumn of 1849 included only 67 subscriptions among the 400,000 inhabitants of Berlin. The worker association in Schwerin, that in October, 1848, had still commanded an impressive count of 873 persons, a year later had declined to 183, *i.e.*, a fifth of its strength.[192] The authorities nevertheless only hesitatingly resolved to dissolve them by force. Saxony and Bavaria, in summer, 1850, undertook the decisive step. In Prussia at that time there were, besides 62 existing societies, 32 liquidated ones. In Wurtemberg the high bailiffs received the order to close the last worker associations in November, 1852, and not until July 13, 1854 did a resolution of the restored Frankfurt Diet bring an end to everything. According to this the federal governments were obliged to abolish within two months all existing worker societies with political, social, and communistic objectives.

Politically, the worker movement had long been dead. It was never really a decisive factor in itself during the revolution. The German journeyman worker had fought the street battle only in alliance with the radical bourgeoisie, he had refused the class struggle, and he had taken up arms in the social struggle in common with the craftsmen. This economic protest of the handworker was directed more against the factory than against the employer, more against the machine than against capitalism, and only in wage questions had he obtained a few successes under his own power. A trade union movement, as originated earlier in England at the end of the 18th century, might also in Germany have been an organic component of a victorious revolution. In the remaining social domains, the resolutions of the journeymen assemblies and the petitions of the worker associations only achieved concrete results through enlightened governmental regulations and the extension of trade laws. There were four areas of major concern about which the worker journeymen and their "central committees" approached the authorities: the improvement of commercial advanced education; aid for the "wandering worker" in the form of reduced railway fares, public assistance funds, and employment bureaus; establishment of trade courts in which masters and journeymen would be equally represented and directed by an expert jurist; finally the limitation of the hours of work and a prohibition on child labor. This last point was significantly controversial among the participants themselves, at least the legal prohibition of Sunday work was rejected by the artisans to a great extent themselves.

It was not the red flag but the green banner with the golden oak wreath about which the delegates of the journeymen's society rallied in Frankfurt. The great worker union that was on their minds, the new social order of federalism which they longed for should include as members artists, intellectuals, merchants, and even factory owners, when they participated in the struggle against the deadly freedom of trade. The request of the worker associations which advanced furthest into principle, the board of trade (*Gewerberat*), was provisionally realized by the Prussian trade regulation of February 9, 1849.[193] The Minister of Trade, von der Heydt, stood up for this with great warmth, and systematically gathered beforehand suggestions of masters and journeymen. In January, 1849 a number of craftsmen were called to Berlin, and their advice, as well as the resolutions of the Frankfurt artisan congress and the work of the trade commission of the Prussian national assembly with its 1600 petitions, was utilized conscientiously in the preparation of the law. The new trade regulation then also found a friendly reception in the circles of craftsmen. It struck a careful middle position between guild compulsion and independent freedom and gave the guild artisans essential protection without limiting entrepreneurial freedom all too much. As a whole the guilds retained the right of examination for their apprentices and were protected from the retail merchandisers who destroyed the schedule of prices for craft work. The fact that journeymen were represented on the examination commission in the same number as the masters appears as a considerable concession to the journeyman movement. Also

STADELMANN: *The German Revolution*

relevant provisions favoring the factory worker were found that in some areas even signified an advance compared to the legal conditions in France and England. Thus the employer was forced to contribute to the disability insurance fund and the communities entrusted with supervision over local provident funds. The pernicious "truck system" was abolished by a law that the worker must be paid his wages in cash, without exception. In other questions like Sunday work, child labor, old age care and unemployment relief, the efforts of the government, which extended into the 1850s, were less sweeping. The obligation of the state for welfare, however, was still vigorously recognized in the first years of the reaction, while the democratic portions of the trade regulation, above all the journeymen's voting rights for the board of trade and their participation in the examination commission were again repealed by the law of May 15, 1854.

A uniform policy of the middle class for small business and factory workers, perhaps together with a generous agrarian reform favoring the rural middle class and a land reform for worker colonies might have been within reach at the moment of the March revolution. If one studies the development of socialism in England, where powers of reconciliation grew from a Christian-humanitarian basis and the extension of political rights to workers prevented the rise of the idea of the class struggle, we cannot acknowledge the inevitability of the tendency of the German worker movement toward Marxism. Insofar as the reactionary period prevented a smooth evolution of the journeyman movement, and let the gap between proletarian and handworker deepen undetected, it contributed to the self-help of the working class being obliged in the 1860s to reorganize from the ground up, first by Lassalle and then after 1868 through the irresistible triumphant march of Liebknecht and Bebel, who in a few years had constructed a strong Marxist labor party. All the same it took twenty more years until the idea of class struggle was able to gain a foothold among the German proletariat, and also the world-historical violence that Marx and Engels predicted at the moment of the March revolution now had to slow down decisively and allow a far reaching "embourgeoisement." Nothing yet verified the dramatic prophesy which especially Frederick Engels had disseminated extravagantly. Neither had the world struggle between the Tsar's eagle and the red flag broken out on

176

German soil, nor was the giant continental war of the liberated European peoples against the tyrant of the world market, England, ignited, which according to Marx and Engels was the necessary presupposition for a successful upheaval of the worker party against its oppressors. The flame of the Hungarian revolt did not join with a new flareup of the social struggles in France, as the leaders of the Internationale still believed in the summer of 1849. The wide social stratum of the working people had other cares and joys than their world revolutionary leaders in London. Another morsel of bread, a little more justice, and a modicum more humanity, that was what the masses longed for, not bloody world wars and the smoke of world-historical battle, out of which the outlines of an untried new social order were supposed to emerge.

The disappointment about the moderate posture of the workers induced bitter invective against their adherents by the authors of the *Communist Manifesto*. If the European working class could not rise to the height of its revolutionary responsibilities, then it might as well perish. A conversation with Marx and Engels is transmitted in which the two friends in August, 1850 announced their intention to emigrate by November at the latest to America, because all the lands of the Old World had proved incapable of social revolution; "They were completely indifferent as to whether this pitiable Europe perished."[194] Could the working class, which clung with every fiber of its consciousness to the bourgeois world and struggled against proletarization, have confidence in men who shook the dust of the old cultural world from its shoes with such contempt, who for the sake of their idea wished a glowing death for the entire world? The German worker in the crisis of 1848 was still far more alone and abandoned than the bourgeois and the Marxist historians dare to admit, and the unclear thoughts and feelings of these participants, generally without historical names, in the journeymen's and workers' congresses of the revolutionary period belong to the most touching witnesses of the history of German social classes. Only a few Christian social politicians and some professional bureaucrats with a consciousness of responsibility had an understanding for the unique needs that the German craftsmen experienced. The bulk of the liberal bourgeoisie ignored them just as thoughtlessly as the two prophets of world revolution, who had only contempt left for them.

XII

THE CIVIL WAR IN MAY 1849

Already during the winter 1848-49, a united movement was initiated on the left that commanded an imposing core in the organization of the "Central March Societies." Founded at the end of November by some delegates of the "Donnersberg," the association, under a strong central direction, branched down through provincial committees to local societies to cover almost all of Germany. It spread communications, publications, and arms, and finally extended to almost a thousand branch organizations and a half-million members. Whether Germany would become a united republic or should find its constitution in a popular empire was not explicit in the general guidelines of the March associations. They were only vigilant against the opportunistic reform group of the liberal center in St. Paul's Church, against the persistently resistant individual states, and above all against Prussia's egotism. Republican endeavours at subversion really first came to the forefront among these leftists when it became clear, through the untrustworthiness of the German courts and by the evasions of the Prussian king, that Germany would never obtain a unitary constitution from the hands of the thrones and their governments. As late as April, 1849 it would have been easy for the princes to have arranged a reconciliation with the revolution if they honestly and without deviation had accepted the Frankfurt constitutional draft. The nation would have even allowed more changes in the Reich constitution favoring the monarchy if it had only materialized at all.[195]

Adoption or refusal of the constitutional draft of the St. Paul's Church was the actual touchstone of the revolution. This is why,

178

in the last phase of the consultations, the constitutionalists and democrats united in Frankfurt in a concerted action and were prepared to make important concessions on individual points. But his realization of precisely this caused Frederick William IV to decline with an almost malicious determination so that the monarchical idea would never cede anything basic. Although the Frankfurt constitutional project contained only a few radical features, it became the field banner of the revolution. It brought together Gagern and Fröbel, but it also brought together south German and north German. The kingdoms became particularistic as a whole, and the Frankfurt delegates became unitary far into the ranks of the right. Even the most extreme left became extremely faithful to Prussia in order that the construction of the national state might be successful and that the entire energy of the revolution would not have been wasted. Even the south German democratic associations signed their internal correspondence "With German greetings" and acknowledged a hereditary imperial Germany with a Hohenzollern prince at its head.[196]

However, all the sensible tactics and all the political wisdom on the side of St. Paul's Church and the Reich ministry were for nought. Frederick William IV refused and even in April declared with cynical pride to the representative of the Reich cabinet, Herr von Beckerath, "Even if the constitution were suitable, I would not accept it, for I am determined to remain King of Prussia."[197] Gagern and Bassermann did their best and almost implored Prussia to name the articles that displeased it and prevented assumption of the supreme authority. It was futile. Frederick William IV did not want to improve the Reich constitution, rather to annul it by his intransigent attitude. All negotiation was pointless, and Gagern's prediction was fulfilled: all of non-Prussian central Germany and the more energetic portions of south Germany rose in rebellion as the collapse of the work on a liberal constitution could no longer be concealed. In Baden and the Rhineland-Palatinate, in Saxony and in the Westphalian industrial district a short but severe ground swell originated which was carried along tangibly more strongly by the social undercurrents than the March movement of a year before. The motive for the insurrections was everywhere the question of the Reich constitution. But the participation of men like Michael Bakunin, Stephan Born, Frederick Engels,

Herman Becker, and August von Willich gave the social-revolutionary undertone to the democratic-Reich-centralistic effervescence, which the governments never again forgot for the rest of the century and which also threw an insurmountable fright into the entire petty bourgeoisie. Assuredly the symbol of the red flag, which now appeared everywhere in imitation of Paris and began to replace the Reich banner (black-red-gold), was not understood in its complete meaning by all of the participants in the May revolts. The rich Hanau peasants, who drove racks pulled by teams of six to the popular assembly in Offenburg and decorated their horses with bouquets of red carnations, definitely would never subscribe to communism. But red had become the color of the continuing struggle of the revolution and gleamed over the land as the beacon of civil war. For many years the idea of democracy throughout Germany would be burdened with the odium of the communist danger which seemed allied to it.

In the Prussian monarchy itself, opinion was divided. While the second chamber was dissolved because they declared support for the Frankfurt draft, Wrangel and the Police President Hinckeldey exercised martial law. Interior Minister von Manteuffel assembled around him the associations of the Electoral Mark and Pomerania loyal to the king and knew how to set the mood by the invented or exaggerated disclosures of alleged lists of proscribed persons whom the democrats would put to the sword. Meanwhile barricades were built in Breslau (Wroclaw), and in the west of the monarchy the armories of the militia (*Landwehr*) had been stormed. A general assembly of militiamen in Elberfeld passed a resolution on May 3 that everyone should stand up "with his person and honor" for the introduction of the German constitution. This was the equivalent of mutiny in the bosom of the Prussian people's army. In Cologne and Königsberg city meetings were held that solidly placed themselves in accordance with the Reich constitution and called upon the perplexed assembly in Frankfurt not to renounce its German task. This patriotic mood was unanimous in the ranks of the bourgeoisie within and outside Prussia's borders. In Kassel the citizen guard was ready to fight for a Prussian empire against a Prussian monarchy. In Dresden an open street battle broke out on the afternoon of May 3, and even in the three Franconian districts of the Bavarian monarchy, the unitary popular movement gained ground

powerfully.[198] The petitions in favor of the Reich constitution piled
up, the territorial conflict between old Bavaria and the Upper Palatinate took on dramatic forms, and on May 2, with immense participation, a gigantic popular assembly of democratic associations,
the citizen guards, and the militia formations of the Franconian
provinces was held on the Maxfeld near Nuremberg, which passed
a resolution that the Pfordten ministry must immediately resign
and the government be forced to accept the Reich constitution,
otherwise Franconia would sever itself from Bavaria. On Sunday
May 13 a second mass meeting took place with an estimated 25,000
in attendance. Under the impression of the rebellions in Saxony
and the Palatinate and goaded by the example of Wurtemberg,
a civil war sentiment also developed in Bavaria, which rose against
the blue-white particularism of the Munich government and defended a Prussian leadership for Germany at the same time as
the achievements of the revolution. A radical peasant association
marched out armed in the Polish manner with 400 scythes beaten
straight. A Nuremberg worker association accumulated a supply
of munitions and prepared themselves for any eventuality. In Erlangen, students, together with soldiers on leave from the fifth
regiment, carried a red flag through the streets and sang the Hecker
song. In trains one could hear soldiers' impertinent language: "that
they would rather shoot down their officers before the regiment
than aim at a citizen." When a Catholic priest near Königshofen
announced from the pulpit, "Better to die Bavarian than to be
ruined by the Frankfurters!" his house was assaulted and demolished. The mood of the local administrative officials was extremely subdued so long as the outcome in Landau, Rastatt, and
Dresden was unsure. The Munich government, to be sure, did not
allow itself to be disconcerted. It marched a gigantic force of troops
together near Nuremberg, and Pfordten dissolved the obstinate
chamber in June. Clashes, even bloody ones, between governmental
troops and radical journeymen were not a rarity in Nuremberg
and Erlangen as late as November, but the hope for a revolutionary
union of the district with the Frankfurt leadership was laid to
rest on June 18 at the latest with the dispersal of the Stuttgart
rump parliament. The elections in July resulted in an overwhelming
movement to the right; the radicals dwindled to a third, and the
right-center of the Bavarian chamber of deputies made its peace

181

with Munich's policy of a separate state. The support from St. Paul's Church at any rate had been unusually slight. Karl Vogt as representative of the central parliament at the Nuremberg mass assembly gave the Franconian rebellion the feeble advice to go home and to fight with legal weapons. If the Frankfurt assembly again had a chance to become a national convention at that moment in May, 1849, it did not make use of it. Meanwhile in Baden, on the Rhine, and in Wurtemberg all eyes were fixed on it. But every territory and every town was obliged, nevertheless, to set forth upon its course in the civil war alone. The domination of the regular military was certainly overwhelming at all of the hot spots of the struggle, and even under a firm leadership the rebels could not have competed. Perhaps a portion of the available formation was sufficient to hold down the insurrection. Only in those places where the troops were unreliable were there seriously uncertain situations.

In Wurtemberg this case arose. The officers and soldiers of the Wurtemberg regiments were of course not so strongly seized by the revolutionary ideas as in Baden, but they felt themselves duty bound to the Reich constitution. Popular opinion and the chamber, the Römer ministry and community authorities of the larger cities forced King William, on April 24, to solemnly acknowledge the Frankfurt constitution. The armed forces held assemblies on their own in which they spoke of their duty *vis-à-vis* the constitutional idea and also subjected their service conditions to a critique. The democratic state committee announced a popular meeting in Reutlingen which imitated the example of the Offenburg assembly. Amid a powerful inrush of the masses this took place during the Whitsuntide holidays. The 20,000 in attendance allowed themselves to be carried away to a revolutionary program by the radical Joseph Fickler from Baden, former editor of the *Konstanzer Seeblätter* and one of the movers of the Hecker rising. They approved an alliance with the rebelling states, an oath of allegiance by the civilians and military to the Reich constitution, and the defense against any hostile traversal through Wurtemberg. In their own state a new constituent assembly should be elected, the feudal burdens abolished without indemnity, an income tax adopted, and the standing army done away with. Military matters like the arming of the people, election of officers up to the rank of captain, and abolition of martial law played a special role. But the arming of the people was no longer a doctrinaire program point, rather a very actual preparation for the struggle. Delegates from all of the administrative districts were to lay out the demands of the people on the following day in Stuttgart, and in case of an attitude of rejection by the governmental agencies, to set prearranged piles of wood on fire in the hills around Stuttgart as a signal for the countryside that it must arise to force the ministry, chamber, and king to take the correct path. There was of course no lighting of signal fires, since the state committee of the people's associations found a mood extremely friendly to the government in Stuttgart, and Minister Römer had posted troops on a plain south of Stuttgart, the Filder. When it was learned that the remaining group of the Frankfurt St. Paul's Church wanted to transfer its proceedings to Stuttgart, the Swabians resolved to hold off with their own revolution and to entrust themselves to this leadership. As far as power relationships were concerned, this meant that in a few days the Stuttgart government was again the complete master of the situation, and those Swabians who were determined to do something for German unity were obliged to rush to aid their brothers in Baden as partisans. On a few occasions, in Riedlingen, Heilbronn, Kirchheim, and Calw, admittedly there were cases of the spontaneous deployment of citizens, or a self-arming of youth as the evil fate became known that the Minister Römer had prepared for his former Frankfurt colleagues in Stuttgart. However, even a Swabian citizen guard was no longer able to assist the rump parliament to get themselves into action again. The brave revolutionary men in the county seats of Wurtemberg were disarmed, the border with Baden was closed, and a Prussian offer of help could be declined with thanks by King William. The monarchy was able to dispose of the civil war mood under its own power. But it should not be forgotten that among the "agitators and screechers" who revolted in those days were included very distinguished individuals, mayors and innkeepers, carpenters and lawyers, and that in many places the city council itself called together the citizens with a roll of the drum and stood ready to fight for the violated Reich constitution in this last hour.[199]

The May revolt of the year 1849 did not pass as bloodlessly and harmlessly in Dresden. It too was not prepared long in advance

183

but, in the words of a radical worker who battled on the barricades, was "nothing else but an angry outbreak of agitated emotions."[200] Against the pressure of the legislative chambers, the communal guard, and the democratic clubs, who demanded the recognition of the Reich constitution by the government and royal house, on the afternoon of May 3 Minister Beust called for preventive aid from a Prussian battalion via diplomatic channels because most of the Saxon troops were in the Schleswig-Holstein theater of war. The Dresden city council in reply organized a committee of public safety, in whose direction the ingenious, restless Russian anarchist Bakunin also meddled, lending a touch of the revolutionary Internationale to the whole affair. Gymnasts, workers, miners, even enthusiastic artists, actors, and musicians enlisted in service of the business at hand. The architect Gottfried Semper, the court conductor Richard Wagner, the music director Röckel, and the famous actress Schröder-Devrient were on the side of the rebels. For four days and nights there were bitter battles from doors and houses and over one hundred barricades. On the second day the king fled on an Elbe steamship to the fortress of Königstein; on the third a Prussian guard battalion under Count Waldersee intervened and strengthened the thin lines of the Saxons, who were not entirely trustworthy, but now were swept into a blood lust that raged even against unarmed prisoners. Over 250 dead were counted on the side of the citizens; the opera house and the natural history collection in the Zwinger were burned to the ground. In the evening of the fourth day when two more battalions came from Prussia the situation was already decided. The commander in chief of the street battle, Lieutenant Colonel Heinze, intentionally allowed himself to be taken prisoner in his colorful Greek uniform, and Stephan Born, the worker leader, to whom the command was transferred, could now only set in motion an orderly retreat of the remaining barricade fighters left in the streets toward Freiberg in Saxony. Those of the leaders of the rebellion who did not escape with the aid of rural inhabitants across the Bohemian border were, after a long trial, broken for life in the infamous Saxon prison Waldheim.

Generally it has been complained that the established burghers held back with their usual caution in this struggle, which had really been a matter of bourgeois ideals, and their places on the barricades were left to workers, artists, and students. Frederick Engels made a similar observation in the industrial district east of the Rhine, where the pious-pietist factory cities of the Wuppertal stood in rebellion since the beginning of May. At the same moment that the Dresden revolt appeared to be gaining the upper hand, barricade battles were reported from Breslau, the grand duke in Karlsruhe had taken flight, and the Hungarian revolt was on the verge of crossing the Leitha, in Elberfeld the prisons were being stormed, barricades built, and the military from Düsseldorf stopped at the city border. The drawing teacher Körner, who would play a role later in North America, and the editor Engels from the *Neue Rheinische Zeitung* drafted plans for insurrection and pondered over how, with the help of the militia organization, they could draw the districts on the left and right of the Rhine into a civil war and create an armed power for the Frankfurt central authority. In spite of all considerations, at this moment even the communists threw themselves into this petty bourgeois revolution and were ready to fight for the Reich authority and the black-red-gold constitution. But the bourgeois left was only moderately pleased with the reinforcements, and the revolutionary committee of public safety in Elberfeld on May 14 announced an abrupt end to the unnatural alliance. "The citizen Frederick Engels of Barmen, with full recognition of his hitherto existing demonstrated activity in this city, is requested to abandon the precincts of the urban community today, in order that his presence should not lead to misunderstandings about the character of the movement."[201] Since Engels had already requested the disarming of the citizen guard and the distribution of the weapons on hand among the rebellious workers, the apprehension was not so remote that the strategist of world revolution intended to use the rising for a general upheaval in which from Paris to Budapest the workers would line up against the bourgeoisie. In truth the civil war in the Berg region showed that it could be very quickly quelled with hard cash, with sensible persuasion, and by means of martial law, so that in no shape or form was Germany prepared for a proletarian revolution. The May revolts everywhere lay firmly in the hands of the Reich constitution men, and the Bassermann-like figures of the street sold their rifles to the citizen guard for a few bottles of liquor.[202]

In the south-western part of the German Confederation the movement without a doubt was most firmly rooted and principally carried by a broad layer of the people. One could here link up with the Hecker myth and the memories of the Baden revolt. The social and democratic slogans were as ever unchanged: Freedom, Prosperity, and Education for All! For the provisional government, as far as possible they clung to the same personalities as in April, 1848. Popular societies flourished everywhere and assembled mayors, innkeepers, peasants, and winegrowers in their ranks. In Offenburg again a great popular assembly met, to which the democrats from the Odenwald, the lands along the Tauber River, from the district of Hanau and the southern Black Forest streamed in hordes. What was new was that this time the garrisons were also sympathetic to the insurgents. Some of the young recruits had taken part in the disturbances a year before, and the new right of assembly had loosened discipline. First from Rastatt, then also from Bruchsal, Freiburg, Lörrach, and Karlsruhe came the news that the soldiers were holding their officers in check and were awaiting the arrival of representatives from the state committee. The minister of war himself could not restore order in the federal fortress and narrowly escaped by a secret sally-port. The Grand Duke of Baden was obliged to be brought to safety in Germersheim on the ammunition box of a cannon. An executive commission, in which the advocate Brentano presided and the former governor of Constance Peter occupied the post of justice, ruled the rebellious land from Karlsruhe.

There was much shuffling in the provisional government, and the situation was already critical by the beginning of June, because the grand duke, who had fled to Frankfurt, joined the alliance of the three kings, and at that two Prussian army corps marched toward the Palatine border. Also Mecklenburgers and Hessians stood prepared to restore expelled dynasties. On the other hand, the insurgents were strengthened by the influx of Swiss, Poles, and French. A foreign legion of 600 men swarmed together. Militarily, of course, generals Hirschfeld and Groben were far superior. Their cavalry alone was almost as strong as all of Baden's "shirted men" (*Blusenmänner*) combined, and the insurrectionaries had no officers except for a few Polish revolutionaries who occupied the higher leadership posts. The Prussian operational army fought its way down from the north and forced the crossing of the Neckar near Heidelberg against Mieroslawski. How bitterly they fought there was described by Gottfried Keller in letters to his mother and sister. The gunners of Baden killed their own wounded so that they would not fall into the hands of the Prussians. But the situation was strategically impossible. The revolutionary army was outflanked through the Rhineland-Palatinate in the west, and from the direction of Germersheim the Prussians were quickly at their rear. Already on June 25 the provisional government was forced to flee from Karlsruhe to Freiburg, and on July 11 Baden was completely occupied by the invading troops. Only the citadel of Rastatt held out for two more weeks, then the drum-head courts martial in Mannheim, Rastatt, and Freiburg began their bloody work. They were made up of members of the Prussian army, but pronounced sentence at the instance of the public prosecutor of Baden and in the name of Baden's reigning sovereign. Twenty-seven martyrs of freedom and the Reich idea, mostly soldiers, were shot. The severe proceedings of the Prussian special courts rightfully bred bad blood, and the two and a half years of expensive occupation of the land by the triumphant military power left no pleasant memories behind. As far as Switzerland they feared a military settling of accounts with all of those who had supported the Baden revolt. The Baden lullaby, written after the manner of a famous model from the Thirty Years' War, preserved an unforgettable memorial to the hatred of Prussia:

> Sleep my child, sleep softly
> There outside go the Pruss'[ians]
> We all must stay still
> Like your father under his stone.

But we may also not overlook the other side. Henriette Feuerbach, the step-mother of the painter, described the entrance of the Prussians into Freiburg.[203] She had, like many professors' families, sought safety in Breisach and observed the stream of thousands upon thousands of refugees, who flowed across the only Rhine bridge open into France. At first it had been the "aristocrats," who fled the provisional government, then came the democrats, who decamped before the reaction, and finally it was peaceful citizens leaving in panic before the Prussians. As the freedom-loving woman returned to her city dwelling in fear after the occupation of Freiburg and passed the Prussian outposts, she had to shed "tears of joy," as she wrote, although she, as a friend of both Herweghs and a relative of the radical philosopher Ludwig Feuerbach, inwardly sympathized with the other side. But the terror and the insecurity of life and property, the barbaric rawness and the helplessness of the revolutionaries, the anger of the unleashed Jacobin powers had been so odious, that one experienced the Prussian occupation as a solution. "It had brought us such an excess of freedom that we did not even know how to act under it." A large number—Frau Henriette maintained three-fourths of the young fighters—were forced to go along or were drawn in by "ruses of lawyers" and gruesome lies about the Prussian massacres. And now the inhabitants of Freiburg experienced a completely different reality. The independent, freedom-loving south Germans certainly sketched no bright picture of the Prussians. Still they were full of praise for them. "They act very humanely and show great sympathy for our poor people's army, that was led into fire so irresponsibly without a plan, and yet still was so upright." The correspondent never tires of praising the courtesy and good manners of the common soldier, the unpretentiousness of the quartered officers, the consideration of the Prussian occupational authorities. The order and discipline, the military bearing and the inner superiority stood in pleasing contrast to the sinister methods of the rebels and to the ragged and theatrical figures of the partisans. Frau Jette Feuerbach remembered with horror the daughter of Robert Blum and the other mounted amazons, who rode before the legion in a black velvet suit, Hecker hat and red feather, with cavalry sabre and dragoon ordinance, carrying a blood-red company flag with the inscription "Revenge for Robert Blum." The most terrible impression, however, was made on her by the bronze-colored faces of the foreign legion, with the strange sound of their southern European tongues, with their red sashes and long beards, with the dreadful emblem of a white skull painted on their black flags. In the clear air of the restored authoritarian state it was like an apparition that Baden had experienced in the short weeks of the *coup d'état*. The disclosure of the insufficient means, of the quarrels in the camp of the insurgents themselves, of the literary bickering over responsibility for the defeat were so unedifying, that even those who had sacrificed their blood for the cause of the people from time to time were unsure whether they had not set their lives on the line for "grandstand clowns and windbags."

The unending chain of treason trials and political convictions which accompanied the crushing of the May rebellions everywhere were certainly the best means to keep the memory undimmed. These proceedings by their abundance and their lack of magnanimity excited a deep exasperation even in the lands where no capital sentences were carried out, as in Saxony and the Bavarian Palatinate. The abyss which had opened up from the penal methods of the reaction had injured an inner conciliation more than all the revisions of constitutions and the limitations on suffrage rights which these years had brought. This gulf between the popular opinion and the police state was only closed over when in the years between 1866 and 1871 the authorities of state and the revolutionary myth were brought together again, and the convicted of 1848-49, men like Gottfried Kinkel, Lothar Bucher, Karl Schurz, and a hundred others shifted to support the work of the foundation of the Reich and its creator. Only on the basis of a common German state could the ideological and spiritual fronts be drawn to reciprocal toleration and respect, since they received a chance to work at the same task, even if as opposing political parties. An excellent deposition of this reconciliation was the chivalrous letter that Bismarck wrote on July 21, 1869 to Gottfried Kinkel as a first sign of peace overture. "When I think back to the mutually harsh position which our parties took twenty years ago, then I think it may be designated as a substantial progress on the way to political maturity when today at least the political parties in Germany no longer deny the sentiment of compatriot homogeneity an influence on their judgment of one another."[204]

XIII

THE RESULTS OF THE REVOLUTION

Was it actually a revolution that took place in Germany from March, 1848 until June, 1849 and never found its way outside the path of loyalty, neither inwardly nor externally ventured onto the road of violence? Was that a revolution, in which the owners of munitions shops, where rifles and sabres were taken, were promised that after the battle these things would be honestly returned, and these promises almost without exception were kept?[205] Was that a revolution, that posted police and authorities everywhere so that no mischief took place and everything maintained its legal form? In truth it was a "Mr. Piepmeyer's revolution", as the Hanoverian representative Johann Hermann Detmold described it and the Düsseldorfer painter Adolf Schröder caught in his drawings. This revolution of puffing and sweating Philistines, who festooned themselves with scarves and daggers and carried their barroom bravado into the street, this revolution of the little man, who could not put aside his inborn submissiveness and devotion and could not hide his deep ignorance of the essence of power, lacked the passionate greatness and the fateful inevitability of a historical thunderstorm. It was hardly chance that German philosophy during this period, with the one exception of Arnold Ruge, concerned itself so little with this experience, because these incidents derived their power neither from a new view of man nor a new conception of history. Even French observers agreed snidely how much the movement of 1848 had borrowed in its speech and its symbols, its ideals and its arguments from the already somewhat dusty memory of 1789 and the example of the Paris February revolution. The barricade and the cockade were of French ancestry. The alliance of student and worker corresponded to the fraternization of the Latin Quarter and the Faubourg St. Antoine. The scythes beaten straight were copied from the Polish revolts. The officers of the civil war had worn Greek uniforms. The civilian guards were an invention of 1789. Jury trials were an arrangement of French judicial process. For the procedure of the St. Paul's Church they studied the parliamentary primer of Jefferson. The bill of rights was to a great extent constructed from a constitutional state interpretation of the habeas corpus act, and English constitutional history remained the unforgettable school of German politicians. All this seems neither elementary nor first hand, not creative nor impressive.

And yet the crisis of 1848-49 was an epoch of German history and psychologically was an actual revolution. Standing midway between Stein and Bismarck, it was a conclusive attempt to build a German state from the powers of the liberal idea. It had undertaken to transform the self-administration idea of Stein from a rural to an urban locale, from a peasant to a bourgeois ideal, and in place of the free landowner to make a mature urban middle class the pillar of the state. It had tried to tear away the principalities from their military and feudal basis and to reconcile them, through the forms of bourgeois parliamentarianism, with the social and economic development of the century. Before Bismarck attacked the problem of the German state from the basis of the old Prussian monarchy and with conservative means of traditional European cabinet policy, the German jurists, authors, and craftsmen undertook creating a liberal national state corresponding to the wishes of the bourgeois majority for unity. They were determined to reconcile the absolute military monarchy and bureaucratic welfare state with the bourgeois constitutional state and to make the feudal state innocuous by legal reforms. The attempt perhaps might have succeeded, if it had attained a solid form at the point when the princes were shaken in their innermost consciences and the Habsburg monarchy was torn apart by the nationality problem. If at that moment a "Coburg prince" had been sitting on the Prussian throne, as Prince Consort Albert of England wished or even as the princess liked to envision William of Prussia, then probably the onslaught of public opinion from Prussia and all of Germany would not have been in vain. When we consider the possibility in March or April, 1848 in Berlin of a truly liberal, and resolutely German-minded ministry under Dönhoff, Eichmann, Arnim, or Bonin, accepted in essence by the king and protected against all influences, then perhaps Berlin might have been able, in spite of the permanent lack of political leadership and judgment in the ranks of the bourgeoisie, to bring the revolution a great deal nearer its double objective of freedom and unity. The wish of the German delegates, which Johann Gustav Droysen formulated in his informative April memorandum in Frankfurt/Main, would then have been carried out without the realization of the fears he expressed at the time.[206] The revolution would have been drawn to a "place of central administration," to a center of power, and the national assembly would have met in the only city which could assume the role of Paris for Germany. With an open cooperation of the Prussian royal house, it was not likely that a "dreadful civil war" or a "laceration of Germany" along the Main River line would have developed from this situation. The fearful hour in which the old powers, even in southern Germany and including even the princely families, the armies, and the bureaucracy, were predisposed to revolutionary enthusiasm, would have been exploited—preferably before March 21 when the "disgustingly ridiculous" imperial parade in Berlin had shaken confidence throughout Germany in the freedom and power of Berlin decisions.[207] The witnesses from the various German federal states leave hardly a doubt that most of the March governments would have been ready to join in a Prussian-German constitutional watchword. Only the option of the German provinces of Austria were really uncertain even then.

With the concessions by princes and the new state governments, with the discernment of the King of Prussia and a decisively liberal course by the Berlin authorities, the point of the revolution would have immediately been broken off, and they could have taken a new evolutionary road that sooner or later would have led to a Victorian constitutional state. Perhaps we have cause for some doubts whether the transformation of Germans from subjects to citizens would have made any progress worthy of mention in this way. Even the benevolent reigning princes, who hurried to accommodate public opinion with freedom of the press, jury trials, and the dissolution of feudal burdens, were incorrigible patriarchs, surrounding themselves in a cloud of His Most High Benevolence

and monarchical self-complacency, and deep within convinced that they had done the utmost and the best if, years ago, they had initiated in their tiny states the right "that every subject could speak to me Sundays and Saturdays."[208] All the good deeds that they now showered out in the March edicts, to their conception were nothing more really than measures of an enlightened despot, as all of their earlier reforms had also been: Abolition of labor service (*Fron*), improvement in the school systems, connection with the Customs Union, introduction of freedom of trade, liberal municipal regulations, and the extension of road building. If the demands of the revolution were proposed and fulfilled in this sovereign sense, then the fundamental condition of the German states had not changed all too much. Then all of the activities of the auspicious spring closed with Philistine cannon salutes by the subjects and majestic exhortations by the sovereigns. A proclamation of the gallant Henry LXXII, Prince of Reuss-Lobenstein-Ebersdorf on March 11, 1848 showed in what spirit the revolution could be overcome, "I trust in you, you Reussen! I rely upon you and say only: Order! Obedience to the law! . . . Draw close in friendship and love with your prince, your fellow subjects, and with this bring an end to yesterday's worker riot that was hardly a compliment to you!"[209]

However, the really German root of the March movement was that it wanted to wrench the nation out of this condition of submission. The beginnings of the reform period of Baron vom Stein were still quite alive, not only in the idea of self-administration and agrarian reform, but also in the promotion of a popular military organization. The Kantian liberalism in East Prussia and west German liberalism in the Rhineland districts had contributed new motives. The constitutional experience of the central German states and the pan-German objective of the 1840s had made their contribution to the revolution. Above all, the powers of both wings of the student associations, the national liberal and the radical democratic, had determined the formation of parties to a great extent. The Hegelian philosophy with its dialectical-historical and political systems had furnished the intellectual background for the extreme poles of the revolution: for the idea of the class struggle here and for the principle of the Christian corporate state there. The old territorial state traditions in many areas had not yet been extin-

193

guished, and only with the challenge of the revolution did they again become a public power. All this bears witness to a deep interlacing of the events of 1848 with German history and stamps it as something inevitable and of long preparation. The March occurrences in Germany were more than mere offshoots of a European storm tide.

But it was also less than a crowning of the German state's constitutional-historical development. If a liberal movement, which was fed by a widespread and powerful intellectual tradition, had triumphed in Germany during 1848, it could have meant the connection of Germany to the west European evolution, and perhaps have led to that ideological community with England, which from a political standpoint would have possibly been the only chance for our development as a national state. As the impetus of the liberal opposition was not sufficient to achieve victory, the consequences of 1848 were more destructive for the external and internal political future of the Reich. The nation had to cover the distance to a modern Great Power without a solid inner support from another European power, and the Germans confronted the economic and social problems of advanced capitalism without a secure connection with its own constitutional-historical past. One cannot deny that Germany at the end of the 18th century was on the verge of cultivating its own governmental character: the enlightened administrative state. This reasonably-led monarchical welfare state was without a doubt constantly in need of reform, but the relation of confidence between the government and public opinion experienced no revolutionary turmoil. After the division had set in, and the government had become a reactionary power, public opinion a revolutionary danger, then the main agents of the enlightened princely state, bureaucracy and the bourgeoisie, were no longer open with each other. The bureaucracy was obdurate, gruff, distant from the masses, pugnacious, and reactionary; the bourgeois society, insofar as it was politically sensitive at all, was irritable, refractory, hostile, inclined to constant criticism, and accustomed to a vicious dualism. The sort of progressive, even enlightened patriarchal administrative official, who embraced the bourgeois ideals of the enlightenment, was among the leaders of his cultural world, and endeavoured to march at the head of the historical development, increasingly died out after 1850 and their places were taken by

rigidly conservative governmental men, who lost contact with the living social process and saw their mission as the suppression of popular currents. In the *Vormärz* era things had still been different. When in the year 1844 Frederick Engels published his disturbing work on the condition of the working classes in England, this book was not merely noticed in the bourgeois weekly press, but the noble high officials also comprehended its full importance. An 1845 report by an exemplary administrator in a small state in Thuringia is preserved in which, on the basis of his reading of Engels, he urged his superior minister that one should use the experiences of a great nation enlarged upon here, and must prevent the development of a working class, for which the germs also existed in Germany.[210] Where in the German administrative state, after the deep incision of 1848, did there still exist the candour and detachment, the consciousness of social responsibility and the faith in itself that such a conception denoted? The miscarried revolution had destroyed the Germans' trust in their state, and abrogated the naive accord with the people in the ruling circles. Only the harsh division into factions of the reactionary period called into question the harmonious existence and the euphony of the enlightened commonwealth, and buried the Germans' pride in their individual constitutional form. The unsettled and wavering political self-confidence of middle Europe was an ominous consequence of the unsettled crisis of 1848, that neither cleansed the atmosphere nor replaced the obsolete and dying with a revolution.

If we call the events of this year, despite many limitations, a revolution, then we are empowered to do so by the appearance of all the currents of a typical revolutionary process. The crisis began as an hour of upheaval and extraordinary experience for the entire nation. From the simple burgher and peasant to the diplomat and minister the feeling was intense that it was a matter of "prodigious occurrences,"[211] that completely new psychic powers were aroused and new times beginning. Even the king declared that a "rebirth" had occurred. No one chose to close himself out of this experience of the community. Only an insignificantly small portion of the court society, the old bureaucracy and the army opposed and detested the uproar even at the very outbreak of the revolution.[212] Everyone else dismissed with indignation the idea that this "profound expression of German idealism" might be brushed aside as a mere street disturbance, as an intrigue of French and Polish emissaries, or as an excess of the "rabble."[213] Students, scholars, artists, artisans, street workers, druggists, taxi drivers, and chamberlains seized the weapons to protect the holy fire of enthusiasm against foreign intervention, against evil-minded reactionaries, against the misuse of the revolution by conspiratorial types. But the second stage of the revolution was immediately imminent. Alongside the enthusiastic youths and the liberal idealists who aspired to a united Germany, free public opinion, and an honorable division of powers in the state, the social motives of the lower classes arose. Peasants and workers moved to assail the feudal right of ownership and to impose on the state a social responsibility that it until then had never supported. Through all sorts of channels isolated splinters of the "communistic" program penetrated into the liberal revolution. Many of these demands were in absolute conformity with the reform objectives of the bourgeois majority and easily integrated into the liberal world of ideas. Arming of the people, the secular state, freedom of education, people's judges, progressive income tax, a unified German state were both liberal as well as social democratic ideals, even though in practice here and there they might assume a different countenance. A second group of social demands might sound unfamiliar to the middle class, but were hardly perceived in their basic meaning. The right to work, state guarantee of a minimum for existence, extended factory legislation, removal of all charges at educational institutions: all of this could be understood idealistically and appeared unobjectionable so long as one did not fully grasp the basic changes in the position of responsibilities for the state. A third group of socialistic programs points, on the contrary, in the eyes of *Biedermeier* Germany, from the very beginning necessarily threatened the foundation of the bourgeois social order and the individualistic ideal of freedom. Among these belonged the nationalization of transportation and credit institutions, the coordination of all bureaucratic categories in wages, the restrictions on inheritance rights, and the confiscation of larger landed estates. Such program points forced the entire bourgeoisie, including the small craftsmen and peasants, to be repelled into the arms of the old powers of order. This then took place visibly during the summer and autumn months of 1848, when the Thermidor mood of October 31 was

196

already growing. The historical authorities: state and army, church and crown, which were gradually recovering their senses, in this atmosphere of fear, could conclude their counter-revolutionary alliance with popular opinion. As reaction converted to the theoretical plane of the opponent and itself became doctrinaire, the leaders evolved an extremely efficacious conservative propaganda, and by using all means of the press, associations, the pressure of the government, and personal publicity, they created a strong reactionary party among broad layers of the people. The revolution was thrown back on the defensive with its own weapons and finally decisively defeated in all the electoral battles.

Only the nationalistic movement dominated by the idea of German unity was still, for the time being, in a state of growth, and in September, 1848, with its abrupt disappointment by the military reverse in Schleswig-Holstein, engendered a second wave of agitation, which to be sure could no longer change the overall fate of a miscarried revolution. That it was the left which then proposed a *levée en masse* and represented revolutionary imperialism can be no surprise. Also in the English revolution of Cromwell's times and in the French Revolutionary War of 1793 it was the radical elements who did not shun military conflict with foreign powers and contemplated expansive objectives. The most passionate spokesmen of a German national war during the orators' battle of September 5 in St. Paul's Church were from among the extreme democrats. A concealed Pan-Germanic note in general resounded in the March revolution. It sounded different in the greater-German camp than in Schwarzenberg's seventy-million plan; it had another pitch among the Kiel professors than with Karl Marx for instance when he protested against the Germans' political and cultural withdrawal from Bohemia. But it was noticeable wherever themes of foreign policy were touched, and furthermore this intensified national self-consciousness has been observed in every people who experienced the exaltation of a revolutionary crisis.

In the final phase of disappointment and animosity over the failure of the revolt, the idea of world revolution was announced, and with this the revolution returned to the internationalism of the initial stage. The exiled social revolutionary Karl Heinzen, in an informative pamphlet, *The Lessons of Revolution* (London, 1850), professed the thought that a revolution must necessarily

197

operate with a dictator at its core intervening in the smallest matter, and in no case could it be fought out on a national but only on the European battlefield. A real revolutionary "cure" was imminent in Europe and would probably cost a few million heads; but that was not too many if it was a matter of the happiness of 200 million people, especially since the sacrifice, as he believed, would only consist of a few million "scoundrels."[214]

Among the Germans who remained behind in the Old World and in the conventional surroundings, the experience of the mis-carried revolution turned very soon into a general scepticism and an astounding political realism. Metternich had once called liberal-ism "the mislearned art of ruling" (*verlernte Regierungskunst*). Now people wanted back the competent art of government at any price. No more impressive witness exists for this than a letter of David Friedrich Strauss, which says the last word on the revolution in the year 1852. The reason for the failure of a movement that he himself had followed with such great expectations, according to his interpretation did not lie in the iniquity or the perversity of any social class or any individual personality; it was not situated among the Junkers and the officers nor among the democrats and the Frankfurt delegates, not even with Frederick William IV or Schwarzenberg, but rather in the fact that Germany hid within itself two state complexes that stood in opposition to one another with historical right, that is with historical might: Austria and Prus-sia. If a German state was ever to arise, then it would have to work itself out of this fissure caused by the two power centers, and only the man who showed the way to do this could really enter a claim for the title of revolutionary. "Alongside of this ques-tion of unity I consider more or less despotism or constitutionalism, Junker or democratic domination in the individual German states as very immaterial."[215] No bourgeois contemporary had drawn a more acute conclusion from the defeat. But after the sad close of the Erfurt union parliament and the wreck of the last hopes of the liberal party many had been converted to this resigned view. In the words of Strauss, world historical expectations confronted us that Bismarck would answer and would determine his path even against his own original will. It was therefore not just a prostration before success and the accomplished *coup d'état* when in 1866 the German professors and the other descendants of St. Paul's

Church recognized Bismarck's mastery. And it was not merely Bismarckian education when the disappointed German middle class turned to a realism of power politics that looked down indulgently upon the idealistic dreams of its fathers. The bourgeois class was shaken too deeply in its self-confidence to still trust itself to solve the German Reich and political problems. Bismarck was almost necessarily the hero of that middle class which in 1848-49 had vainly attempted the same question. In the rooms of the simple craftsman after 1870 one would see Bismarck's powerful head hanging in the same place once honored by a cheap lithograph of Hecker's portrait or the bill of rights of the German people in a black-red-gold frame. The political road that the intimidated bourgeoisie in Germany entered upon was basically no worse than the path that the French middle class followed after the June Days. To avoid the dictatorship of the proletariat, the burgher class in France by a gigantic majority submitted to the illegitimate power of Louis Napoleon, his army, and his successful foreign policy. Order here could only take the form of caesarism, a democratically elected tyranny, since the legitimate monarchy had been disposed of by the bourgeoisie itself. In Germany the party of order, when it appeared threatened by the left-radical current, threw itself into the arms of the powers of the legitimate authoritarian state, the princes, their ministers, and their officer corps. And they made their peace with it a second time when they at least secured a national state from Bismarck's victorious foreign policy. Thus the March revolution, by the hopes that it awoke and the reality it could not produce, was likewise a preparatory stage for 1871.

But we would do an injustice to the movement of the year 1848 if we insisted on judging merely its shortcomings, reverses, and the indirect results. Only as we pursue the history of manners and customs, institutions and social groups, legal conditions and social esteem, can we measure how deeply it really reached into German life; it was not even annihilated by reaction in all areas. The Berliners certainly joked that the only permanent accomplishment of the revolution was the permission for a person to smoke tobacco in a public street. Such police regulations and barriers of etiquette were indeed often abolished; such triumphs of bourgeois self-reliance were accomplished in abundance. Whether "*Sie*"* was now intro-

*Formal "you" address, corresponding to French "vous."

duced in the army for the protection of human dignity or the differentiation between *Demoiselle* and *Fräulein* was dropped in the future, whether a university for women could be opened in Hamburg, or in Austria from now on the Protestant churches might also have a bell tower—similar claims of tolerance and equality of customs neither before nor after in Germany found such rapid and lasting realization as in the revolutionary year, 1848. Admittedly constitutions were made retrogressive, and in Austria, on December 31, 1851, the constitution was even completely suspended, but in every land inextinguishable traces of a new legal order remained behind, brought by the years 1848 to 1850. Even in the Habsburg monarchy the work of peasant emancipation had taken a permanent step on the road to more just conditions of ownership and state regulations of burdens. By a statute labor law of 1849 the absolutist Danube state created even more balanced and tenable rural conditions than Prussia had once acquired by the Stein reforms, and the honor for this falls to the last effective resolution by the revolutionary Viennese Reichstag of September 7, 1848.

If we trace the history of the reaction in north Germany, then indeed Frederick William IV and the Junker party reversed a series of beneficent laws of the revolution after 1852, but in the area of the constitution of justice, court procedures, and substantive law, the years of disturbance continued to point the direction for the future. The actual Palladium of the feudal epoch, the manorial jurisdiction, was not restored, although the police power of the lord of the manor again made its appearance in 1856. Entail and manorial privileges were resurrected in the old form, but the Junker right to hunt on other's lands was not restored after it was replaced in 1850 by a proprietary hunting law. The very well-considered rural communal arrangement of 1850, which enveloped the entire east, was inexcusably abolished again a little later. The self-administrative organs for the county and districts expired after two years of revocation. But there still remained a lasting accomplishment of the Prussian commonwealth introduced through the law of 1849 in a new criminal law code for the entire state, and after this time oral prosecution, indictment by a special magistrate, and judgment of guilt by a jury belonged to the permanent components of the Prussian constitutional state. In the criminal law book of 1851 many basic tendencies of the French *code pénale* were adopted without including its particular harshness. Corporal punishment was abandoned, the death penalty was limited to a few crimes, the execution of punishment directed in new milder ways, and the old-fashioned sentences of deportation, confiscation, and civil death were removed from the Prussian criminal law book.[216] When one considers also that the protracted work on peasant emancipation in Prussia finally came to an end with the law of March 2, 1850, and the establishment of revenue banks with the state as intermediary in the loan system between the lord of the manor and the peasant, and one regards further that in the area of commerce too, the state adhered to a beneficial policy, and since 1850 numerous credit institutions, producers' cooperatives, cooperative stores came to the aid of small business, then one must say that the powerful peasant and artisan movement of the revolutionary year was not entirely in vain.

But the material benefits and the political consequences of the revolution do not exhaust its historical meaning. No matter how small and petty bourgeois it may have been, the courage of sacrifice and the devotion, the enthusiasm and the love of the fatherland that was intense in every revolutionary fighter were really lasting and undying. Karl Schurz later, in his reminiscences, set down in words for posterity this meaning of the March revolution, that carries with it the imprint of actual experience:

> What should make the memory of the spring, 1848 especially esteemed by the German people was the enthusiastic willingness to make a self-sacrifice for the great cause which spread through almost all social classes with a rare unanimity. . . . I knew in my surroundings many honest men, scholars, students, burghers, peasants, workers, with or without wealth, more or less dependent on their daily work to insure themselves and their families a decent livelihood, devoted to their profession not alone from interest, rather also by preference; but at that time prepared at any moment to risk their position, possessions, prospects, life, and all for the freedom of the people and for the honor and greatness of the fatherland. We respect those who were prepared to sacrifice their lives for a good and great idea. And everyone, whether as an individual or as a nation, that experienced such moments of self-sacrificing enthusiasm in his life, may he honor the memory of them.[217]

NOTES

INTRODUCTION

1. Karl Griewank, *Deutsche Literatur Zeitung* (Berlin), LXXI (1950), 376-78.
2. This term is from the outstanding study by Fritz K. Ringer, *The Decline of the German Mandarins: The German Academic Community, 1890-1933* (Cambridge, Mass., 1969).
3. Hermann Heimpel, "Rudolf Stadelmann und die deutsche Geschichtswissenschaft," *Historische Zeitung*, CLXXII (1951), 285-307; Eduard Spranger, *Rudolf Stadelmann zum Gedächtnis: Akademische Trauerfeier am 21. Januar 1950 im Festsaal der Universität Tübingen* (Tübingen, 1950), pp. 10-12, 17-18, 25-26.
4. *Die Bildungswelt des deutschen Handwerkers um 1800: Studien zur Soziologie des Kleinbürgers im Zeitalter Goethes* (Berlin, 1955).
5. Foreword to the German edition of this book.
6. George Rudé, *Debate on Europe 1815-1850* (New York, 1972), p. 189.
7. Werner Boldt, *Die Anfänge des deutschen Parteiwesens: Faktionen, politische Vereine und Parteien in der Revolution 1848* (Paderborn, 1971).
8. For the most eloquent rejection of this apology for Frederick William see Friedrich Meinecke's scathing review article of Felix Rachfahl's book, "Friedrich Wilhelm IV. und Deutschland," *Historische Zeitschrift*, LXXXIX (1902), 17-53.
9. Frederick de Luna, *The French Republic under Cavaignac, 1848* (Princeton, 1969), pp. 345 ff.; James Chastain, "Jules Bastide et l'unité allemande en 1848," *Revue historique* 511 (Juillet-Septembre 1974), 51-72.
10. Stadelmann speculated, probably correctly, that the failure of the German 1848 revolution was caused largely by the *lack* of a foreign threat. Since there was no outside threat to German unity, the Germans did not have a devil to fight, an external focus of hatred as a nucleus of unity; for more recent literature see James Chastain, "French *Kleindeutsch* Policy in 1848" (University of Oklahoma, doctoral dissertation, 1967); Günther Gillessen, *Lord Palmerston und die Einigung Deutschlands: Die englische Politik von der Paulskirche bis zu den Dresdener Konferenzen (1848-1851)* ("Historische Studien," No. 384) (Lübeck, 1961), cf. Lawrence Jennings, *France and Europe in 1848: A Study of French Foreign Affairs in Time of Crisis* (London, 1973) and Robert Hahn, "The Attitude of the French Revolutionary Government toward German Unification in 1848," (Ohio State University, doctoral dissertation, 1955).
11. This problem of the development of the idea of class struggle has been the object of a great debate among German historians; for a discussion of the important literature on this question see Walter Schmidt and Rolf Dlubek, "Die Herausbildung der marxistischen Partei der deutschen Arbeiterklasse," *Zeitschrift für Geschichtswissenschaft*, XIV (1966), 1282-333; Theodore Hamerow argued that the artisans were the real proletariat of 1848, since their economic position was in reality lower relative to the better-paid factory employees, even if their social standing was in theory superior; he emphasized the inherent social conflict between

the artisans and the upper bourgeois "March ministries" whose economic goal of *laissez-faire* destruction of the guilds clashed directly with the artisan's desire for guild protection of handicrafts; this left the way open, Hamerow showed, for the reactionaries to champion the cause of the artisans against the liberals and split the united bourgeois front of the March revolutions. *Restoration, Revolution, Reaction: Economics and Politics in Germany, 1815-1871* (Princeton, 1958).
  12. A. J. P. Taylor, *The Course of German History* (New York, 1946-62), p. 68.

CHAPTERS I-XIII

  1. A very interesting attempt to explain historical transformations in this manner was made by Max Wundt, *Aufstieg und Niedergang der Völker* (Munich, n. d.).
  2. Cf. my essay, "Deutschland und die westeuropäischen Revolutionen," in the collection of articles, Rudolf Stadelmann, *Deutschland und Westeuropa* (Laupheim, 1948).
  3. *Auszug aus der Saulgauer Pfarrchronik* (Saulgau, 1851), p. 57.
  4. Cf. Karl Biedermann, *Deutschland im 18. Jahrhundert* (2d. ed.; Leipzig, 1880), I, 230 ff.
  5. Even the convinced republican Joseph Fickler from Constance computed in the year 1848 for the thirty-four "cannibalistic monsters" of the reigning German princes only around 1300 further parasites, who lived from the sweat and blood of the subjects; that comes to an average of not quite forty courtiers for each princely throne. F. Lautenschlager, *Volksstaat und Einherrschaft* (Constance, 1920), p. 95.
  6. Biedermann, *Deutschland im 18. Jahrhundert*, II, 1153.
  7. The statistics are from the tables of Gustav Schmoller, *Zur Geschichte des deutschen Kleingewerbes* (Halle, 1870), pp. 65 and 71.
  8. Karl Biedermann, *Deutschland im 18. Jahrhundert*, I, 384 f.
  9. Interesting excerpts from this pamphlet literature in Jürgen Kuczynski, *Die Geschichte der Lage der Arbeiter in Deutschland von 1800 bis zur Gegenwart* (Berlin, 1947), I, 54 f., 79 ff. Especially striking was the information of the Mainz district judge Friedrich Dael concerning the wage rates for the artisan classes in Rhine-Hesse, *Zeitschrift des Vereins für deutsche Statistik*, I, (1847), 840 ff., who calculated the yearly income of a man at 220 fl. and in 1846 an annual deficiency of 122 fl. for a family household. An unnamed Swabian statistician worked out for Wurtemberg that almost a third of the working population, all the winegrowers, and the third portion of the small peasants and industrially employed did not reach the subsistence minimum of 300 fl. a year, rather existed on an average income of 200 fl. *Ibid.*, I, 1077. However, for Hamburg, Bremen, Lübeck, and Frankfurt, Reden offers a much more favorable picture of the relationship between prices and wages, *Ibid.*, I, 1046. The figures deviate greatly, often from the same author! Cf. *Ibid.*, I, 568 f., 840 ff., 1038 ff., 1076 ff. The income surplus for unexpected disbursements, that 1787 in Berlin amounted to around a quarter of wages, by 1846 certainly had vanished completely (*Ibid.*, p. 569), but the standard of living correspondingly improved.
  10. The wage data from Wurtemberg and Saxony which Kuczynski quoted certify that the increase in pay was sustained. A Swabian tailor, who in 1820 earned an hourly wage of 1.11 M. rose to 1.34 M. in 1850, and the press worker improved between 1820 and 1840 from 1.89 to 2.14 M. Miners' wages show a more vigorous

growth: those in the Saar district ascended, 1820: 1.23, 1830: 1.57, 1840: 1.75, and 1850: 2 M.; *Geschichte der Lage*, I, 81.

11. Reuter, "Verhältnisse und Lage der landarbeitenden Volksklassen in den deutschen Gegenden des mittleren Rhein- und unteren Main- und Neckargebietes," *Zeitschrift für deutsche Statistik*, I, (1847), 378.

12. *Neue Zeit*, III (1885); in addition Gustav Schmoller, *Grundriss der allgemeinen Volkswirtschaftslehre*, and Veit Valentin, *Geschichte der Deutschen Revolution von 1848-49* (2 vols.; Berlin, 1930-31).

13. The numbers seem to me strongly exaggerated, as the following consideration shows. For Berlin the total of workers was given for 1847 as 10,000. That was 1/40 of the entire population of the city. How should the entire monarchy amount to the relationship of 550,000: 16,000,000, that is 1/30 of the entire population consisting of workers, if this average number was not even reached in the largest industrial city of the country! And the figures for Berlin were certainly not too low, since they come from the socialist Dronke, who had an interest in proving the proletarian character of Berlin. Cf. Heinz Pflaume, *Organisation und Vertretung der Arbeitnehmer 1848-49* (University of Jena, doctoral dissertation, 1934), p. 18 f.

14. Wilhelm Kaiser, "Anfänge der fabrikmässig organisierten Industrie in Baden," *Zeitschrift für Geschichte des Oberrheins*, XLVI (1933), 626 ff. Until 1850 the number grew only to 12,800 factory and 4,400 home workers, although in Baden during this period larger concerns like the spinning mills of Ettlingen and the machine factory of Karlsruhe already employed 1150 and 600 workers respectively. The figures for craftsmen from Gustav Schmoller, *Zur Geschichte des deutschen Kleingewerbes*, p. 104.

15. Johann Daniel Georg von Memminger, *Beschreibung von Württemberg* (Stuttgart, 1841), p. 419; for 150,000 masters and journeymen there were 10,000 workers; that results (without the home workers, who are included in the statistics from Baden) in a relationship of 15:1 favoring craftwork.

16. Gustav Schmoller and Max Sering (eds.), *Staats- und sozialwissenschaftliche Forschungen* (Leipzig, 1880), II, Heft 2 and 3.

17. *Ibid.*, II, H. 3, 55.

18. *Ibid.*, II, H. 3, 153.

19. *Ibid.*, II, H. 2, 115.

20. Ernst Dronke, *Berlin* (2 vols.; Berlin, 1846); Ernst Violand, *Die soziale Geschichte der Revolution in Österreich* (Leipzig, 1850); Bettina von Arnim, *Dies Buch gehört dem König* (Berlin, 1857).

21. H. Wollheim, *Versuch einer medizinischen Topographie und Statistik von Berlin* (Berlin, 1844).

22. Instructive for this is the work of Siegfried Kuhn, *Der Aufstand der Kleineisenindustriearbeiter in Solingen am 16. und 17. März 1848* (University of Munich, doctoral dissertation, 1938) (also *Zeitschrift des Bergischen Geschichtsvereins*, 1938); in the same periodical vol. 20 (1913) and vol. 54 (1923-24) are works concerning the social question in Wuppertal.

23. Clara Wittenstein, "Die Entstehung der sozialen Frage im Wuppertal," *Zeitschrift des Bergischen Geschichtsvereins*, LIV (1923-24), 177.

24. Oldwig Leopold Anton von Natzmer, *Unter den Hohenzollern* (Gotha, 1889), IV, 281.

25. Wilhelm Wolff, *Gesammelte Schriften*, Franz Mehring (ed.) (Berlin, 1909), p. 44.

26. Friedrich Harkort, *Bemerkungen über die Hindernisse in der Zivilisation und Emanzipation der unteren Klassen* (Elberfeld, 1844) p. 8.

27. On this relationship between political and social uncertainties see the very

informative Johanna Köster, *Der rheinische Frühliberalismus und die soziale Frage*, ("Historische Studien," No. 342) (Berlin, 1938).

28. Georg Friedrich Knapp, *Die Bauernbefreiung und der Ursprung der Landarbeiter* (Leipzig, 1887), I, 149 ff.

29. The results of this survey of various Prussian provinces were communicated in the publication of Alexander von Lengerke, *Die ländliche Arbeiterfrage* (Berlin, 1849). The point of view of the east Elbian landowner, who was only too favorably inclined to make the "moral conditions," the love of display, luxury, enjoyment of brandy, and the laziness of the people responsible for social misery was evident throughout the reports of the agricultural societies. Nevertheless, a rather objective picture of the living conditions of the rural worker emerged, as well as the evidence of divided, completely opposing suggestions for reform coming from interested circles. The call for state help was there along with the defense against all invasions of the public hand, the demand for expansion of elementary school instruction beside the cry for its simplification and dismantling.

30. Erich Jordan, *Die Konservative Partei* (Berlin, 1914), p. 60. The same ratio was reported from Lippe. Whereas in 1772 there were only 5-6 renters (Einlieger), in 1846 these numbered 110. The number of landowners remained constant at around 40. Until the mid-18th century the younger peasant sons could settle on uncultivated places of the commons and "heaths." Cf. Georg Funke, "Über die Verhältnisse der Einlieger in den Fürstentümern Lippe-Detmold und Schamburg-Lippe," *Zeitschrift des Vereins für deutsche Statistik*, II (1848), 1104 ff.

31. Karl Reis, *Agrarfrage und Agrarbewegung in Schlesien im Jahre 1848* ("Darstellungen und Quellen zur schlesischen Geschichte," XII) (Breslau, 1910), pp. 12, 26, & 138; Johannes Ziekursch, *Hundert Jahre schlesischer Agrargeschichte* ("Darstellungen und Quellen zur schlesischen Geschichte," XX) (Breslau, 1912), p. 372.

32. Georg Friedrich Knapp, *Die Bauernbefreiung*, I, 268.

33. A vivid description of peasant conditions in Germany outside of Prussia is contained in the work of Wilhelm Engel, *Wirtschaftliche und soziale Kämpfe in Thüringen von dem Jahr 1848* ("Zeitschrift des Vereins für Thüringische Geschichte") Beiheft XI) (Jena, 1927), pp. 20 ff.

34. Freiherr von Wöllwarth private archive, Essingen bei Aalen, Wurtemberg.

35. Wilhelm Wolff, *Gesammelte Schriften*, p. 113.

36. Elli Lehmann, *Die Spiegelung der deutschen revolutionären Ereignisse von 1848-49 in der schweizerischen Presse* (University of Bern, doctoral dissertation, 1935), p. 23.

37. Since Treitschke no one has presented these accomplishments in a single work; individual biographical studies: F. & P. Goldschmidt, *Das Leben des Staatsrat Kunth* (Berlin, 1890); Paul Wentzcke, *Justus Gruner* (Heidelberg, 1913); G. Hasse, *Theodor von Schön* (Leipzig, 1915); H. von Petersdorff, *Friedrich von Motz* (2 vols.; Berlin, 1913).

38. Cf. the vivid description from the liberal side, "Das Königreich Württemberg bis zum März 1848," *Die Gegenwart*, IV (1850).

39. This is the basic thesis of Otto Bähr, *Das frühere Kurhessen* (Kassel, 1895).

40. Karl Biedermann, *Deutschland im 18. Jh.*, I, 158.

41. Adolf Rapp, "Uhland im politischen Leben," *Württembergische Vierteljahreshefte für Landesgeschichte*, XXXIII (1927), 58 f.

42. Ludwig Uhland, *Briefwechsel* ed. Julius Hartmann (Stuttgart, 1914), III, 368 f.

43. Friedrich Harkort, *Bemerkungen über die Hindernisse*, p. 27.

44. Cf. Stüve's letter of July 6, 1842, Gustav Stüve (ed.), *Johann Karl Bertram Stüve nach Briefen und persönlichen Erinnerungen* (Hanover, 1900), I, 323.

45. A highly characteristic testimony for this old bourgeois self-confidence was

205

contained in a letter of the Bremen Mayor Smidt. When he was informed of the intended engagement of his daughter to the Baden diplomat Baron von Blittersdorff, he wrote from Frankfurt, the meeting place of the German Diet delegates, "We would only in an extreme case give our approval to an engagement with a non-Bremer, least of all with a nobleman. I would prefer any shopkeeper in Bremen. A free burgher in our cities, even if he were only a good craftsman, is ten times better off than a Prussian official of the first rank. I circulate here daily with the most trusted and respected servants of emperors, kings, and princes, but they all are and remain more or less servants, and I would trade places with none of them." Hermann Entholt, "Bürgermeister Smidt und seine Korrespondenten," *Bremisches Jahrbuch*, XLII (1942), 15 f.

46. The memorandum of 1830 was published in David Hansemann, *Das preussiche und deutsche Verfassungswerk* (Berlin, 1850), especially pp. 14 & 33.

47. Otto Wagner, *Mitteleuropäische Gedanken und Bestrebungen in den vierziger Jahren (1840-48)* (University of Marburg, doctoral dissertation, 1935).

48. Rudolf Stadelmann, *Moltke und der Staat* (Crefeld, 1948), p. 102.

49. Cf. George W. F. Hallgarten, *Studien zur deutschen Polenfreundschaft* (Berlin, 1928) and Eberhard Maier, *Die aussenpolitischen Ideen der Achtundvierziger* ("Historische Studien" vol. 337) (Berlin, 1938), pp. 17 ff. & 63 ff.

50. Rudolf Haym, *Aus meinem Leben* (Berlin, 1902), p. 166.

51. Lewis B. Namier, *1848: The Revolution of the Intellectuals* (London, 1944).

52. When Friedrich Harkort learned in Brussels the news of Louis Philippe's abdication and his host suggested that the revolution could spread to Germany, the Westphalian liberal jumped up in the greatest excitement and replied with unaccustomed harshness, "We revolution? We in Prussia? This is completely impossible. We in Prussia want peaceful popular reform and a liberal constitution, but under no circumstances revolution!" Ludwig Berger, *Der alte Harkort* (4th ed.; Leipzig, 1902), p. 335 f.

53. It appears interesting for a social historical explanation of the revolution that the depression 1846 and 1847 was far below the intensity of the depression of 1817. The grain prices for matters of comparison were for a *Simmeri* of cereal in 1817, 11 Gulden; 1847, 4 Gulden. *Saulgauer Pfarrchronik*, pp. 54 & 58.

54. A. Bernstein, *Revolutions- und Reaktionsgeschichte in Preussen und Deutschland* (Berlin, 1882), II, 79.

55. Leopold von Ranke (ed.), *Aus dem Briefwechsel Friedrich Wilhelms IV. mit Bunsen* ("Sämtliche Werke," L) (Leipzig, 1887), p. 462.

56. "Das deutsche Vorparlament," *Die Gegenwart*, II (1849), 686.

57. Egon Caesar Conte Corti, *Anonyme Briefe an drei Kaiser* (Leipzig, 1939), p. 118f.; the police reports Julius Marx utilized testify that material causes also did not matter decisively in the Habsburg monarchy. Where a social exacerbation arose, it turned against Jewish factory owners, not against the Metternichian state. "Die Wirtschaftslage im deutschen Österreich vor Ausbruch der Revolution 1848," *Vierteljahresschrift für Sozial- und Wirtschaftsgeschichte*, XXXI, (1938), 242 ff.

58. The most illustrative source about the flight of Metternich were the letters of his companion, Count J. B. Rechberg, in Edgar Stern-Rubath, "Sturz und Flucht Metternichs," *Deutsche Rundschau*, CXCIX (1924), 286 ff.; especially characteristic for Metternich's inner resignation before the events of the times was his letter to Tsar Nicholas I. of March 14, 1848, *Aus Metternichs Nachgelassenen Papieren* (Vienna, 1883), VII, 605.

59. Pronouncement of the Tübingen Chancellor von Wächter, who himself was a member of the fifty, *Die Gegenwart*, IV (1850), 423.

60. Paul Boerner, *Erinnerungen eines Revolutionärs* (Leipzig, 1920), I, 82.

61. "Berlin in der Bewegung von 1848," *Die Gegenwart*, II (1849), 545.

62. According to a source quoted from a manuscript by Max Lenz, it was no demonstrating street mob, rather many people who were walking home to change into dress clothes for this festive occasion; Max Lenz, *Geschichte der Universität Berlin* (Berlin, 1918), II (2), 208.

63. Karl Gutzkow, *Rückblicke auf mein Leben* (n. d.), p. 336.

64. Unpublished diary of Baron von Hiller, entry of March 18, Family archive of Baron Hiller von Gärtringen; an especially reliable picture of the events of March 18 was outlined by M. Schasler in his "Tagebucherinnerungen eines alten Achtundvierzigers," *Vossische Zeitung*, 1892, Sonntagsbeilage No. 638, quoted extensively by Wilhelm Liebknecht, *Robert Blum und seine Zeit* (2d. ed., Nuremberg, 1889), pp. 297 ff.

65. An informative testimony for the popularity of the pre-romantic Prussian administrative state until 1840 was given by the revolutionary medical student Paul Boerner, "The dead king was respectable and kind to the people, in spite of the bony mechanism of his bureaucratic-military government." Paul Boerner, *Erinnerungen*, I, 99.

66. Ludwig Bergstraesser, "Neue Beiträge zur Geschichte der Berliner Märztage," *Historische Vierteljahrsschrift*, XVII (1914), 79 f.

67. Karl Haenchen, "Flucht und Rückkehr des Prinzen von Preussen im Jahre 1848," *Historische Zeitschrift*, CLIV (1936), 32 ff.

68. An especially clear picture of the composition of the crowd was traced in the report of a First Lieutenant von Reibnitz, who had the duty to protect the castle Monbijou on the afternoon of March 18 and the following night with a detachment of guards. He dealt cool-headedly with the leaders of the mob which demanded of him as from all the watchposts of Berlin the delivery of weapons. The first time it was a young worker with a hatchet and a large iron nail in his hand who confronted him; then it was almost always students with whom he had to parley. There were remarkably reasonable and protracted dialogues. The students were easily seized and then brought around from the point of view of honor. The crowd, among whom were not a few former militia soldiers, were impressed by the determination and devotion of the officer, who actually was only carrying out his orders. The only outlook that fascinated the crowd was solidarity with the attacked comrades. "The soldiers murdered my brothers; I must hurry to save them or to die with them, and for that we must have weapons," was the argument preferred in greatest excitement by the young worker who led the group. As the cleverly negotiating officer sent his watch into the caserne without giving over the weapons, the students brought forth a thundering cheer for him, and the crowd joined in frantically as Reibnitz passed the cheer on to the king. Only one of the leaders spoke with a Polish accent; and the most heated clash was between Reibnitz and a young Westphalian, who he thought was a student. That was the approximate sociological data repeated by all the unbiased witnesses. Mass psychological conformity with the law drowns out any political motivation or social individuality. The report was published by Karl Haenchen, "Neue Briefe und Berichte aus den Berliner Märztagen," *Forschungen zur brandenburgischen und preussischen Geschichte*, XLIX (1937), 271 ff. The plentiful eyewitness accounts are included in Adolf Wolff, *Berliner Revolutionschronik* (3 vols.; Berlin, 1849-54) & Dr. Würth, *Album der Geschichte des Jahres 1848 in Europa* (n. p., n. d.).

69. Reported from the Moscow central archive by Valentin, *Geschichte der deutschen Revolution 1848-49*, I, 435.

70. Eduard Bernstein, *Geschichte der deutschen Schneiderbewegung* (Berlin, 1913), I, 68 f.

71. The important letter of Frederick William IV to Camphausen of May 13, 1848 in Karl Haenchen, *Revolutionsbriefe 1848* (Berlin, 1930), p. 97 f.

72. Very instructive for the popular mood in Berlin was an utterance transmitted by Paul Boerner. During the king's ride on March 21, the brother of the monarch, Prince Albrecht of Prussia, was also drawn into the stream of people. A worker took him by the left arm and a well-known satirical writer by the right, and the proletarian on the left spoke to him highly outspokenly in a broad Berlin worker dialect. "It's good that your brother made peace, royal majesty! I'll tell you, otherwise it would have been sticky, real nasty. We was all for the republic if that there shootin' hadn't quit. Yeh, now everything is hunkydory. We think if everyone was to keep his word, then we'd stay nice 'n cozy." Paul Boerner, *Erinnerungen*, I, 218.

73. Nevertheless the revolution in Karlsruhe also occurred during the worst weather. As on March 1 a grey rainy day was brewing, certainly the 20,000 men who were expected for the demonstration in the capital stayed away in this number. But from Mannheim, Heidelberg, and Offenburg hordes came streaming in and were met by a crowd of a thousand at the Karlsruhe train station. On the castle square, to be sure, the guards stood sullen and with bad grace, umbrella in one hand and rifle in the other, and did not allow matters to take a stormy course. Cf. Wilhelm Zimmermann, *Die deutsche Revolution* (2d. ed.; Karlsruhe, 1851), pp. 32 & 35.

74. From Tarde and Le Bon to Grabowsky and Baschwitz much has been written on this problem, admittedly not in the first line from the historical point of view; useful stimulation is offered by Paul Reinwald, *Vom Geist der Massen* (2d. ed.; Zurich, 1946); the book by Theodor Geiger, *Die Masse und ihre Aktion* (Stuttgart, 1926) contains less than its title promises.

75. Wilhelm von Kügelgen, *Lebenserinnerungen des Alten Mannes in Briefen an seinen Bruder Gerhard*, Otto Freiherr von Taude (ed.) (Leipzig, 1942), pp. 172 ff.

76. Cf. Franz Engler, *Revolution und Reaktion in Anhalt-Dessau-Cöthen* (University of Halle, doctoral dissertation, 1929), pp. 12 ff.

77. A good presentation of the governing methods in the state of Bernburg, where more than a fifth of the income was squandered on the maintenance of the court, was given in an anonymous article in *Die Gegenwart*, IV (1850), 133 ff.

78. Letter of February 9, 1847, Kügelgen, *Lebenserinnerungen*, p. 181.

79. January 23, 1848, *Ibid.*, p. 201.

80. David Friedrich Strauss, *Ausgewählte Briefe*, Eduard Zeller (ed.) (Bonn, 1895), p. 204. The end of the letter already allows a hint that this fiery spirit just five weeks later would change to a tone of deepest disappointment with the revolution and would disgustedly wish a return to the strong protection of the police state. The letter to Rapp on March 29 closed with especially desperate gaiety. "It can be that with the events that await us we shall often look back with regret to the quiet of bygone days; possibly we shall receive too much motion where we until now have not had enough; however, for that reason it still remains true that too much here is healthier than too little. And also more amusing if one only understands himself rightly."

81. Letter March 4, 1848, Kügelgen, *Lebenserinnerungen*, p. 202.

82. *Die Gegenwart*, IV (1850), p. 271 & Veit Valentin, *Geschichte der deutschen Revolution*, I, 416 f.

83. March 18, 1848, Kügelgen, *Lebenserinnerungen*, p. 202.
84. *Ibid.*, p. 203.
85. March 21, 1848, *Ibid.*, p. 204.
86. May 9, 1848, *Ibid.*, p. 211.
87. Hermann Entholt, "Bürgermeister Smidt und die Zeit der Deutschen Revolution," *Bremische Weihnachtsblätter*, Heft VIII (1938), 6.
88. April 28, 1848, Kügelgen, *Lebenserinnerungen*, p. 210.
89. Stephan Born, *Erinnerungen eines Achtundvierzigers* (Leipzig, 1898), pp. 116 f.
90. Strauss, *Ausgewählte Briefe*, p. 207.
91. Letter April 3, 1848. *Ibid.*, p. 206.
92. Cf. the penetrating research of George Lefebvre, *La Grande Peur* (Paris, 1932).
93. Theodor Bunz, *Der Franzosenfeiertag 1848* (Reutlingen, 1880).
94. Report about Königsberg, *Die Gegenwart*, IV (1850), 501 f.
95. Violand, *Die soziale Geschichte der Revolution in Österreich*, pp. 77 f.
96. Ernst Viktor Zenker, *Die Wiener Revolution 1848 in ihren sozialen Voraussetzungen und Beziehungen* (Vienna, 1879), pp. 111ff.
97. "Nassaus politische und soziale Zustände," *Die Gegenwart*, V (1851), 283.
98. Friedrich Lautenschlager, *Die Agrarunruhen in den badischen Standes- und Grundherrschaften im Jahre 1848* (Heidelberg, 1915); Karl Hoffmann, "Der Bauernaufstand des Jahres 1848 im badischen Bauland," *Neues Archiv für die Geschichte Heidelbergs*, V, Heft 2.
99. Hella Mohrdieck, *Die Bauernunruhen in Württemberg: Ein Beitrag zur Geschichte des Revolutionsjahres 1848-49* (University of Tübingen, doctoral dissertation, 1949).
100. "Das Märzministerium in Württemberg," *Die Gegenwart*, VI (1851), 95.
101. Count Bernsdorff, Report of March 15, 1848, Berlin, Geheimes Staatsarchiv, in Veit Valentin, *Geschichte der deutschen Revolution*, I, 397.
102. Reis, *Agrarfrage und Agrarbewegungen.*
103. Report of *Grenzboten* in Walter Reinöhl, *Revolution und Nationalversammlung 1848* (Stuttgart, 1919), p. 50.
104. Outstanding material for the history of the revolt in Solingen was contained in the work of Sigfrid Kuhn, *Der Aufstand der Kleineisenindustriearbeiter*; his sources refute without exception the dramatic conclusions which he draws from them; among other investigations of the worker disturbances are noted: Hans Pflaume, *Organisation und Vertretung der Arbeitnehmer in der Bewegung von 1848* (University of Jena, doctoral dissertation, 1934); Karl Rüdinger, *Die Arbeiterbewegung in Bayern 1848-50* (University of Munich, doctoral dissertation, 1934); W. Koeppen, *Die Anfänge der Arbeiter- und Gesellenbewegung in Franken* (University of Erlangen, doctoral dissertation, 1934); & Alphons Thun, *Beiträge zur Lehre von den gewerblichen Betriebsformen: Solinger und Remscheider Industrie* (Dorpat, 1880).
105. Karl Haenchen (ed.), "Bericht des Leutnants von Kalben vom 4. März 1849," *Forschungen zur brandenburgischen und preussischen Geschichte* XLIX (1937), 266.
106. Ludwig Häusser, *Denkwürdigkeiten zur Geschichte der badischen Revolution* (Heidelberg, 1851), p. 113.
107. *Ibid.*, p. 114.
108. [Missing]
109. Henriette Feuerbach, *Ihr Leben in ihren Briefen* (Berlin, 1912), pp. 136 & 143.

110. Marcel Herwegh (ed.), *Briefe von und an Georg Herwegh* (Paris, 1896), p. 257.
111. Emil Rothpletz, *Militärische Erinnerungen 1847-95* (Zurich, 1917), pp. 52 ff.
112. *Briefe von und an Georg Herwegh*, p. 301.
113. Born, *Erinnerungen*, p. 134.
114. Freiherr von Wöllwarth private archive, Essingen bei Aalen, Wurtemberg, Rep. B9.
115. Veit Valentin, *Geschichte der deutschen Revolution*, I, 447 cites the eyewitness report of the Russian Ambassador von Meyendorff (Moscow central archive).
116. Ludwig Bergsträsser (ed.), *Das Frankfurter Parlament in Briefen und Tagebüchern* (Frankfurt, 1929), p. 269.
117. H. J. A. Körner, *Lebenskämpfe in der Alten und der Neuen Welt* (Leipzig, 1865), I, 417.
118. Julius Fröbel, *Ein Lebenslauf* (Stuttgart, 1890), I, 202.
119. Julius Fröbel, "Die Bourgeoisie und das Volk," *Wiener Studentenkurier*, No. 65, September 3, 1848, printed in Fröbel, *Lebenslauf*, I, 196 ff.
120. See the excellent report about the situation in Königsberg, *Die Gegenwart*, IV (1850), 504 ff.
121. Sigmund Neumann, *Die Stufen des preussischen Konservatismus* ("Historische Studien," No. 119) (Berlin, 1930), pp. 112 f.
122. Hermann Wagener, *Erlebtes* (Berlin, 1884), I, 34.
123. *Ibid.*, I, 17.
124. *Ibid.*, I, 20.
125. Franz Schnabel, *Der Zusammenschluss des politischen Katholizismus in Deutschland im Jahre 1848* ("Heidelberger Abhandlungen," XXIX) (Heidelberg, 1910), pp. 50 f.
126. On the activity of the left associations there is remarkably little consideration in historical writing beyond the work of Gertrud Lüders, *Die demokratische Bewegung in Berlin im Oktober, 1848* (Berlin, 1909).
127. Election manifesto of the democratic party for Germany of April 16, 1848, Walter Neher, *Arnold Ruge als Politiker und politischer Schriftsteller: Ein Beitrag zur deutschen Geschichte des 19. Jahrhunderts* ("Heidelberger Abhandlungen," LXIV) (Heidelberg, 1933), p. 172.
128. Peter von Meyendorff, *Politischer und privater Briefwechsel 1826-63*, Otto Hoetzsch (ed.) (3 vols; Berlin, 1923).
129. *Ibid.*, II, 37.
130. Haenchen, *Revolutionsbriefe*, p. 23.
131. The attempted interpretation by Felix Rachfahl was not sustained by the sources, *Deutschland, König Friedrich Wilhelm IV. und die Berliner Märzrevolution* (Halle, 1901).
132. Haenchen, *Revolutionsbriefe*, p. 32.
133. Theodor Schiemann, *Geschichte Russlands unter Kaiser Nikolaus I.* (Berlin, 1919), IV, 140 f.
134. Harold Temperley and Lillian Penson, *Foundations of British Foreign Policy* (Cambridge, 1938), pp. 156 f.
135. Hans Precht, *Englands Stellung zur deutschen Einheit 1848-50* ("Historische Zeitschrift," Beiheft 3) (Munich, 1925), pp. 37 ff.
136. Prince Schwarzenberg to King Leopold I of Belgium, August 1, 1851, *Haus-, Hof- und Staatsarchiv*, Vienna, quoted in Eugen Franz, "Leopold I., Fürst Schwarzenberg und die deutsche Frage 1848-52," in *Stufen und Wandlungen der deutschen Einheit: Festschrift für Karl Alexander von Müller*, Kurt von Raumer & Theodor

NOTES

Schieder (eds.) (Stuttgart, 1943), p. 243; Schwarzenberg's statements sound decidedly different during the year 1850 in Johann A. von Rantzau, *Europäische Quellen zur schleswig-holsteinischen Geschichte im 19. Jahrhundert* (Breslau, 1934), p. 217.

137. Franz Wigard (ed.), *Stenographische Berichte über die Verhandlungen der deutschen konstituierenden Nationalversammlung zu Frankfurt am Main* (Frankfurt, 1848), III, 1885.

138. Precht, *Englands Stellung*, pp. 77 ff.

139. *Ibid.*, p. 69.

140. Palmerston's instructions for the English representative at the Diet already made these conditions on March 25, 1848, when the founding of a German state was designated simply as the *"Garantie de la paix générale,"* Vicomte de Guichen, *Les grandes questions européennes et la diplomatie des puissances sous la Seconde République française* (Paris, 1925), I, 81.

141. Leading the way was Erich Marcks with his stimulating essay, "Die europäischen Mächte in der Achtundvierziger Revolution," *Historische Zeitschrift,* CXLII (1930), 73-87, and with the presentation in the first volume of his historical work, *Der Aufstieg des Reiches* (Stuttgart, 1936); this thesis was more thoroughly continued by Alexander Scharff, *Die europäischen Grossmächte und die deutsche Revolution: Deutsche Einheit und europäische Ordnung, 1848-51* ("Das Reich und Europa," II) (Leipzig, 1942); two further articles by the same author deal principally with the Schleswig-Holstein question, "Schleswig-Holsteins Erhebung und die europäischen Grossmächte," *Kieler Blätter,* 1942, pp. 100-17 & "Europäische und gesamtdeutsche Zusammenhänge der schleswig-holsteinischen Erhebung," in the *Festschrift K. A. von Müller,* pp. 196ff.

142. Guichen, *Les grandes questions,* I, 167 f.

143. Alexander Scharff had at the time of publication indicated a study of his own; D. M. Greer, *L'Angleterre, la France et la Révolution de 1848* (Paris, 1925).

144. Michael N. Pokrovsky, *Historische Aufsätze* (Vienna, 1928), pp. 95 ff.

145. Cf. Louis Rosenbaum, *Herkunft und Beruf der deutschen Abgeordneten, 1847-1919* (Frankfurt, 1923).

146. Cf. Robert Heller, *Brustbilder aus der Paulskirche* (Leipzig, 1849).

147. Diary entry of Hallbauer, January 11, 1849 in Bergsträsser (ed.), *Das Frankfurter Parlament,* p. 228.

148. *Ibid.*, pp. 107 f.

149. Heinrich von Srbik, *Deutsche Einheit* (2d ed.; Munich, 1936), I, 362.

150. *Ibid.*, I, 370 f.

151. Adolf Rapp, *Grossdeutsch-Kleindeutsch* ("Der deutsche Staatsgedanke") (Munich, 1922), p. 65.

152. As recently noted by Alexander Scharff, *Die europäischen Grossmächte,* p. 111.

153. Cf. the judgment of Hans Erich Feine, *Vom Werden des deutschen Staates* (Stuttgart, 1939), p. 151.

154. Heinrich von Srbik himself admitted this, *Deutsche Einheit,* I, 412.

155. Leopold of Belgium's position was very reserved, E. C. C. Corti, *König Leopold I.* (Vienna, 1922), pp. 148 ff.; Memorandum of the Prince Consort Albert of March 28 in Ernst von Coburg, *Aus meinem Leben und aus meiner Zeit* (Berlin, 1887), I, 273 ff., Memorandum of Christian Baron von Stockmar of April, 1848 in his *Denkwürdigkeiten* (Brunswick, 1872), pp. 489 ff.; Memorandum of Stockmar and Bunsen of August 15, 1848, Haenchen, *Revolutionsbriefe,* pp. 156 ff.; Memorandum of Prince Consort Albert of February 22, 1849, *Ibid.*, pp. 357 ff.

156. Stockmar, *Denkwürdigkeiten,* p. 528.

157. Haenchen, *Revolutionsbriefe,* pp. 156 ff.

158. Scharff, *Die europäischen Grossmächte*, p. 106; it is that much more incomprehensible that Scharff, following in the steps of Erich Marcks, on page 112, again spoke of a "bloody solution" (*blutige Lösung*) by which the King of Prussia would have been without allies if he had accepted election as emperor.

159. Letter of Gustav Rümelin, May 2, 1849, in Bergsträsser, *Das Frankfurter Parlament*, p. 127.

160. Karl Marx, *Revolution and Counter-Revolution*, E. M. Averling (ed.) (New York, 1891, 1971), p. 41; this work was a common effort of Engels and Marx.

161. *Ibid.*, p. 73.

162. Bergsträsser, *Das Frankfurter Parlament*, p. 143.

163. Karl Friedrich Vitzthum von Eckstädt, *Berlin und Wien 1845 bis 1852* (Stuttgart, 1886) in letters to his mother and his uncle gave an illustrative picture of revolutionary Vienna.

164. Fröbel, *Lebenslauf*, I, 192.

165. Very informative for the mood of the rural population is the description by the Silesian peasant's son and young champion of peasant liberation, Hans Kudlich, *Rückblicke und Erinnerungen* (Vienna, 1873), III, 76 ff.

166. Letter November 1, 1848, evening 10 p.m., Vitzthum von Eckstädt, *Berlin und Wien*, pp. 180 ff.

167. Boerner, *Erinnerungen*, I, 233 f.

168. Haenchen, *Revolutionsbriefe*, p. 207.

169. With this the neuralgic topic of the Prussian bourgeois monarchy is touched; cf. the memorandum of Frederick William IV, November 8, 1848 in Friedrich Frahm, "Entstehungs- und Entwicklungsgeschichte der preussischen Verfassung," *Forschungen zur brandenburgischen und preussischen Geschichte*, XCI (1928), 273 f.

170. New material from the Waldeck papers was presented in the biography by his grandson, Wilhelm Biermann, *Franz Leo Benedikt Waldeck* (Paderborn, 1928), pp. 153 ff.

171. Haenchen, *Revolutionsbriefe*, p. 338.

172. Bruno Bauer, *Die bürgerliche Revolution in Deutschland* (Berlin, 1849), pp. 294 f.

173. On the development of the artisan class from the 18th to the 19th century see Rudolf Stadelmann & Wolfram Fischer, *Die Bildungswelt des deutschen Handwerkers um 1800: Studien zur Soziologie des Kleinbürgers im Zeitalter Goethes* (Berlin, 1955).

174. Werner Sombart in 1906 wrote an ingenious work that today is still worth reading, *Warum gibt es in den Vereinigten Staaten keinen Sozialismus?* (Tübingen, 1906).

175. Johann Georg Hoffmann, *Das Interesse des Menschen und Bürgers bei der bestehenden Zunftverfassung* (Königsberg, 1808).

176. Cf. the illuminating presentation by Hermann Schlüter, *Der Anfang der deutschen Arbeiterbewegung in Amerika* (Stuttgart, 1907).

177. Born, *Erinnerungen*, p. 122.

178. Draft by head of sub-department of July, 1850, Documents of Ministry of Interior, Wurtemberg State Archive, Ludwigsburg, E 146-149, fasc. 1960.

179. Wurtemberg State Archive, E 146-149, fasc. 1960.

180. For Weitling an extensive monographical literature exists; the best is certainly that of Ernst Barnikol in the volumes of the series "Christentum und Sozialismus," (Kiel, 1929 ff.).

181. On Schlöffel cf. Max Lenz, *Geschichte der Universität Berlin*, II (2) *passim*.

182. Karl Griewank, *Friedrich Wilhelm Held* (University of Rostock, doctoral dissertation, 1922).

NOTES

183. Wilhelm Friedensburg, *Stephan Born* ("Beiheft des Archivs für Geschichte des Sozialismus") (Leipzig, 1923), pp. 63 ff.; Eduard Bernstein, *Die Geschichte der Berliner Arbeiterbewegung* (Berlin, 1907), I, 54 ff.; Pflaume, *Organisation und Vertretung.*
184. Eduard Bernstein (ed.), *Dokumente des Sozialismus* (Stuttgart, 1903), III, 40 ff.
185. Valentin, *Geschichte der deutschen Revolution,* I, 532.
186. A complete presentation of the Frankfurt journeymen's assembly was given by Wilhelm Eduard Biermann, *Karl Georg Winkelblech* (Leipzig, 1909), II, 270 ff.; in addition Veit Valentin, *Frankfurt und die Revolution von 1848* (Stuttgart, 1908), pp. 304 ff.; more recently Pflaume, *Organisation und Vertretung,* pp. 36 ff.; [Theodore S. Hamerow, *Restoration, Revolution, Reaction, Economics and Politics in Germany, 1815-1871* (Princeton, 1958) & P. H. Noyes, *Organisation and Revolution: Working-Class Associations in the German Revolutions of 1848-49* (Princeton, 1966) pp. 176 ff. supersede all earlier studies]; the text of two pamphlets which contain the "decisions" of the Frankfurt worker congress and a "memorandum" for the draft of an industrial code adopted by the artisan masters meeting at the same time were printed completely as appendices I & II in Biermann's detailed biography of Winkelblech, II, 441 ff.; minutes of the meetings apparently were not made; a collection of petitions drawn up by the workers and artisans and sent to the Frankfurt assembly and a second collection of petitions sent to the artisans' congresses can be found in the city archives of Frankfurt.
187. The figure 12,000 was named by Weitling's worker newspaper, *Der Urwähler,* Bernstein, *Die Geschichte der Berliner Arbeiterbewegung,* I, 84; the number of 12,000-15,000 members of the worker "brotherhood" (*Verbrüderung*) was given in a memorandum of the Prussian government from June 8, 1850, Wurtemberg State Archive, E 146-149, fasc. 1960.
188. Articles from this publication, *Die Verbrüderung,* were collected by Max Quarck, *Die Arbeiterverbrüderung* (Frankfurt, 1900).
189. The impulse for this forced savings fund originated with the surveyor Schwenniger, who reported of a concern in Westphalia where such an experiment was already being carried out, Born, *Erinnerungen,* pp. 166 f.
190. The confiscated papers of the Wurtemberg worker associations were collected for the most part in the documents of the Wurtemberg Interior Ministry, Wurtemberg State Archive, E 146-149, fasc. 1959-1961; there is also a series of excellently collected reports of the *Oberregierungsrat* Camerer; some material in the police files of the *Oberämter* Ulm and Göppingen.
191. A vivid description of life in the Franconian worker associations in Ludwig Brunner, *Politische Bewegung in Nürnberg 1848-49* ("Heidelberger Abhandlungen zur Mittleren und Neueren Geschichte," XVII), pp. 109 ff.
192. Bernstein, *Geschichte der deutschen Schneiderbewegung,* pp. 82 f.
193. An outstanding examination of its origins exists, written from the sources by Margaret Tilmann, *Der Einfluss des Revolutionsjahres 1848 auf die preussische Gewerbe- und Sozialgesetzgebung* (University of Berlin, doctoral dissertation, 1935), pp. 35 ff.
194. Gustav Mayer, *Friedrich Engels* (Berlin, 1920), I, 396.
195. This opinion even Karl Schurz expressed, *Lebenserinnerungen* (Berlin, 1906), I, 191.
196. As example see the descriptions from the Bavarian-Wurtemberg border region in the richly documented dissertation by Hermann Kessler, *Politische Bewegung in Nördlingen und dem bayrischen Ries während der deutschen Revolution 1848-49* (University of Munich, doctoral dissertation, 1939), pp. 246 ff.
197. Valentin, *Geschichte der deutschen Revolution,* II, 459.

213

198. The following according to Koeppen, *Die Anfänge der Arbeiter- und Gesellenbewegung*, pp. 64 ff.

199. For example, the valiant village mayor Neidlein in Saulgau in the Danube district of Wurtemberg, who—to honor Swabian reaction let it be said—was not even replaced because of his taking the law into his own hands, rather remained for further decades in office. Documents of the Wurtemberg Interior Ministry, Wurtemberg State Archive, E 146-149, fasc. 1929 & 1933.

200. Born, *Erinnerungen*, p. 207.

201. Mayer, *Friedrich Engels*, I, 425.

202. *Ibid.*, I, 360.

203. Hermann Uhde-Bernays (ed.), *Henriette Feuerbach: Ihr Leben in ihren Briefen* (Munich, 1920), pp. 151. f.

204. Otto von Bismarck, *Gesammelte Werke* (Berlin, n. d.), XIV (2), 751; another letter of Bismarck to Kinkel of July 1, 1869 was published in the *Deutsche Allgemeine Zeitung*, April 1, 1930.

205. *Die Gegenwart*, II (1849), 552.

206 "If Frankfurt were a city like Paris or if the assembly were held in Vienna, Berlin, in a place of central administration, then possibly an extemporized reestablishment of Germany could have emerged: a reestablishment undoubtedly that would have awakened a Vendée, destroyed more than a Lyon in a frightful civil war, would have been put down in a complete dismemberment of Germany." Frankfurt, April 29, 1848, Johann Gustav Droysen, *Politische Schriften*, Felix Gilbert (ed.) (Munich, 1933), p. 125.

207. What sort of reaction in mood the news of March 21 evoked Stüve described in a retrospect manuscript, Gustav Stüve, *J. C. Bertram Stüve*, II, 4.

208. Proclamation of Prince Heinrich LXXII of Reuss-Lobenstein-Ebersdorf from March 11, 1848, Karl Adam, "Kulturgeschichtliche Streifzüge durch das Jahr 1848-49," *Zeitschrift für Kulturgeschichte*, III (1896), 259.

209. *Ibid.*

210. The report that the *Oberamtsmann* Alfred von Bibra of Römhild in August, 1845, directed to the Minister of Interior von Meiningen after the study of the writing of Engels, dealt with by Wilhelm Engel, "Wirtschaftliche und soziale Kämpfe in Thüringen vor dem Jahr 1848," *Zeitschrift für thüringische Geschichte*, N. F. XI (1927), 132.

211. Cf. the letters of March 23-25, 1848, of the young ambassadorial attaché Kurd von Schlözer from Berlin to his parents. Kurd von Schlözer, *Jugendbriefe* (Stuttgart, 1920), pp. 119 ff.

212. *Ibid.*, p. 121.

213. Even men of the extreme right were moved by the current of the times. There is a letter from Bismarck of March 28, 1848, which is usually falsely interpreted and from which it is clearly apparent that even the Brandenburg Junker and his royalist wife were still convinced at the end of March that one must give in and set up a German parliament at the Diet, even if one could not foresee what line the Austrian power might take in this case, or whether it might lead to war. The knighthood of the Mark on this point agreed that a "peaceful" (*friedfertige*) mood of the king, friendly to developments, would not provide for the wishes of all Germans. Bismarck, *Gesammelte Werke*, XIV (1), 102.

214. Hans Huber, *Karl Heinzen* ("Berner Untersuchungen zur allgemeinen Geschichte," VI) (Bern, 1932), p. 85.

215. Strauss, *Briefwechsel*.

216. Eberhard Schmidt, *Einführung in die Geschichte der deutschen Strafrechtspflege* (Göttingen, 1947), p. 293.

217. Karl Schurz, *Lebenserinnerungen*, I, 129 f.

Selective Bibliography of Works by Rudolf Stadelmann

BOOKS:

Der historische Sinn bei Herder (1928)
Vom Geist des ausgehenden Mittelalters: Studien zur Geschichte der Weltanschauung von Nicholas Casanus bis Sebastian Franck (1929, 1966)
Das Jahr 1865 und das Problem von Bismarcks deutscher Politik (1933)
Scharnhorst und die Revolution seiner Zeit (1938)
Vom Erbe der Neuzeit (1942)
Deutschland und West Europa: Drei Aufsätze (1948)
Soziale und politische Geschichte der Revolution von 1848 (1948, 1962, 1970, 1973)
Moltke und der Staat (1950)
Scharnhorst: Schicksal und geistige Welt: Ein Fragment (1952)
Geschichte der englischen Revolution (1954)
jointly with Wolfram Fischer, *Die Bildungswelt des deutschen Handwerkers um 1800: Studien zur Soziologie des Kleinbürgers im Zeitalter Goethes* (1955)
"Reformation," in *Handbuch der deutschen Geschichte* edited by Rudolf Stadelmann et al., II, 303-465 (1936-42, 1952)

EDITED:

Otto von Bismarck, *Erinnerung und Gedanke: Kritische Neuausgabe*, in Bismarck, *Die gesammelten Werke*, XV (1932)
Jacob Burckhardt, *Weltgeschichtliche Betrachtungen* (1949)
Grosse Geschichtsdenker: Ein Zyklus Tübinger Vorlesungen (1949)

Suggestions for Additional Reading

The best bibliography of works on 1848 is contained in Veit Valentin, *Geschichte der Deutschen Revolution von 1848-1849* 2 vols. (Berlin, 1930-31). Articles and books on 1848 are listed in a yearly bibliography of German history, the *Jahresberichte für Deutsche Geschichte*. Andreas Dorpalen searchingly describes the East German view of 1848 in "Die Revolution von 1848 in der Geschichtsschreibung der DDR," *Historische Zeitschrift*, CCX (1970), 324-68 and compares the Marxist and non-Marxist positions of "The Revolutions of 1848," in *Marxism, Communism, and Western Society: A Comparative Encyclopedia* (New York, 1973), VII, 244-53. The views of major historians are analyzed by Theodore S. Hamerow, "History and the German Revolution of 1848," *American Historical Review*, LX (1954), 27-45 and Kurt Schwerin, "The Revolution of 1848 and German Historians." Ph.D. dissertation, Columbia University, 1955.

Fine recent accounts covering the period of the revolution include, in addition to Valentin, Jacques Droz, *Les Révolution Allemandes de 1848 d'apres un manuscript et des notes de E. Tonnelat* (Paris, 1957), Karl Obermann, *Deutschland von 1815 bis 1849* 3d. ed. (Berlin, 1967), and Theodore S. Hamerow, *Restoration, Revolution, Reaction: Economics and Politics in Germany, 1815-1871* (Princeton, 1958).

Karl Obermann has edited two good collections of documents, a group of pamphlets, *Flugblätter der Revolution: Eine Flugblattsammlung zur Geschichte der Revolution von 1848/49 in Deutschland* (Berlin, 1970), and *Einheit und Freiheit: Die deutsche Geschichte von 1814-1849 in zeitgenössischen Dokumenten* (Berlin, 1950). Hans Jessen, *Die Deutsche Revolution 1848/49 in Augenzeugenberichten* (Düsseldorf, 1968) brings the age to life with eyewitnesses.

Marx and Engels' standard account *Revolution and Counter-Revolution* (London, 1896), has been supplemented by their *The Revolution of 1848-49: Articles from the Neue Rheinische Zeitung* (New York, 1972), Oscar J. Hammen, *The Red '48ers: Karl Marx and Friedrich Engels* (New York, 1969) and Gerhard Becker, *Karl Marx und Friedrich Engels in Köln: Zur Geschichte des Kölner Arbeitervereins* (Berlin, 1963). Frank Eyck, *The Frankfurt Parliament, 1848-1849* (New York, 1968) and Rolf Weber, *Die Revolution in Sachsen, 1848/49* (Berlin, 1970). P. H. Noyes, *Organization and Revolution: Workingclass Associations in The German Revolution of 1848-49* (Princeton, 1966), R. John Rath, *The Viennese Revolution of 1848* (Austin, Texas, 1957), Ersebêt Andics, *Das Bündnis Habsburg-Romanow: Vorgeschichte der zaristischen Intervention in Ungarn im Jahre 1849* (Budapest, 1963), and Karl Obermann, *Joseph Weydemeyer: Ein Lebensbild, 1818-1866* (Berlin, 1968) are examples of fine specialized studies that have appeared since this book was written in 1948.